CORPORATI

GAMES THAT'LL BLOW YOU AWAY

BRUTAL ENGINE

THE DRAGON AWOKEN

JAMES NORBURY

ALSO AVAILABLE FROM BRUTAL GAMES
Corporation - Core Rules
The Eastern Bank
Machines of War - Technology Guide for Corporation

You need the Corporation Core Rules to use this book.

CORPORATION: THE DRAGON AWOKEN
2009 © James Norbury, Brutal Games

MGP 6155
ISBN 978-1-907218-13-2

www.corpgame.com

Disclaimer
Unfortunately the Ai-Jinn DO exist, their Agents are everywhere and their methods merciless. There really are only two choices, join them or pay the price.
V1.0

WE NEED NO LONGER SQUABBLE WITH BARBARIANS OVER BLACKENED EARTH. OUR FUTURE LIES AMONGST THE STARS.

FROM *EIGHT NEW PRECEPTS*
ATTR: YUAN QINGZHAO - AI-JINN CEO

ADDITIONAL DEVELOPMENT
Matthew Keevil

ADDITIONAL FLAVOUR TEXT
Petroc Wilton

PROOF READING
Ruth Norbury, Petroc Wilton, James Norbury

KEY PLAY TESTERS
Ruth Norbury, Matthew Keevil, Paul Arran, Hugo Marchent, Jon Dore, James Norbury

FORUM SYSADMIN
Gareth Larter

Special Mention to Hubert Cumberdale

ART
Ian Norbury
Mark Beer - logan619@hotmail.co.uk
Factory Map - Iain Stark - agentdaniq@googlemail.com
James Norbury
Stock Models - Mr. Jumpman V.2, The Germanator, HustlerJohn

CONTENTS

CONTENTS

INTRODUCTION

We are despised in some quarters because we do not aspire to beauty. What our detractors fail to realise is that our design ethic represents an efficiency of the most fundamental kind. If it takes me two days to make a sword, and it takes you three days to make a beautiful sword, then on the morning of the third day I will take my sword and cut you down while you are still working at your forge. Now I have two swords, and two forges with which to make more. Thus we prevail.

attr: Juan Meng, Mountain Lord of the Hong Kong White Lotus Society

Welcome to the Dragon Awoken. This book will give you great insight into the clandestine, industrial machine that is the Ai-Jinn. All manner of information can be found within these pages, from new Trainings and cybernetics to factory plans and pleasure orbitals. A wealth of new character options are presented which are intended to make your Agents far more 'Ai-Jinn' and really differentiate them from the other Corporations.

The Ai-Jinn, although an Asian based corporation, take their Agents from all over the world. They are the least ethnically selective of the corporations and their divisions are the most culturally diverse. You will find thick-necked British gangsters alongside Japanese yakuza, Jamaican yardies and Russian mobsters. This range of backgrounds makes the division extremely adept at working on a global scene as, unlike a Shi Yukiro division, they are more likely to understand a greater range of international customs and methods.

This can of course be a disadvantage as the division may not always get along to eye. An exiled German surgeon who has joined the Ai-Jinn may well have trouble seeing eye to eye with an African-American gang-banger. Nevertheless, the security the Ai-Jinn offer to their Agents can have a mellowing effect and strange combinations can find themselves getting on like proverbial houses on fire.

Another advantage to the Ai-Jinn's recruitment methods is the sheer range of professionals they seem to net. No matter what job you're in, if the UIG come down on you hard you may well find yourself knocking at the Ai-Jinn's door, offering your skills and life in exchange for money and safety. This open door policy has to be carefully managed though; the possibility of infiltrators can be a significant problem. To reduce this, before being made active Agents, recruits are required to betray those they were previously loyal to. This is normally a sizable action which anyone who retains a vestige of loyalty would be reluctant to perform.

The division are normally set to perform each of these purification

missions as a whole so before the Division is assigned proper Ai-Jinn missions, they will typically spend their first 4 or 5 outings making brutal strikes against their former employer's assets. In cases where there is not a former employer, the Agents are simply required to go along and help. This also gives the Ai-Jinn power over their Agents should they falter at some point in the future. More on this on page 110.

Being essentially a pack of thieves, murderers, extortionists, and gangsters the Ai-Jinn need to maintain order within the ranks like no other Corporation. This tends to be done through the concept of loyalty and by using a tried and tested system of enforced comradeship the Ai-Jinn are able to weed out potential trouble very early on. More on this on page 110.

AI-JINN: THE SHADOW BUSINESS

All the corporations have dark secrets, no entity as massive and monolithically powerful as a corporation-state can exist without acquiring a few, but while most have them at the very highest levels of command, the Ai-Jinn has them at all levels. No other corporation has as many skeletons in their closet, though E.I. probably would if they bothered with cover-ups, and none even come close to having the degree of illicit knowledge the Ai-Jinn possess. Most of these secrets are fairly petty affairs, at least on the scale at which the corporation-states operate, involving street-level crime, racketeering and extortion, but others are posed to smash the world into shards.

Where did the technology for the FarDrive come from?

What are the future plans of the UIG?

What lurks out in deep space?

How many trusted Agents are actually spies for rival organisations?

Why did the rogue Archons defect?

The Ai-Jinn may not know the definitive answer to all or even any of these questions, but they know more than anyone else and, for the time being, they're keeping their cards close to their chest. The power of the Ai-Jinn is twofold; the members are ultimately loyal to the Corporation and they are everywhere. No city, town or spire is without its criminal element, and every seemingly disorganised gang of hoodlums might be reporting back to the Ai-Jinn, sometimes they might not even know it themselves. Much as the other corporation-states might like to dismiss the Ai-Jinn as a rabble, they have learned through harsh experience that when the Ai-Jinn make a move, it's best to watch them very closely. Of course, when it's for something that truly matters, it's as though the Ai-Jinn were never there.

STYLE

The Ai-Jinn build to last. Whereas the Shi Yukiro and E.I. may build with a certain amount of flair, the Federation with fearsome purpose and Comoros on a budget, the Ai-Jinn tend to build with scale and durability in mind.

One of the most obvious examples of this is in their vehicles. Whether it's a hulking FarDrive craft or a sub-orbital shuttle, the design will be as simple as possible, the materials as strong as attainable and the aesthetics thrown out of the door. Even their FarDrive crafts, which you might expect to be streamlined, elegant pieces of art, give absolutely no quarter to styled appearance.

This is something that is worth remembering and can add a strong feeling of consistency to your game. If you try to remember that anything built by the Ai-Jinn is likely to be solid, dependable and down-to-earth, it can help to keep the corporation's various styles distinct. When the players need to visit an Ai-Jinn spire the lack of frills and chunky, no-nonsense construction will be a familiar sight. If they are E.I. or Shi Yukiro Agents, then they may be a little disdainful and will be looking forward to getting back to their own, more refined cities.

GRIME AND CRIME

Another of the key themes you should try to keep in mind when running a game involving the Ai-Jinn is the concept of 'grime and crime'. Simply put, anything or anyone in the Ai-Jinn world is metaphorically only a few feet from the seedy world of crime and ugly, hulking structures of heavy industry. Take, for example, the Maitabo Restaurant in the Enlight Archology; yes, it looks beautiful; its interiors cascade with sparkling waterfalls, exotic plants and magnificent fountains and it serves some beautiful food.

It would not take long however to discover the Maitabo is run by D-Company, essentially an Indian Mafia. You had better be sure of yourself because by walking through its doors you enter a world of gambling, extortion, bootlegging, murder, and blackmail. If you sit down and flash the cash, someone will take notice, in a weeks time you may be approached with an 'unmissable' business deal or you may be asked for some inside information on your company's operations. And this trend continues throughout all Ai-Jinn assets; nothing is as it seems.

If you see an Ai-Jinn backed charity you can be sure that for every credit donated, 75% goes directly towards the purchase of armaments and drugs.

And the grime? Well, that refers to a more literal filth and lack of grace. The Ai-Jinn maintain nothing that does not need it. If you were to take a look behind the scenes of a Shi Yukiro spire, you'd find order, cleanliness and efficiency. In an Ai-Jinn spire things are only cleaned if there is a practical reason; if not it can wait. Even the wealthy areas are nothing like a typical E.I. residence, hygiene is not the reason the rich come to live in such places. As long as the Ai-Jinn continue to offer their discreet, no-questions service, they will always have a broad client base. The no-frills, oppressive, industrial environments which characterise Ai-Jinn structures are here to stay.

I DON'T LIKE THE CEO

This book pins down many aspects of the Ai-Jinn corporation such as its leaders, methods and many of its assets. This is not meant to hamper your game and make your carefully designed CEO or Spire City redundant. It's for three main reasons.

1. To add consistency to the world.

2. To save you the job of making them up so you can concentrate on plot etc.

3. To present ideas you may not have thought of.

You should not be at all concerned about disregarding any aspect of this book and instead using your own NPCs, weapons, tactics and buildings.

RULE AMMENDMENT

Note that this change was made to severing body parts in July 2009.

When you sever a body part (except the torso), you only deal as much damage as needed to sever the part in question.

For example, if you deal 50 damage when severing the arm, the target will only take 10.

The reattachment of a severed body part replaces the hit points lost. So in the example above, when you reattach the arm, you regain 10HP

THE FORMATION OF THE AI-JINN

Historically speaking, one of the largest obstacles to China's continued development was the transit of resources around its massive landmass. It was therefore no surprise that the company which developed and built the Trans-Asian magna-rail was going to be pivotal in the formation of the Ai-Jinn Corporation.

At the time, the Lang Transit Conglomerate was an industrial giant building most of Asia's cars, trains, planes and roads. The magna-rail was ingenious because of the low cost involved in taking the rail to any part of the country. It was therefore possible to build rails going all over East Asia for a relatively modest sum. The technology was owned by Lang but they leased the rail to anyone wishing to use it for the transportation of goods. It was easily the cheapest form of transport for private, commercial and industrial customers. The Lang Conglomerate was fast becoming a super-corporation and the government were rightfully concerned that the entire country was completely dependent on Lang and consequently subject to its whims.

The Chinese government, headed by Chairman Cho Yun, was unable to do anything about the situation legally. Their attempts at trying to force Lang to split into smaller units were crushed by armies of lawyers. Rather than pursue more fruitless court cases, Cho Yun established a task force who were instructed to put control of Lang into the government's hands via any means necessary. They were given access to essentially unlimited government resources and granted immunity from prosecution.

The task force initially attempted a range of methods including espionage and sabotage but Lang's immense resources were still insurmountable. Eventually the task force approached Asia's less savoury elements such as the Yakuza, Triad, Tong and Snake heads. By transferring their own immunity and resources onto these organised criminals they rapidly created the largest, most comprehensive army of ruthless, immoral and devious soldiers ever made.

The organised criminal groups took no prisoners bringing Lang to its knees. Hundreds of high-up employees were murdered and terrorised until all of Lang's executives were too terrified to maintain their positions. Within months the company began to crumble but the results were not as Cho Yun had predicted.

The task force, who had named themselves Ai-Jinn, were not about to relinquish the power they had acquired and by continued alliances with the criminal organisations were able to make sure a sizable amount of Lang's wealth and assets ended up, not with the government, but with the task force and their new allies.

This combination was phenomenally successful and the government were powerless to do anything about it. Any investigations were called off when those in charge ended up dead or missing. If any of the Triad or yakuza bosses were placed on trial, members of the jury would be intimidated or judges would be murdered.

Unusually, however, the collapse of the Chinese government did not lead to chaos among the citizenry. The Ai-Jinn became the new government, using the Triads, Yakuza and Tongs as a form of police. The streets were not patrolled in the traditional manner but anyone engaging in crime without the permission of the local clans would be dealt with in the time honoured manner. Over time the Ai-Jinn, building on the framework of the shattered Lang Conglomerate, rose not only as the head of a criminal empire but as an industrial giant. There was one final event which would seal the Ai-Jinn's place among the greatest Corporations of all time.

THE DISCOVERY

The newly formed Ai-Jinn did not take long to become the foremost industrial force on the planet. So efficient and successful were they that even the other Corporations were forced to accept it was cheaper and more productive to get the Ai-Jinn to build their structures and mine their ores than it was to do it themselves.

It was during such a mining operation in Antarctica that a massive anomaly was detected deep beneath the ice. The operation was immediately halted and the Ai-Jinn ferried in several war ships, transporters, battle class cyberlins and heavy excavators. After months of painstaking work the fruits of their labour were transported home spread over three cargo barges. Although many images exist of the operation, there is no hard evidence to reveal exactly what they found down there. The most likely answer is some kind of space-travelling vessel. This supposition is backed up by the fact that nine months after the discovery the Ai-Jinn began their first test launches of a new breed of shuttle capable of travelling through sub-space, cutting journey times significantly.

Many attempts have been made to find out what the Ai-Jinn discovered that day. It is common knowledge that the item was taken around the coast to the Xa Men factory complex but the use of SatBlankets and cyberlins was sufficient to make sure it was not tracked to an exact location. The general consensus is that it was taken underground into a specially constructed vault and is probably still there. The force of cyberlins stationed at Xa Men and the array of synchronously orbiting war satellites suggest that this supposition is correct. Aside from the FarDrive and their illegitimate GET station, the Ai-Jinn show no other signs of abnormally advanced technology suggesting that whatever they did find; its secrets have either been fully realised or are, at this time, beyond comprehension.

Ranger Class Cyberlin - *Fire from Heaven*.
This mech is equipped with environmental seals so that it can hide in swamps and lakes.

SECTION 2
CHARACTER ADVANCEMENT

The four Agents lurked in the shadowed recesses of the antechamber; the tumult of the heated board meeting was a subdued murmur behind the heavy door. Division leader Han grinned, teeth flashing white and chrome in the gloom, and addressed his kill-team in a sibilant whisper of subvocalised Mandarin.

"The degenerate cowards believe they can hide their Corporate lapdogs behind arrays of ion shrouds and weapons scanners. They cannot understand that we need no weapons – that we are the weapons! On my command, my brothers, we will surge through that door and slaughter every living thing behind it with the Scarlet Tiger finger claw technique, that all the corrupt El barbarians may witness the cost of their incursions on our territory in the Eastern Bank!"

Han turned to face the door, drawing in a deep breath, narrowing his awareness down to a lethal point. But then Agent Peng hissed back in heavily accented Cantonese, entirely throwing off his concentration. "Scarlet Tiger will never leave a clear enough message, Division Leader. Let us demonstrate the seven point nerve block of Raging Monkey, that the expressions on the faces of their dead shock the gwailo into repenting of their transgressions. I have been practising."

Han opened his mouth to respond but was forestalled by Agent Harris's angry response in badly mangled pidgin Shanghainese. "You say gwailo cannot fight? Raging Monkey style is old men and children fighting! We best use decimating throat strike of Blind Drunken Ox style. El bastards choke repentance in last breathing!"

The conference room beyond the door had now fallen completely silent. None of the Division noticed, because the normally taciturn Agent Yasuda now weighed into the debate in broken English, disdaining Mandarin and having long since despaired of the Division's ability to master his native Japanese. "It's Five Dragon karate for best quickly of kill," he opined softly. "Let's mutilating all corpses after killing, for our most splendid intimidation results. Get! Hammer hand reverse strike!"

The door swung open and an enormous El Nuke lumbered out into the antechamber to see what all the fuss was about, peering into the shadows and idly weighing a frag grenade in one hand. Han cursed, leapt up towards the doorway and grabbed the top of the steel doorframe single-handed, pivoting smoothly back down to kick the Nuke in the chest with both feet. As the massive Agent toppled back into the chamber Han grabbed the grenade now tumbling through the air, flicked the activator, lobbed it in after the Nuke and swivelled to slam the door closed again with a sweeping roundhouse kick before cartwheeling away.

The explosion, devastating in the confined space, blew the door off its hinges and back into the antechamber, clanging off the opposite wall before crashing to the ground where it lay with the occasional ping of cooling metal, the only sound that broke the sudden silence. Han turned to stare admonishingly at Peng, who sighed, unclipped a small dental records matcher from his belt, and walked gingerly through the ravaged doorway into the charnel house that had until recently been a conference chamber. "This would never have happened with Raging Monkey," they heard him mutter as he vanished into the haze of greasy smoke.

TRAININGS

Below are presented a range of new trainings. Although a few are exclusive to the Ai-Jinn and their sects most can be used for any Corporation Agent.

NEW RULE - CRASH COURSE

Sometimes an Agent needs to learn a new Training but does not have the time or means to go through learning all the prerequisite Trainings. In such a situation he needs to go on a crash course. This represents learning all the key aspects he needs in order to master the final technique.

System
You may pay 5XP extra to acquire a Training without possessing one of the prerequisite Trainings. You must pay 5XP for each Training you wish to skip in this way. You must still meet all other prerequisites.

Note that you are NOT considered to possess the skipped Training and you will have to pay to skip it again.

Example
You wish to buy the Knife Man Training but you do not own the Machines of War supplement so don't have access to 'Twist the Knife'. Instead you can pay 15XP for the Knife Man Training. You still need Mastered Weapon (knife), Attitude 7, Close Combat 7, and Reflexes 8.

You will NOT get any benefits from the 'Twist the Knife Training.'

CORE TRAININGS

Some Trainings are fundamental and cannot be skipped. These are referred to as 'Core Trainings'.
Those in existing books are listed here. In future books it will be stated in their description.

Telepath
Telepathic Adept
Metahuman
There is Only Ai-Jinn
Conviction of One
Undivided Focus

Corporation or Group Specific Trainings can only be skipped by people in that group. Such trainings include Ai-Jinn Mechanic, Ai-Jinn Heavy Vehicle Pilot, Comoros Reverse Engineer, Eurasin Inc. Medic, Shi Yukiro Ion Smith, Shi Yukiro Ion Weapon Specialist, Shi Yukiro Master Ion Swordsmith, Shi Yukiro Shuriken-Do and Dynasty Strain Trainings.

TRAINING UNDER A SHI YUKIRO MASTER

A prerequisite for some Trainings.

This is a rarity indeed and only advanced Shi Yukiro Agents are permitted to train with the 3 or 4 true masters within the ranks of the Shi Yukiro. It is not something that can be requested, and it is only offered to those who show true dedication and promise.

COMBAT TRAININGS

ADVANCED COMMAND
Shandian Shuài

A Shandian Shuài member may spend a Conviction point and make a 'Presence + Attitude' roll as a full action, if successful their XS on the roll is converted into temporary Conviction points that may be divided among any Ai-Jinn or allied troops (including Agents) within earshot.

A Shandian Shuài may not benefit personally from any Conviction generated in this way. Unspent temporary conviction are lost at the end of the scene.

Note that some other character types may be able to take this training. This will be noted where appropriate. In this book only the Shandian Shuài make take it.

ADVANCE UNDER FIRE
Ling Kao Strain
Athletics 8
Agility 8
Ling Kao are not good in fire fights. It is imperative they close on the enemy as fast as possible. They use this training to advance quickly, hopefully dodging the hail of gunfire that is sure to rain down.

System
When closing on an enemy the Ling Kao may use Full Dodge. This should not normally be possible as Full Dodge assumes you are heading into cover and dodging bullets, not charging the enemy.

CLANGER
Ai-Jinn Agent
In true Ai-Jinn tradition you enjoy using extremely heavy armour and have become adept in its use. The Maximum Agility score associated with any armour granting an AV of 4 or more is increased by 2.

Example, on page 45 of the Core Rules you can see that Heavy Combat Armour, Powered Tactical Armour and Tactical Assault Armour would all be valid armours for the training.

CYBERLIN PILOT
Mechtronics 3
Combat Pilot (Training)
Drive 5
Pilot 5
You are skilled in the piloting of cyberlins. The mechanical monsters are yours to command. This allows you to pilot all classes of cyberlin and smaller mechs such as MAG Tanks.

GRAPPLE HOOK COMBAT
Personal Grapple
Athletics 4
Agility 7

Commonly used by the pirates of the Cai Qian (page 106) this training represents the ability to use the personal grapple (page 59) as a combat weapon. It allows the following moves.

Firing the grapple in combat uses 'Perception + Light Firearms' The grapple ignores shields and deals 1 point of damage. It can embed itself into anything with AV 20 or less.

Pre-emptive grapple
Before initiative is worked out the user should make an attack roll. If he hits then the grapple embeds into the target and the grappler can pull them off balance. This gives the target -6 to initiative and they are considered attached to the grapple. Everyone then rolls initiative as normal.

Reel In
The grapple can reel in 400kg at a speed of 20 metres per second. The user can reel in a target as a free action so if the target was less than 25 metres away they will be considered to be in close combat.

If they wish to, the attacker and the target should make opposed

---

Agent Marx squared his shoulders and raised the railgun; checking the sight he could see, between two large factory units, a single target exactly 907 metres distant. Marx dropped to one knee and, steadying his hand, levelled the crosshair at the solitary figure. He squeezed the trigger and smiled.

The smile disappeared as soon as it had come as Marx saw the figure now running at him, its sprint broken by the occasional leap or flip. Marx levelled the gun again, took careful aim and fired. No hit. "Shit!"

Marx dropped the LEAW and hauled the M50 off his back. Putting in a fresh clip he stood up and held down the trigger. A torrent of bullets sprayed from the weapon, concrete was shattered and torn apart, windows exploded and flurries of dust erupted from every impact point. Marx flicked on his thermal to check for life signs. The figure was now only a few hundred yards

away, leaping off low walls and rolling under transit piping.

"What the.." Marx slammed a new clip home and slowly backing up along the potholed road, opened up on the advancing target, thermal still active. The figure was just 50 metres off, dodging every bullet as though they were in slow motion.

Marx dropped the M50, and went to draw his sword. As he did so the figure, now clearly identifiable as a woman wearing a heavy black cotton robe tied with a red cloth belt, leapt high in the air and drew a straight bladed qi jian. She landed in near silence directly behind him, placed the sword against his neck and spoke a single word of Mandarin.
Marx just had time to mentally translate before his head fell from his shoulders.

"Coward."

'Strength + Athletics' rolls. The loser is dragged to the winner. The GM may give either side a bonus / penalty if appropriate.

Quick Escape
When fleeing combat the user gains +4 to their roll as long as there is an object they can grapple to facilitate their escape.

GRAPPLE HOOK COMBAT (ADVANCED)
Grapple Hook Combat
Light Firearms 4
Close Combat 4

This builds on the existing 'Grapple Hook Combat' Training to present more options.

Wrestling Bonus
Someone with this training gains +4 to all wrestling rolls as they are able to use the wire to restrain and impair their opponent. Wrestling is covered on page 145 of the Core Rules.

Steal Item
As long as your opponent is 5+ metres away you can fire your grapple hook at their carried item in an attempt to steal it.

Roll 'Perception + Light Firearms' with a modifier.

Coin Sized	-12
Pistol	-6
Rifle	-4

If you hit you attach the grapple to the object. The opponent must pass a 'Strength + Endurance' roll with a penalty equal to your XS or lose it. When you reel in the grapple you can spend a free action to detach the grapple and take the object.

GUAN YU USE
Mechtronics 1
Access to a Guan Yu Suit.
Guan Yu Instructor

Anyone can learn to use Guan Yu Armour. As long as you have access to a suit to practice you can purchase this Training at the normal cost. Note that all Ai-Jinn Agents gain this Training for free at character creation.

If you do not have an instructor you can still learn to use the suit but it requires another 10XP and an additional 4 weeks of downtime.

Without this training the suit is unusable.

> *Know that the suit was named for a humble warrior of ages past, whose formidable prowess and unflinching fidelity resulted in his elevation to godhood. Remember his example whenever you stride to war in this armour, that you too may one day carve your way into legend with strength of arms and strength of loyalty.*
>
> *attr: Hang Ying Wa, Guan Yu instructor.*

IAIDO
Ling Kao Strain or Trained Under a Shi Yukiro Master
Reflexes 9
Close Combat 9

This represents the fast draw and instant use of swords. Either for self defence or as a pre-emptive strike. This training only applies to swords of longsword / katana length. Not to enormous two handed swords or short swords.

Offense
When the first round of a combat scene is announced, instead of rolling initiative, the Iaido practitioner gets a single free attack before combat officially begins. Opponents gain no Defence against this attack. Once this has been completed combat begins and the practitioner must roll his initiative as normal.

Defence
If the practitioner is surprise attacked in close combat there is a chance he can draw his sword with incredible speed and thus retain his defence.

He must roll 'Reflexes + Close Combat' with a penalty equal to the attackers XS on his attack roll.

For example, the attacker sneaks up and tries to assassinate the Ling Kao. He passes his roll by 4. The Iaido practitioner must pass a 'Reflexes + Close Combat' roll at -4 to block the assassination attempt. Combat then resumes as normal.

Looking Good
After using Iaido against an NPC without the Iaido Trainining you may make a 'Presence + Looking Good' roll. If you pass the opponent is so intimidated that he receives a -1 penalty to all rolls until the end of the scene

IAIDO HAKANAI
Ling Kao Strain or Trained Under a Shi Yukiro Master
Iaido Training
Looking Good 5

This training builds on the basic Iaido training to allow the practitioner to draw the sword, cut the target, clean the blade and replace the sword in a single smooth action. This training functions in the same way as Iaido (above) with the exception of the Looking Good aspect which is boosted.

Offense
When the first round of a combat scene is announced instead of rolling initiative, the Iaido practitioner gets a single free attack before combat officially begins. Opponents without Iaido gain no Defence against this attack. Once this has been completed combat begins and the practitioner must roll his initiative as normal.

Defence
If the practitioner is surprise attacked in close combat there is a chance he can draw his sword with incredible speed and thus retain his defence.

He must roll 'Reflexes + Close Combat' with a penalty equal to the attacker's XS on his attack roll.

Looking Good

After using Iaido Hakanai against an NPC without the Iaido Hakanai Training you may make a 'Presence + Looking Good' roll. Note your XS and consult the table below.

IAIDO HAKANAI

Pass	Intimidation Level
0-4	The opponent receives a -2 penalty to all rolls until the end of the scene.
5-6	The opponent receives a -4 penalty to all rolls until the end of the scene
7+	The opponent runs from combat unless there is a critical reason for him to stay. If he stays he receives -6 to all rolls until the end of the scene.

Note than any character with conviction can spend 1 conviction point to ignore these effects for a scene.

Ai-Jinn Legacy Operative

Ghosting silently amidst the network of bulky iron girders that reared above the conference chamber, Agent Marcel 'Shiv' de Cour found himself at last within sight of his target. Just metres away, back turned and all attention fixed on the room below, stood Agent Maowei Tang, aka Ka Cha Xiansheng – 'Mr. Click'. A simple bodyguard, but responsible for more confirmed kills than any other Ai-Jinn operative in recorded history; Tang's reputation alone now served to dissuade most would-be assassins from attacks on his wards.

But de Cour was here not for Tang's charge, a petty extortionist occasionally adding his tremulous, wheedling tones to the babble of Mandarin below. De Cour had been sent for the specific purpose of eliminating Tang himself, mainly as a message to the Ai-Jinn that EI's cadre of Assisted Retirement Executives – assassins being a rather passé term – simply could not be intimidated, and most certainly not by a grubby little bodyguard.

So de Cour, with his customary attention to detail, had spent six months studying the dreadful little man. He knew that Tang eschewed armour, preferring cheap and tasteless fabrics; knew that Tang refused to use any weapon apart from his infamous sword, which currently hung at Tang's side with his right hand resting lightly on the grip; knew that Tang appeared to subsist on the kind of rudimentary diet that he, de Cour, would only lower himself to even consider were starvation the only other option. The only thing de Cour had not been able to ascertain in six months of painstaking research, to his slight irritation, was exactly why Tang had acquired the ridiculous nickname of Mr. Click.

Well, reflected de Cour, it hardly mattered anymore. Soundlessly closing the distance to within two feet of the little man's back, he drew back his left hand; the slim dagger it held was tipped with an elaborate, rapid, and very expensive poison. His lip curled in a sneer.

Out of nowhere erupted a sudden and very brief confusion of silent movement that de Cour, somehow, couldn't quite follow. He blinked, and saw that Tang remained in his original position: his back still turned, all his attention still fixed on the argument going on below. Tang's right hand, though, appeared to have shifted slightly and was now easing his sword back into its sheath, from which it unaccountably seemed to have emerged by a few inches. As the weapon slid home, it made a quiet but very distinctive sound –

– click –

– and then, as de Cour glanced down and saw his insides tumbling out in a scarlet jumble from the cut that ran from his shoulder to his hip, as the taste of blood drowned his next breath, as the world began to fade around him, then he finally understood.

KNIFE MAN / BUTCHER
Attitude 5
Close Combat 7
Reflexes 8
Twist the Knife (Machines of War)
Mastered Weapon (Knife)

Some would maintain there is no such thing as a good knife fighter; if you're that good it's more of an assassination than a fight. However, in this day of augmentation, your traditional killing strike is not always so effective.

This training represents your skill in fast, aggressive knife work. A significant part of these attacks is in the mind-state. The close up, visceral slashing and stabbing requires a certain disposition to pull off effectively.

System
When using a single knife as your attacking weapon you automatically win initiative and your first attack each round deals double total damage.

MARTIAL APTITUDE
Close Combat 9

You are highly skilled at picking up new martial skills. Any Combat Training with Close Combat applications can be purchased for only 8XP instead of 10. If you are going to 'Crash Course' a Close Combat training as on page xx, you pay 4XP instead of 5.

The GM may need to arbitrate which trainings have geniuine close combat applications.

MOTORBIKE AND SWORD COMBAT
Combat Pilot or Combat Driver depending on vehicle used.
Mastered Weapon (Relevant Sword)

In true *bosozoku* style you have mastered using your sword from the back of a motorcycle (or jet bike / anti-grav bike). Any attacks made with a sword whilst on the back of a moving motorbike have your Drive score added to the damage (or Pilot on jet / anti-grav bikes).

Note; this stacks with damage from speed detailed on page 149 of the Core Rules.

At the GM's discretion other weapons could be used such as axes, kama, clubs or flails.

STRIKE OF THE COBRA
Ling Kao Strain
Close Combat 10
Medicine 7

The Ling Kao can make a single unarmed strike against a target with a natural cardio vascular and nervous system. The attack is made at -4 and any Defence must also be taken into account. If it hits, the target is instantly reduced to 0HP. This attack has a rate of 1. Agents, Malenbrach, most Cultists etc. are all immune to this kind of strike.

TRIAD BLADE / JACK OF ALL BLADES
Close Combat 7
Mastered Weapon - Knife

In keeping with the code of the Triads you have ensured you are adept with a range of light bladed weapons so that you need never be far away from a suitable weapon. You can treat any small item which possesses a blade-like quality as though it were a knife.

In normal circumstances you can therefore always lay your hand on a make-shift knife. Examples include:

Cleavers, broken chair legs, melon knives, pen knives, pocket knives, kitchen knives, apple corers, roofing knives, prison shanks, smashed bottles, potato peelers, cut throat razors, scissors, craft knives, box knives, stilettos, punch daggers, shards of metal, sharpened credit chips, sharp sticks, sharpened pencils, trazors (toothbrush / razor), etc.

This means if you have any trainings which pertain to knives you may use these trainings with any improvised blade without any penalties. Example trainings include:

'Mastered Weapon – Knife'
'Dual Weapon Use – Knives'
'Knife Man'

Triad Blade is the term used when this training is applied to Ai-Jinn characters. Outside the Ai-Jinn it is Jack of All Blades.

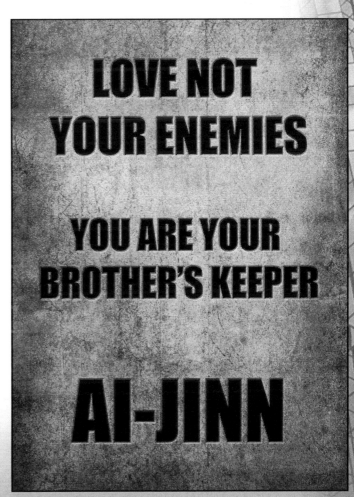

LOVE NOT YOUR ENEMIES

YOU ARE YOUR BROTHER'S KEEPER

AI-JINN

NON COMBAT TRAININGS

AI-JINN CULTURE
Arts & Culture 3

The Ai-Jinn have a rich culture which takes many influences from ancient Eastern mythology and lore, particularly that of Chinese origin. This training represents your familiarity with these ways and how they relate to the modern corporate machine.

This includes such things as how to correctly address VIPs of varying status, dining protocols and gift etiquette. It also grants knowledge of many old myths and legends which are important to the principles of the Ai-Jinn.

> -"So you've met him before eh? This 'Purple Cloud' guy. What's he like? I gotta say, he sounds like a shirtlifter."
>
> -"Well it's funny you should say that, I thought the same thing. And when I first saw him I nearly pissed myself. He was wearing some ancient pink gown with flowers on it, had a beard down to his nuts and eyebrows like a schnauzer."
>
> -"So what does he do exactly?"
>
> -"Well seems he's some kind of uber-telepath, saw me smirk and threw me across the room like a rag doll. Said I was unworthy to attend and had the manners of a pig.
> I wasn't hurt or anything but I missed the meet and failed the mission. So this time...we don't fuckin' laugh!"
>
> The last words of Agent Chris Banks (E.I.) to Agent Paul Harris (E.I.)
>
> Both lost at the notorious E.I. / Ai-Jinn Border Talks at the Khan Spire.

CONVICTION OF ONE
Ai-Jinn Agent

This Training has no effect unless everyone in the division purchases it. You cannot have 3 out of the 4 members using it. It represents the divisions members' steadfast trust in one another. If one member decides not to be a part then it shows the division are not really that well bonded.

Effect
The Division has a floating pool of conviction from which any Agent can draw points. The pool is replenished when the division succeeds as a whole entity. For example, at the end of a heated gun battle where Agents have aided each other and everyone has played an important part, the GM could replenish the pool by 1 or 2 points. At the end of a completed mission the pool may gain 3 or 4 points. The pool has a maximum number of points equal to the number of active division members.

Any member of the division may draw conviction from the pool at any time though you still cannot spend two conviction points in one round.

If a new member joins the Division he will need to invest 10XP into the Training. Until he has done so the floating pool cannot be used by anyone.

DYNASTY KNOWLEDGE
Arts and Culture 4

You are aware of the existence of the Metahuman Dynasties and know about their genegineered physiologies. You can make an 'Intelligence + Arts and Culture' check to know various details about the dynasties. The GM should apply a modifier based on the obscurity of the information.

Example Modifiers

Where is a family located?	+2
How many members in a family?	+0
What are their goals / modifications?	-1
What dark deeds have they done recently?	-2
Recognising members faces / names.	-4

JOINT DISLOCATION
Trained under a Shi Yukiro or Ling Kao Master (or Tao Strain)
Agility 8

By learning to dislocate joints the Agent can slip free from any wrestle during his turn. This takes a full action but ends the wrestle immediately. In addition you gain +4 to perform feats such as squeezing through narrow gaps, escaping restraints, or avoiding having your arm broken.

KINETIC FIELD REPAIR
Survival Training
Jury-Rigging Training
Relevant Firearms Skill at 3+
Mechtronics 2

When in the field you can repair any kinetic firearms which you are skilled in the use of. (Relevant Skill must be 3+.) You don't need tools or spares, you can just use anything to hand to get the weapon functioning. This is commonly used by Ai-Jinn Tigers (page 34) who often need to spend weeks at a time in the jungles salvaging broken weaponry.
System: Roll 'Intelligence + Mechtronics' and note your XS.

You can automatically repair a weapon and get it working in one hour. The weapon is reduced to a condition level equal to your XS. If your XS was equal or greater than its existing condition, it does not decrease.

If you fail the weapon works for the next scene and is then broken beyond any repair.

A weapon cannot be reduced below condition 1, however, if you roll a double while using a condition 1 weapon it dies irrecoverabley and cannot be fixed. It is considered important parts have snapped, been lost or just exploded.

For example, Agent Pak finds an old rifle (condition 6) in a river bed. He spends one hour and passes his 'Intelligence + Mechtronics' roll by 4. The weapon is thus reduced to condition 4.

If he had passed by 6 or more the weapon would not reduce in condition at all.

MISSION OFFICER
Corp. Knowledge 6
Intelligence 6
Rank 4

You have taken and passed the Mission Officer's Exam. You can now act in the capacity of a Mission Officer. Whenever you oversee a mission you are paid an additional 500¢ per level of your Rank with the possibility of a bonus if all goes well. If it goes badly you are held partially responsible. It is possible to act as a Mission Officer while in the field and receive transmissions from your acting Division.

PICK POCKET
Crime 4
Agility 6

You are skilled at relieving a mark of small items of property with skilful sleight of hand. You must observe the mark for at least one round (3 seconds) before making a move.

Roll 'Agility + Crime' with a penalty equal to the mark's Crime score.
The GM should feel free to add other modifiers if appropriate.

Circumstance	Modifier
Mark is drunk or very distracted	+4
Crowded, bustling area such as subway car	+2
Mark is wary of pickpockets	-2
Item is large or well secured	
such as a neck tie or handbag	-4

Success indicates you have taken the item from the mark without alerting them.

Failure means you have the item but have been spotted by the mark.
Obviously most targets have little or no knowledge of crime and so taking a wallet from a businessman in a crowded street is fairly easy. Lifting a weapon from a UIG officer at a guard post would be another story.

REDMAN
Hacking Training
Computers and A.I. 9
Corp Knowledge 5
Medicine 2

You know how to operate as a Redman and can program illegal licenses, download them into chips and install them into clients. This work is highly illegal and punishable by a standard removal of 50 rank points + 10 for each provable offense. More information on this can be found on page 21.

You will normally need redman software, redman chips, a computer and hypodermic gun to run your business.

System
Roll Intelligence + Computers & A.I. with a penalty equal to the level of the license to be created. Success means you create the chip and can inject it without a problem. Multiple licenses require multiple rolls.

SUBCONSCIOUS COERCION
Hien Strain
Presence 9
Psychology 10

By engaging someone in a seemingly unrelated conversation you can subtly implant minor suggestions in their subconscious, biasing them to a particular course of action.

After spending a few minutes speaking with the target of this training, you may make a 'Presence + Psychology' roll opposed by your targets 'Perception + Intelligence'

If you are successful then they must make a second 'Perception + Intelligence' roll with a penalty equal to your XS the next time a situation relevant to the suggestion arises or carry out the suggested course of action.

Suggestions made must be fairly minor, 'accidentally' leaving a door unlocked or absent-mindedly speaking a password aloud next time they type it are okay, shooting someone or jumping out a window are not. In general, a suggestion can be anything that can be accomplished in a free action or through simple inaction.

TELEPATHIC MIGHT
Comoros Agent, Order of the True Faith or Ang Fen Strain

Once per day the telepath can spend a conviction point and double his score in a single telepathic power. The costs for activating the power are also doubled. Ang Fen do not have to spend a conviction point to use this power but they can still only do it once per day.

For example, your Assault score is 7, once a day you can double this to deal 14D6 at a range of 140 metres. It would cost 14 TE points to activate.

THERE IS ONLY AI-JINN
Ai-Jinn Agent

This training represents your total dedication to the Ai-Jinn and your deep-set belief that what they stand for is undeniably right. Although this can be taken at character creation the GM should feel free to temporarily remove the training if there are signs your loyalty is wavering. The training has the following effects.

Loyalty Warning
If you are about to perform an action that will annoy your Ai-Jinn superiors the GM should inform you.

Betrayal Resistance
If you are ever forced to betray the Ai-Jinn in any way you receive a +4 / 20% bonus to resist. This could be a roll to resist torture or a penalty to a psychogenic's roll. The GM should adjudicate this bonus.

Detect Sedition
You are adept at spotting disloyalty in others. If you spend five minutes chatting with an individual who is supposed to be loyal to the Ai-Jinn you can make a 'Presence + Psychology' roll to determine whether the seeds of betrayal are taking root in the

individual. The results are not 100% certain but will give a good indication.

If the individual is actually trying to fool you and pretending to be loyal when they are not, they can roll 'Presence + Lying & Acting', if they gain more XS than you the results of your chat are inconclusive. You gain +4 if you have the Interrogation training.

Staunch Agent

Your allies, subordinates and superiors respect your steadfast loyalty to the corporation. You are not seen as a snivelling toady, rather a solid and dependable member of the corporation who can be trusted with delicate tasks and sensitive information.

THOUGHT RESONANCE

Must be Hien Strain
Presence 10
Psychology 10

Some rare Hien are able to hone their natural abilities to perform true feats of mind reading by picking up 'neural resonance images' from those they interact with, an undeniably psychogenic ability that would be grounds for instant execution if discovered.

However, a Hien is not simply able to read thoughts from anyone, they must first create a psychic 'back door' by getting the target of their ability to give some gesture of trust. What this is can vary, for example, getting the target to accept an item of food - even just a stick of gum or a candy - or confide a fact about themselves such as their date of birth or favourite colour.

If the criteria can be met the Hien need only expend a conviction point in order to read a specific neural resonance image, which should be phrased as a question such as "what is your password?"

or "did you meet Tex Calahan last night?". If the person does not know what they are attempting to read then the conviction is wasted.

TOSS THE PLACE

Crime 2
Perception 4

You are skilled at rifling through an area to find items of interest. For example, turning over an office for incriminating evidence or searching a dwelling to find where the resident hides their car keys and savings.

No roll is needed if you possess this training; you will succeed. The only issue is time so roll 'Perception + Observation'. Failure means the search takes 10 minutes.

Success indicates you have been speedy and the search takes (5-XS minutes) with a minimum of 30 seconds.

Example: you pass your roll by 3, the search therefore takes 2 minutes.

WHEELMAN / GETAWAY DRIVER

Drive 7

You are a legend behind the wheel and are no stranger to driving backwards at 60mph, crashing through market stalls and jumping over moving bridges. When evading or pursuing in a land vehicle you gain a temporary conviction point which lasts one scene and may only be spent on rolls related to driving.

For example, you can spend the point to help bank the car onto two wheels and squeeze through a tight alleyway. You could not use it to gain +4 to fire a pistol out of the window.

LICENSES

REDUCING THE DOWNTIME ON LICENSE APPLICATIONS

Have you ever wanted a license but just can't get the time off? To remedy this situation the UIG have recently granted access to their state-of-the-art neural patterner in Stockholm which enables a subject's brain to be programmed with the necessary information at a faster rate than they could normally learn it.

Access to the Neural Patterner is in high demand so anyone with a poor relationship with the UIG had better hope they are feeling generous.

System: Normally a level 5 license requires 5 weeks of downtime to acquire. For each week of downtime you want to skip you must pay 1000¢ x License Level. You cannot reduce the time to less than one week so using this system on a level 1 license is pointless.

For example, if you want to reduce the downtime on a 5 point license as much as possible you could knock 4 weeks off by paying 5000¢ per week. That's a total of 20,000¢ and 1 week in the patterner. You also need to pay the standard fee on top (500¢ per level).

The total cost for learning a level 5 license in this way would be 22,500¢ and 1 week of downtime.

ASO CHIP LICENSE (AUTHORISED SCAN ONLY) (5)
Rank 3

The user is fitted by the UIG with a variant on the standard ID Chip. This new chip is known as an ASO Chip and cannot be scanned without the owner's permission, which is granted via a neural pulse which places the chip into a readable mode for 3 seconds.

Ai-Jinn Agents may take this modification but it only affects the primary ID chip. Their alternate ID cannot be upgraded to be an ASO Chip.

Cost: The upgrade costs 4000¢ and must be performed at a UIG Clinic (located in most cities and spires).

The UIG are free to decline this license to anybody they feel may be intending to abuse it.

Unauthorised scans will detect the presence of a legal chip, but none of the information on it.

RESPONSE DRIVER (I)
Drive 8
Law Enforcement License (All Agents already have this.)

You are licensed to utilise flashing emergency lights on any vehicles you drive when responding to emergency situations. Most Marshals, Rangers and Agents with this license carry a small, powered, portable unit (see page 58) which they can simply attach to the roof of their vehicle when needed. It emits a 130db siren and utilises flashing strobes, typically in blue.

Under normal circumstances traffic will part for the responding vehicle dramatically reducing travel times.

System
Although some GM discretion is required you can generally gain a +4 modifier to drive rolls when pursuing if you use the sirens and lights. The GM may award you a bonus to evade as well but you will typically make life easier for your pursuer too.

Note: UIG squad and patrol cars all have sirens and lights equipped. All UIG officers automatically gain this license for free.

CYBERUN APPROPRIATION LICENSE (4)
Cyberlin Pilot Training
Public Appropriation License
Rank 3

You are licensed to commandeer a cyberlin in order to enforce the law. Abuse of this license is met with extremely harsh punishments; typically removal of all cyberlin related licenses and the loss of 20 rank points. This is not to mention any punishments that may arise from the havoc you cause while rampaging around in the metal monster.

ILLEGAL LICENSES

License information is held in the primary UIG datavaults. When an ID chip is scanned the chip initiates a microscopic subspace rift, pulls the data from the vault and displays it on the chip scanner. This process is incredibly secure and up until recently only the Ai-Jinn have managed to find a way to interfere with this process and force the scanners to display erroneous information. This forms the foundation of the second identity held by all Ai-Jinn Agents. (More information on this can be found in the Eastern Bank.)

More recently however other wily individuals have moved into creating illegal licenses. The process does not use the same high end subspace routing that the identities use and instead involves inserting a tiny chip under the ID chip which creates an extremely convincing augmentation to the genuine UIG scan.

The chip is extremely limited but can essentially fool the scanner into finding a few additional pieces of information on the subject in the form of licenses. The chip is covered in crystal weave making it undetectable by scanners and is so small a surgical search would only stand a 5% chance to find the device.

The main drawback to this method is that the information is not as foolproof as that carried by an alternate ID and therefore every time you are scanned there is a chance your deception will be discovered. On the plus side, anyone with criminal contacts can try to get themselves an illegal license.

TIME NEEDED

The process requires no downtime but you will need to spend time setting up the meeting and getting the chip injected. The GM should rule on this but a day should normally be sufficient.

THE PROCESS

Once you have a meeting set up you will need to choose the license you want. The quality of the contact can influence the level of the license you can get but this is up to the GM. Payment is made and the vendor, commonly known as a Redman (due to his cutting through the red tape) will use a computer to create a customised license for you. This information is downloaded onto a redman chip which is then placed into a hypodermic gun and injected into the target just under the ID chip. Up to 10 licenses can be installed on a single chip.

The target is scanned a few times to check the license is working and the job is finished.

If you are having a second lot of illegal licenses installed at a later date another chip is injected. It makes no real difference if you have them one at a time or on multiple occasions. You cannot edit the existing chip once it is installed, its easier just to intall another.

ILLEGAL LICENSE COSTS

Firstly you need to have a link to the criminal world. The quality of this link can affect the price.

Price

Underground Operations Training	x1
Contact (Criminal*) at 6-10	x1
Contact (Criminal*) at 1-5	x1.5
A friend has the contacts	x2
No link, just asking around etc.	x3

*This could be contacts with a gang, organised crime unit, hit man etc. Any contact which is essentially criminal in nature.

Payment is almost always upfront unless you are trusted by the contact.

There is generally a 1000¢ handling fee which is in addition to the cost below.

Cost = Level of License^2 x 500¢

Example: you want a level 3 license and have the Underground Operations training.

This will cost (3x3) x 500 = 4500¢.
Add to this the one thousand credit handling fee for a total of 5500¢.

If you are having multiple illegal licenses you only pay one handling fee.

GETTING CAUGHT

The production of illegal licenses is an extremely serious crime and the punishment for having them is severe. As regards getting caught, the less illegal licenses you have the better. Because the UIG A.I. must check billions of license scans every day it 'skims' most of them and doesn't go into much detail. However, some situations are set to trigger a more in-depth scan.

The most common of these are an excessive number of licenses for a particular type of person. For example, a high ranking agent would be expected to have several whereas a spurky vendor might only have one or two. Opposite are listed the basic chances of getting caught with illegal licenses.

You should add up all the relevant percentages and write the on your character sheet. Every time you are scanned the GM should roll a D100. If he gets equal or lower than the stated percentage the person scanning the chip is aware of the fake.

Don't bother to roll for automated scanners on spire doors or in nightclubs etc. They only perform superficial ID checks. Automated UIG scanners such as those on customs checkpoints or contraband checkers may require a roll.

Always a chance

> Note that the GM can use this system to add great tension to a situation. Even if he has decided the scanner is not doing an in-depth scan, he can ask everyone their 'illegal license %' and roll some dice just to get everyone worried.

A roll of 01% when checking should always result in the target getting caught. Even if his percentage chance is -5% there should always be a small chance that the UIG A.I.s have stumbled upon the anomaly.

Example
A citizen of rank 1 has a single illegal level 2 license.

Rank 1	*-5%*
One illegal license	*5%*
Level 2 license	*5%*

Each time he is scanned there will be a 5% chance of getting caught.

CITIZENS / OUTCASTS

Number of illegal licenses	Chance of getting caught
1	5%
2	10%
3	25%
4	50%
5	75%
6+	90%

Level of Illegal License	Chance of Getting Caught
1	0%
2	5%
3	10%
4	15%
5+	20%

Use the value of the highest level illegal license you have.

Rank	Chance of Getting Caught
0	0%
1	-5%
2	-10%
3	-15%
4	-20%
5	-25%
6	-30%
7	-35%
8	-40%
9	-45%
10	-50%

AGENTS / UIG

Number of illegal licenses	Chance of getting caught
1	0%
2	5%
3	10%
4	25%
5	50%
6	75%
7+	90%

Level of Illegal License	Chance of Getting Caught
1	-5%
2	0%
3	0%
4	5%
5	10%
6	15%
7+	20%

Use the value of the highest level illegal license you have.

Rank	Chance of Getting Caught
0	-5%
1	-10%
2	-15%
3	-20%
4	-25%
5	-30%
6	-35%
7	-40%
8	-45%
9	-50%
10	-55%

MISCELLANEOUS FACTORS

Within a Capital Code Zone such as the Eastern Bank	+10%
UIG are on high alert	+5%
License is totally inappropriate	+5%
Ai-Jinn Agent	-10%
The person scanning is highly distracted	-5% to -10%
Archon or Powerful A.I. connected to the scanner	+50%

PUNISHMENT

For acting as a Redman you can expect a removal of 50 rank points if you get caught. You will also suffer a further loss of 10 rank points per provable redman offence. For holding illegal licenses you can expect the removal of 10 rank points per level of the illegal licence held. More if you have been using it inappropriately.

THE AI-JINN AND ILLEGAL LICENSES

Illegal licenses do not use subspace technology and as such the Ai-Jinn do not have a monopoly on this field. However they are extremely well connected in the criminal world and so their handling fee for obtaining illegal licenses is waived.

In addition they have access to a much better choice of redmen so can choose from the best. For this reason they start with an innate -10% on their chance to get caught. This means if the current stack of illegal licenses would lead to a 25% chance of getting caught, an Ai-Jinn agent would only consider this to be a 15% chance.

AI-JINN RANK BONUSES

Page 81 of the core rules contains information on bonuses you gain as you increase in rank. These are generic for all corporations and quite basic. The ones listed are more detailed and specific to the Ai-Jinn. These bonuses replace those in the core rules, they do not supplement them.

COMPULSORY UNARMED TRAINING

Although the Ai-Jinn Corporation holds great stock in heavy ordnance they believe that an Agent himself is the most powerful weapon available. There are sadly very few everyday problems which can be solved with a cyberlin or heavy p-tank. In line with this philosophy the Ai-Jinn insist that their Agents are competent combatants, even when completely unarmed.

Over the last 100 years since the inauguration of Dragon's Head Kuan-Yin Liang a policy of unarmed martial proficiency has been implemented. This involves each Agent having to spend a certain amount of their time practicing unarmed martial arts such as boxing, muay thai, kung fu, wrestling, wushu etc.

The hours demanded are not high and don't eat into an Agent's downtime. Each Spire has a wealth of instructors on hand whose services are available freely for all Agents.

System
All Ai-Jinn Agents reduce the cost to increase their Close Combat skill by 1 point (to a minimum of 1). If an Ai-Jinn Agent chooses to spend a downtime action practicing his martial arts he gains 3xp to spend on the Close Combat skill instead of 2 as described on page 82 of the Core Rules.

NOTES

Rank Loss Reductions
The Ai-Jinn defend their Agents fiercely against UIG prosecutors. This results in reduced sentences for Ai-Jinn Agents.

At ranks 2, 4, 6 and 8 you gain reduced rank point loss. You only get the newest reduction, not all of them added together.

For example, at rank 4 your loss is reduced by D6, not D4+D6.

Assets
Ai-Jinn Agents are awarded assets such as vehicles, clothes etc. If you destroy the asset it will be replaced for free next time you increase in rank.

NEW RANK BONUSES
The table on the opposite page details the new rank bonuses awarded to Ai-Jinn Agents. Note that as you increase in rank any bonuses maked with an * will be lost when a better version becomes available.

For example, your small apartment at rank one will be replaced by a moderatly sized apartment at rank 3.

Your D6 rank point loss at rank 4 is replaced with a 2D4 rank point loss at rank 6.

ROLEPLAYING RANK BONUSES
Although there is no requirement to role-play the acquisition of assets the GM may deem that it may occasionally be appropriate.

For example, at Rank 3, upon acquiring 3 points of contacts with a criminal group, the Mission Officer could introduce you to Mr. Kang who is to be your contact.

Alternatively the players could be given contacts in a criminal group they have already had dealings with.

DIVISION LEADER

The division leader gains more than the other members of the division. This is for two reasons, the first is based on the extra responsibility he carries and is by way of a reward. The second is to facilitate his work and takes the form of assets which are to be used by the division as a whole.

As the division leader increases in rank he augments his existing assets.

The division leader gains the benefits from the list on page 23 and the one on page 23 unless he is effectively getting an upgrade.

Examples

If he is given a larger office it effectively replaces the smaller one.

If he gains a heli-pad that will be in addition to the parking space.

At rank 1 the division leader gains a medium apartment instead of a small one.

In essence the Agent will always get the best deal.

RANK BONUS

1   *Small apartment
    *Small spire parking space
    Standard issue business suit
    Compulsory Unarmed Training (see opposite)
    Guan Yu Use Training for free

2   Sedan Car - Bronze Stallion - (see page xx)
    VIP pass to all Ai-Jinn owned clubs
    *All rank point losses are automatically reduced by D4
    1 free frag grenade each mission
    Small workshop or lab.

3   Motorbike (dirt bike or sports bike)
    *Moderately sized apartment
    Spacious covere garage in the spire.
    VIP pass to all Ai-Jinn owned casinos and house credit to 10,000¢
    3 points of contacts in a criminal group such as the Triads
    Heavy grade weapons locker installed into apartment

4   Access to mid range VIP lounges
    *All rank point losses are automatically reduced by D6
    Suit of heavy combat armour
    1 heavy explosive charge each mission
    Another 3 points of contacts in a criminal group such as the Yakuza
    Large workshop or lab

    Choose from the following trainings for free. You must have the prerequisities though.

Cyberlin Pilot (Machines of War)	Clanger
Combat Driver	Motorbike and Sword Combat
Combat Pilot	Dynasty Knowledge
Ai-Jinn Heavy Vehicle Pilot (Machines of War)	Ai-Jinn Culture
Ai-Jinn Mechanic (Machines of War)	There Is Only Ai-Jinn
Mastered Weapon (Heavy Firearms)	Triad Blade

5   Ownership of a level 5** local business with criminal ties
    Access to all but top level Corporate Lounges
    *Large spire apartment
    Suit of Guan Yu Armour (see page 52)
    The Agents gain the services of a Rank 1 (green) Division who they can use to do trivial work such as collecting cash, stealing tech or performing recon. An Agent with the Mission Officer training (page 25) is elected to be their Mission Officer and is responsible for assigning missions to them and ultimately for their success or failure.

6   *All rank point losses are reduced by 2D4
    Free Port Splitter for your Guan Yu Armour.
    Another 3 points of contacts with a criminal boss such as Tong leader
    Third identity on your ID chip if required

7   Access to all Ai-Jinn VIP Lounges
    Large luxury spire apartment

8   All Rank Points losses are automatically reduced by 2D6

Rank 9 and 10 do not follow the same system and essentially take whatever they need.
*See New Rank Bonuses section opposite.
** A Level 5 business is described in the Eastern Bank, if you don't have it then the business would be like a chop-shop / small brothel.

I direct your attention to the footage on screen 6; this has been compiled from various cameras, droids and sat images to give a comprehensive picture of the incident.

At 23 hundred hours, the Ai-Jinn division known to us as Red Sky arrive at our supposedly secret Capetown reverse engineering lab. You'll notice the ease with which they gain entry suggesting they had inside help; itself a deeply concerning revelation. Our early defence droids may as well not have been there, such was the efficiency of their EMP gunner. As you can see they proceed with infuriating calm towards the labs where we have been studying the subspace device, again alluding to some kind of insider assistance.

Now, at this point we do have the upper hand, unknown to them an Essence division led by a psychogenic, are assisting with the analysis of the device and are in fact waiting in the lab. You'll see that with relative ease, the Ai-Jinn intrusion specialist bypasses the door lock and they enter the lab.

The ensuing scuffle is quite something, with surprise on our side you can see it quickly goes our way. The psychogenic seems to be having difficulty influencing their minds but as we know, the Ai-Jinn training is extremely effective in strengthening their resolve.
I'll just pause the video at this point and explain what's about to happen. You'll see these four Ai-Jinn Agents here are going to leave cover and charge, essentially sacrificing themselves while the woman at the back here, activates an invisibility field, takes the device and flees. I'll resume the video.

And now the big surprise, you'll see the larger man on the left muttering under his breath; our speech analysts tell us it's some kind of Ai-Jinn death chant, a vestige of another time. And now we are forced to switch to the satellite feed as the explosion took out all nearby cameras.

The woman, who we have subsequently identified as Sun Li Kang, the division's leader, having passed the device onto a contact waiting outside, now re-enters the burning building. We can only guess at what went on inside but one by one she carries out her dying division and applies medical aid; from what we can see only one of them died, though all were mangled, missing limbs and unconscious. Our own Agents were found dead, their heads cut from their bodies.

What I find most concerning about this event is the willingness of the Ai-Jinn operatives to sacrifice themselves at the behest of their leader. By looking at the damage done to the room the chance of death was high and almost certain for the individual carrying the bomb. That a rabble of criminal dogs should show such a profound level of trust, loyalty and obedience is far more concerning than any technological advance they may have acquired from the wretched Archons.

DIVISION LEADER BONUSES

RANK	BONUS
1	Medium apartment in the spire, probably with a window.
	Small lounge / office where the division can meet and discuss mission plans.
	Large parking space. This will be big enough to accommodate a lorry or tank.
	Workstation computer connected to the WDN. This should NOT be used for hacking as it is located in the division's office.
	Tai-Lan Pinko Car
2	Three large parking spaces.
	Large office and a lounge.
	Snack machine and TV in the lounge.
	Workshop or Lab
	Large off-road vehicle - Tai-Lan Bison (see page 87)
3	Heli-Pad if the division has access to a heli or hovercopter.
	Large van which can seat 6 or accommodate a large load
	Workshop AND Lab
4	Aircraft hanger at the nearest shuttle bay
	Ability to requisition a standard 4 door saloon car from any Ai-Jinn asset currently in possession of one. You cannot take the car from a superior officer unless she agrees.
5	A hovercopter, generally with no offensive capabilities
	Armoured Personnel Carrier
	Mission Officer Training, providing the prerequisites have been met.
6	Access to a shuttle and pilot to chauffer the division around the Earth.
7	Mag Tank (page 91)
8	Battle Class Cyberlin providing someone in the division is licensed and trained to use it.

GREEN DIVISIONS

AT LAST - MY OWN DIVISION!

Rank 1 divisions fresh out of training have a number of nicknames, none of which tend to sit well with new Agents who generally have elevated feelings of self worth and importance. Some common names include:

Greenhorns (Greens), Juniors, Virgins, Recruits, Tryos

The most common term used is Greens and is not considered TOO demeaning. Don't forget to use these terms for new player character divisions just to wind them up a bit.

When a Division Leader reaches Rank 5, if he has been division leader for at least 3 complete missions the prerequisites he automatically acquires the Mission Officer Training; originally appearing in the Eastern Bank on page 11 but reprinted here for convenience.

MISSION OFFICER
Corp. Knowledge 6
Intelligence 6
Rank 4

You have taken and passed the Mission Officer's Exam. You can now act in the capacity of a Mission Officer. Whenever you oversee a mission you are paid an additional 500¢ per level of your Rank with the possibility of a bonus if all goes well. If it goes badly you are held partially responsible. It is possible to act as a Mission Officer while in the field and receive transmissions from your acting Division.

Your Division then gain command of a newly trained Rank 1 Division. If there is more than 1 Agent with the Mission Officer Training you should decide between you who will be the executive Officer for the Rank 1 Division. If you cannot decide the GM should play the part of the Corporation and decide for you.

WHAT DOES THE JUNIOR DIVISION DO?

Anything you want really; the important thing is to put them into the action so they can get some hands-on field experience. The difference between an NPC division and a player division is that the missions of the NPC division can be boring, mundane and fruitless. For example, staking out a club for 10 days and finding nothing of interest would be a tedious mission for player characters but would be a fair use of your NPC division.

Appropriate missions might include:

Collecting resources such as money or equipment
Surveilling areas and collecting intelligence
Acting as backup on aggressive missions
Cleaning up parts of old cities which the player's Division intend to occupy later
Advance scouting in enemy cities
Acting as intermediaries with contacts
Kidnapping civilian-level characters

Inappropriate missions might include:

Raid the UIG weapons testing facility and bring back some prototype tech
Assassinate a guarded VIP, Agent or UIG Officer
Complete a section of a mission allocated to the PC (player character) division
Clean the Agent's weapons (i.e. spend their downtime on belittling tasks)
Infiltrating a Canathikta people-hunting ring
Missions involving entering Relic Cities without Order consent
Testing valuable experimental or illegal tech

CREATING THE DIVISION

When creating your Green Division it is not necessary to detail every skill and stat. Rather you should attempt to describe their area of expertise and general style. There are 3 ways you can create your Green Division.

1. Get each player to design a level one Agent (or more if required)
2. The GM should design the division.
3. Use the Random Agent Generator

1 and 2 are self explanatory, the Random Agent Generator is detailed on the next page. Re-roll any conflicts or rolls for which you do not possess the appropriate books.

You can obviously introduce other factors or fields when you generate the agents. You don't have to adhere rigidly to any one of these systems.

RANDOM AGENT GENERATOR

Gender (D10)
1-5	Male
6-0	Female

Area of Speciality (D20)
1	Heavy Firearms (Nuke)
2	Social Interactions
3	Assassin
4	Mechtrician
5	Psychologist
6	Medic
7	Scientist
8	Robotics / Cybernetics
9	Driver / Wheelman
10	Criminal
11	Gladiator / Weltball
12	Industrial Thief
13	Saboteur
14	Street Specialist
15	Computer Specialist / Hacker
16	Animal / BIO Handler
17	Intrusion Specialist
18	Weapons Expert
19	Businessman / Lawyer
20	Cultural Specialist

Preferred Combat Style (D8)
1	Heavy Firearms
2	Light Firearms
3	Tactical Firearms
4	Telepathics
5	Close Combat
6	Droid
7	Support
8	Toxic

Field of Science (D10)
1	Biology
2	Cybernetics
3	Chemistry
4	Physics / Subspace
5	Xenotech
6	Neurostatics (Machines of War)
7	Artificial Intelligence
8	Computer Science
9	Environmental Science
10	Crime / Forensics

Positive Attitude Traits (D12)
1	Honest
2	Self Reliant
3	Hard Working
4	Clever
5	Witty
6	Empathic
7	Charismatic
8	Positive Mental Attitude
9	Lateral thinker, problem solver
10	Good team skills
11	Generous
12	Brave / Good leadership skills

Negative Attitude Traits (D12)
1	Dishonest
2	Negative attitude / Moans a lot
3	Lazy
4	A bit thick
5	No sense of humour
6	Distant / Removed
7	Irritating personality
8	Greedy
9	Cowardly
10	Poor team skills
11	Shoot first, ask questions later
12	Sexist, womaniser / maneater

REWARDING AND PUNISHING YOUR DIVISION

As an MO it's your job to reward or punish a division under your command. You can select rewards and punishments as stated in the Core Rules such as reduction of privileges or extra cash.

The results of these carrot and stick measures are listed below. Bear in mind if you hand out unjust punishments the green division may go above your head to higher ranking Agents and ask for an appeal of some kind. Too many rewards and the accountants will be asking questions. A good MO should be able to get results by working with his division and setting them appropriate tasks.

Some punishments can be found on page 83 of the Core Rules.

Mild
Reward	50% extra pay / free clothing / weapon upgrade
Punishment	30% pay reduction / 'Under the Eye' / temporary license restriction
Result	20% chance of gaining a Competence level

Moderate
Reward	100% extra pay / free equipment / lifestyle bonus
Punishment	60% pay reduction / lifestyle reduction / 'Stripped' / small rank reduction
Result	50% chance of gaining a Competence level

Strong
Reward	200% extra pay / free vehicle / new accommodation
Punishment	Take all pay for next 3 missions / heavy rank reduction / license removal
Result	90% chance of gaining a Competence level.

GREEN DIVISION SUCCESS

The GM can simply decide on the success or failure of any mission given to the greens but if you want to add an element of the unknown you can use the system outlined below.

GREEN DIVISION SUCCESS

Roll a D6 and add any modifers.

1   Critical Failure
The mission was an abysmal failure and everything went wrong.

D4 division members died irrecoverably and those remaining are in either enemy or UIG custody (50/50 chance). It will cost the Corporation 60,000¢ to free each UIG imprisoned Agent and the Mission Officer will be docked D6 rank points unless he can justify the catalogue of disasters. The Agents will be replaced but if such an act happens again he may lose his status as Mission Officer. The Corporation may insist the PC Agents recover their captured allies if they are in enemy hands.
There is also a good chance that severe political or diplomatic damage has been done and the Mission Officer will be expected to make a full statement to his superiors as to why such a heinous fuck-up was made.

2   Botched mission
Most aspects of the mission went wrong. D2 Agents died and another D2 are in UIG enemy custody (50/50 chance). The Mission Officer will be docked D4 rank points and the Corporation may insist that the PC division recover any Agents in enemy hands.

There was likely some political and diplomatic fallout which will have to be dealt with.

3   Failed Mission
The mission was a failure. Although no lasting harm has been done the green division will be demoralised and the Mission Officer's superiors will not be pleased. There is a 20% chance that a single division member was caught by the UIG or an enemy.

4-5   Marginal Success
The mission is a success but only just. There is a 10% chance a division member was captured and may need to be recovered.

6-7   Success
The mission went according to plan and everything happened the way it should.

8+   Total Success
The mission went perfectly and additional objectives were completed. The green division gain an extra point of competence. The PC division also gain more than they had asked for be it in terms of items, intelligence, money etc.

MODIFIERS

You should be very strict on these modifiers and not apply them unless directly pertinent. It is thus beneficial to send your Green Division on missions they are suited for.

MODIFIERS FOR SUCCESS

Area of Speciality
+1 for each Agent whose speciality relates directly to the nature of the mission. For example, if the mission is to sabotage a small factory and one of the Agents is a saboteur then you'll gain a +1 bonus.

Attitude
+1 for each Agent whose attitude will be extremely useful in achieving the mission. For example, if you are trying to gather information from the families of a murderer, an Agent with 'Empathy' will be a useful asset.

General
-1 for each Agent whose personality or style may directly conflict with the nature of the mission. For example, you need to attend a diplomatic conference and one of the Agents is a massive nuke who has an innately irritating personality.

GM Discretion
The GM can add other modifiers if she sees fit but they should be used VERY sparingly.

GREEN DIVISION COMPETENCE

PASS - Each time a mission is passed the division gain one level of Competence

FAIL - Each time a mission is failed the division lose one level of Competence

Competence may be used to automatically complete the following tasks with no need for roleplaying.

1. Get a division member out of UIG custody (legally)
2. Prevent a division member dying on a future mission
3. Allow a single re-roll on the 'Green Division Success' table (only once per mission). You must take the new roll.

The total accrued competence is an indicator of how successful a division is and somewhat akin to 'Level' in PC Agents. Although you may spend competence points, you should also keep a running total earned to date.

AI-JINN SECTS

INTRODUCTION TO SECTS

Like all corporations the Ai-Jinn have a number of sub groups (or sects) which perform specific functions. When you join a sect it does not mean your entire division need to be in it. For example, if you are a member of the Kabuki-Mono you may still operate in a division made up of normal Agents.

The GM may require you to come up with a reason that you are not with the rest of your clan but this should be seen as adding character and depth to the Agent, not making weak excuses.

For example, imagine you want to play a member of the Kabuki-Mono, a wild and terrifying sect, the following reasons could all be used to explain your placement into a standard division.

1. The division are considered to be in need of some more spontaneity.

2. The rest of your clan was killed.

3. Your particular skill-set is lacking in the division.

4. Your clan believe you need some 'outside training' to expand your horizons.

5. The division you are joining have need of someone versed in anti-authoritarian activities.

6. The target of your missions is also of interest to your Kabuki-Mono clan.

Sects are designed to add interest and direction to your character. If a sect requires you to behave in a certain way you should be able to use this to enhance your gaming experience rather than detract from it.

LEAVING A SECT

This is really for the GM to rule on. If you have acted against the interests of your sect then you be expelled or worse. The severity of the action will depend on what happens to you. For example:

If you steal from the sect you will most likely be expelled and disgraced.

If you sabotage the sect's actions you will probably be maimed, disgraced, stripped of upgrades and kicked out of the sect and out of the Ai-Jinn.

If you kill another member you will need to explain yourself to the rest of the sect. If they are not convinced that your actions were justified you may find yourself executed.

If you want to voluntarily leave a sect then good luck. Once you join you become privvy to some very sensitive information and are consequently expected to remain loyal until death.

So have fun with the sects. If your group want to all play Kabuki-Mono and run riot around the streets, scaring the crap out of the locals then go for it. If you'd rather add depth to your long-term character by having them apply to be in the Hattamoto-Yakko then give it a go.

And as a final note, if you're the GM don't forget to make some of your NPCs into sect members to make them more memorable and interesting.

ENTERING A SECT

Acquiring entry to a sect is requires no XP or downtime,a though the prerequisites are rather stringent . However, the benefits of being a member of a sect are not something that can be acquired in a vacuum, they are the result of entering into an organisation within an organisation and members may be expected to undertake work on behalf of their sect as well as their corporation.

Though all sects will be loyal to the corporation itself they nonetheless all have external motivations and their own spheres of influence to govern.

Sect members often have access to information that less well connected employees don't, just one of the perks of being a member of an inner circle, this is represented by the following rule;

SECT CONNECTIONS

Members of a sect gain an automatic contact rating within their sect allowing them to acquire internal information relating to activities the group might be involved in. The contact rating starts at 3 and increases or decreases whenever the GM decides that a character's actions have been beneficial or detrimental to the mission of the sect. This is a special contact not available to those outside of the sect and may not be purchased or increased with downtime.

> It's about time law enforcement got as organized as organized crime.
>
> *Rudolph W. Giuliani*

HATTAMOTO-YAKKO

AKA: Hatters, Untouchables, The Serpents Teeth

Prerequisites
Arts & Culture 6, Looking Good 6, Corp. Knowledge 7, Close Combat or Light Firearms 8, Rank 5
Commendation for loyalty from your mission officer, must have never suffered formal reprimand for insubordination.

As personal servants to the CEO of the Ai-Jinn, the Hattamoto-Yakko occupy one of the most prestigious and coveted positions within the entire corporation. Having the ear (and, more importantly, the gratitude) of one of the most powerful people on the planet has its advantages, after all.

The Hattamoto-Yakko command respect. They are selected from among already highly distinguished Agents and represent the ideal of self-sacrificing Ai-Jinn loyalty. The Ai-Jinn looks after its own and loyalty never goes unrewarded. Members of the sect are highly paid and well looked after by the corporation, even to the point of arranging fall-guys and manufacturing alibis when the UIG gets on their back.

A good thing too, considering how the Hattamoto-Yakko are often involved in some of the Ai-Jinn's shadiest business and take their orders directly from the CEO herself, who under no circumstances can be allowed to be implicated.

Missions & Duties
As the eyes, ears and hands of the Ai-Jinn's leader the Hattamoto-Yakko are called in on missions where discretion and absolute, unwavering allegiance are needed. Most often this means transporting sensitive information, bodyguard duty for V.I.Ps or performing the kind of jobs the corporation would rather nobody find out about; assassinations, mass-killings and no-witnesses attacks against UIG assets being prime examples.

Uniform & Equipment
One of the jobs of the Hattamoto-Yakko is to represent their corporation and its ideals well, they are highly paid and are expected to look like it; slovenliness is not tolerated. They are most commonly seen wearing obscenely expensive tailored suits (off-the-rack just won't cut it) in flashy styles and colours, formal enough to do business in but cut so as not to impede their movement when the bullets start flying. Many also sport extensive symbolic tattooing or cybernetic skin modifications modelled after the gang-tats of the various organised crime groups that make up the Ai-Jinn.

Membership Benefits
The Ai-Jinn will throw the full weight of its legal department in your defence, reducing any rank point deductions you suffer to 1/4 (rounded down) of what it should be for your crimes. Being reduced below rank 5 may still lead to you being temporarily discharged from the Hattamoto-Yakko.

Example. You are looking a a loss of 13 points for various crimes. Because you are Hattamoto-Yakko this is reduced to 3.

In addition, you can effectively ignore the universal chain of command when on a mission for the CEO within the Ai-Jinn corporation. This means you could search a Rank 8's house without his permission even if you are only Rank 5.

Finally, your pay-grade and corporate perks are increased as though you were one rank higher than you actually are, to a maximum of 9...for now.

> *The CEO of the Ai-Jinn is a shrewd woman but she's no genius. If we take her out someone will just pop up to replace her. What stops the whole house of cards tumbling down is the Hattamoto-Yakko.*
> *They've acted as the CEO's private go-to guys for hundreds of years and that collective knowledge is still held within the sect. They have a wisdom far in excess of any other group in the Ai-Jinn and have been privy to almost every major corporate operation since its establishment.*
> *If we could take them out it would set the Ai-Jinn back a hundred years.*
>
> *attr: Agt. Daniel Gigerman, E.I. Counter-Corporate Specialist*

KABUKI-MONO

AKA: Kabuki, Crazy Ones
Prerequisites
Street Culture 6, Attitude 7, Close Combat 8, Mastered Weapon (Long Sword or Katana), Perform an initiation task for a Kabuki-Mono clan.

The Kabuki-Mono form the street-level enforcement arm of the Ai-Jinn, ensuring that nobody challenges the corporation's supremacy in the criminal underworld. Their methods are usually deterrent-based; making a single, gruesomely bloody example of those who try to muscle in on Ai-Jinn operations often does more than a dozen relatively clean hits.

Organising themselves into extremely close-knit gangs, which they refer to as 'clans', the Kabuki-Mono represent a living nightmare for the authorities; street toughs with corporate backing. Local security and even the UIG are often rendered impotent by these well-equipped, well-financed and utterly unreasonable hoodlums.

Some of the most sadistic and aggressive Agents find their way into the Kabuki-Mono, random acts of unsolicited violence are their instrument of choice for keeping a neighbourhood under control and so it makes an ideal channel for an Agent that might otherwise prove problematic, as well as teaching them the value of brotherhood.

Missions & Duties
Divisions of Kabuki-Mono Agents are often given long-term mission assignments within individual cities and largely left to their own devices by the Ai-Jinn. As long as they keep the Ai-Jinn's street-level operations running smoothly, and make sure that concerned locals, rival gangs and the authorities are too terrified to try and stop them, the corporation is largely content to just send resources their way and let them get on with it.

Before joining, a potential Kabuki-Mono must perform a mission on behalf of their clan. Often this is done as much as to bloody their hands as it is to test their skills. Some examples include:

1. Kidnapping, torturing and executing a UIG officer who has been

making trouble for the clan, then leaving the body where the UIG will find it.

2. Fighting to the death in an illegal underground competition such as a bare knuckle boxing match or strap-fight against a superior opponent, for exmaple a machina cultist.

3. Joining the clan on an arson-spree, bonus credit is awarded for suggesting interesting or amusing targets.

4. Springing a clan member from prison in a UIG compound and making sure the officers responsible learn the magnitude of their mistake.

5. Killing twenty members of a local gang who have been muscling in on Ai-Jinn territory...in one night.

6. Beating up and terrorising the family of a problematic official, then kidnapping his wife or children if he refuses to back down.

7. Stealing twenty thousand credits, either in slip or equivalent goods, and donating it to the clan.

Uniform & Equipment
Kabuki-Mono members are immediately recognisable by their signature style of dress, favouring bright colours, often in neon shades, and wild hairstyles. But the real uniform of the Kabuki-Mono is the sword, all members are frighteningly competent either with the Chinese *jian* (straight blade) or Japanese *katana* and carry them at all times, the blade being the sect's preferred weapon. Indeed, a common saying among the Kabuki-Mono goes; *"It's just not a Friday night without some arterial spray."*

Membership Benefits
The Kabuki-Mono inspire fear in any sane person, their habit of killing random bystanders for no other reason than their own amusement is well documented and most people who know about them will treat a Kabuki-Mono member much like they would a rabid dog.

Sect members gain a +4 bonus on all Attitude and Psychology rolls related to intimidation. The GM could increase this bonus if the GM decides the targets are familiar with the Kabuki-Mono.

Almost all those who join the Kabuki-Mono are, at least to a degree, psychotic. Those that aren't soon end up that way. Forming close bonds with their similarly deranged clan-mates means that these tendencies often become reinforced, making the Kabuki-Mono into fearless and nihilistic killers.

Sect members are immune to fear effects and gain a +4 bonus to resist coercion, including psychogenic coercion, due to their warped mindstates.

The Kabuki-Mono have strong links to the Yakuza. As a result their sect contact can be used not only with the sect itself but to acquire information and assistance from Yakuza syndicates as well. Halve your contact level when dealing with the Yakuza.

Their attire is marked by a nauseating riot of colour, texture and style; their communications are broken with the shrieking, desperate laughter of the clinically insane; and their kills are made with the unpredictable, savage frenzy of a pack of wild dogs. I have seen groups of these lethally dangerous clowns take down Malenbrach in full Erabite armour, interrupting their hectic, lunatic dances only long enough to drive their blades repeatedly into joints and eyeguards while our officers' weapons do nothing but scorch garish silks.
The idea of a clean kill is utterly foreign to them. If you are called to a crime scene where the Kabuki-Mono have been involved, bring many large guns and heavy reinforcements, in case they have not yet departed; and bring mops and buckets, in case their work is already finished.

attr: UIG Colonel Grant Forterin, address to Eastern Bank recruits

MACHI-YAKKO

AKA: Bakuto, Wiseguys
Attitude 6, Crime 7, Street Culture 8, Underground Status Training*. Infiltrate a spire city or archology within rival corporation territory and operate there for a month.

Featured in The Eastern Bank supplement, replace requirement with both the Underground Operations and Surveillance trainings if book is not available.

Where the Kabuki-Mono are the Ai-Jinn's iron fist, the Machi-Yakko are its silken glove. The Machi-Yakko are the undisputed masters of manoeuvring through the criminal underworld, often for the purpose of finding dissent against the Ai-Jinn and cutting it off at the root.

Experts at infiltration, their preferred tactic is to insinuate themselves into organised crime groups not affiliated with the Ai-Jinn and after a lengthy period of observation decide whether they are worth bringing into the Ai-Jinn fold. Most are deemed too inconsequential to take any action for or against, but for those groups that might prove valuable or dangerous to corporate interests the only options are kill or convert.

Missions & Duties
In addition to their work as underworld secret-police, the Machi-Yakko form the intelligence service of the Ai-Jinn corporation; wherever there is spy-work to be done they are the first called in. Like the Shi Yukiro's Clan Hitori, the Machi-Yakko favour a relatively low-tech approach to subterfuge, relying on personal competence over technological superiority.

Machi-Yakko have self-sufficiency to rival a Comoros survivalist, and any mission that requires Agents to spend protracted amounts of time separated from the support network of the corporation will typically be delegated to the Machi-Yakko.

Uniform & Equipment
The Machi-Yakko implicitly do NOT have a preferred style of dress, they are spies and disguise-artists and have no problem adopting the dress of other groups if it furthers their aims.

If anything could be considered standard it would be casual, moderately stylish civilian gear and nothing corporate-issue anywhere on their person. Most Machi-Yakko ditch their standard Agent equipment the first chance they get and buy everything they need from fences and unlicensed dealers, knowing that even the gun at your hip can be part of your disguise.

Membership Benefits

All sect members will cultivate a web of underworld contacts, either directly or through their sect connections, that ensures they can always find what they need, when they need it. Be it drugs, guns, illegal cyberware or simply information, if someone in the underground has it then a Machi-Yakko can acquire it.

The number of times per session that they may make use of their Underground Operations training is equal to half their Presence score, rather than simply one.

Machi-Yakko receive a free retrofit of their Agent cybernetics to make them undetectable to conventional scanning and physical inspection. Their process socket is made to hide seamlessly and all cybernetic components are sheathed in scan-blocking crystal weave mesh.

A Machi-Yakko's Agent upgrades are undetectable by normal means, this does not apply to any of their other cybernetics, such as cyberlimbs or an alloy skull, but such augmentations are freely available to civilians anyway and so can be easily explained away. They will still have to adopt certain behaviours to pass as a normal human, suffering a grievous flesh wound without even flinching will tend to give the game away.

> It is no secret that organized crime in America takes in over forty billion dollars a year. This is quite a profitable sum, especially when one considers that the Mafia spends very little for office supplies.
>
> Woody Allen

SHANDIAN SHUAI

> 'Computer, load music-file Wagner oh-two, "Ride of the Valkyries". Play it loud.'
>
> - attr. Ai-Jinn Tank Commander Yu Shai Tung, during the third New Korea Pacification.

AKA: Iron Dragons, Storm Commanders
Prerequisites
Rank 2, Drive 6, Assess Tech 6, Heavy Firearms 7, Attitude 8, Command Training, Vehicle License (Military), must have been division leader during at least ten separate combat encounters versus significantly superior forces.

The Ai-Jinn possess vast armoured infantry forces, the largest land-army of all the corporations. At the head of these forces is the Shandian Shuài, the corporation's military command branch. The Shandian Shuài are possibly the most renowned armoured battalion commanders in the world, having earned the fear and respect of the world during the Corporate Wars. Their use of heavy armoured vehicles as moving fortresses made the Ai-Jinn army almost impossible to turn back once it was dug in, thwarting even the attempts of the legendary E.I. air fleet on several occasions.

Missions & Duties
The first duty of the Shandian Shuài is obviously to lead the Ai-Jinn's armies into battle. With the (perhaps temporary) end of open hostilities between the Corporation-states their operations have been somewhat reduced in scope but the Shandian Shuài are still valuable to the Ai-Jinn in dealing with the multitude of small skirmishes that break out from time to time. With groups such as the Cult of Machina becoming ever more sophisticated and well equipped, often to the point of being able to field their own heavy armour and cyberframes, even the UIG can't deny the efficacy, and even the practicality, of a tank-brigade in breaking up terrorist operations.

Uniform & Equipment
The Ai-Jinn military possesses its own uniform, ironically modelled on that of the pre-Corporate Chinese People's Liberation Army. Officers dress in the Ai-Jinn colours of teal and oxide-brown, with all levels of the army possessing notably more and better armour than that which is provided to troops from other corporation-states.

In the field, the Shandian Shuài uniform consists of officer-pattern light body armour, armoured greatcoat and peaked hat, though many will possess their own distinctive suit of Guan Yu armour instead.

Membership Benefits
Shandian Shuài receive the 'Advanced Command' Training that allow them to motivate and coordinate corporate forces with great efficiency.
The core of Ai-Jinn military tactics is the application of heavy armour. As such, members of the Shandian Shuài gain a +4 bonus on all drive rolls associated with tanks, armoured cars and APC's. As long as they can observe the terrain and make contact with other drivers, they may also confer a +2 drive bonus on a number of other drivers equal to their Presence score.

Finally, all Shandian Shuài of rank 3 or above receive a free suit of Guan Yu armour (page.52).

NEW TRAINING

ADVANCED COMMAND
Shandian Shuai

A Shandian Shuài member may spend a Conviction point and make a 'Presence + Attitude' roll as a full action, if successful their XS on the roll is converted into temporary Conviction points that may be divided among any Ai-Jinn or allied troops (including Agents) within earshot. A Shandian Shuài may not benefit personally from any Conviction generated in this way. Unspent temporary Conviction is lost at the end of the scene.

LEGACY OPERATIVES

To wear weak flesh but not be shackled by it is a sublime stride towards the pinnacle. How have they done this? The question drives a yearning to taste these morsels.
Many iterations will be granted to any who bring one alive into the Embrace. Only the mind need live, for it is the fate of all flesh, even when transcended, to be sloughed away.

-attr: Charnel, haruspex of the Cult of Machina

AKA: Men in Black, Legates, Sword of Hyperion, Legacy Agents
Prerequisites
Arts & Culture 6, Assess Tech 6, Mechtronics 7, Science 8, Xenotech training*, Contact (Hyperion) 10; selection for the position by Hyperion.

Featured in the 'Machines of War' supplement, if you don't have this book see the Crash Course Rules on page 11.
Legacy Operatives are an anomaly within the Ai-Jinn Agent program in that their allegiance to the Corporation is secondary to another higher authority; the Archon Hyperion.

Part of the pact the Ai-Jinn made with the rogue Archon is that Hyperion has free rein to choose Agents from among their ranks to serve his incomprehensible whims. Those Agents that Hyperion selects receive a summons to the Changsha facility, making them the only human beings to set foot inside the hyperfactory since its construction. What happens inside is a mystery perhaps even to the highest levels of the Ai-Jinn but, whatever it is, it leaves the Agents... changed.

Though some are organised into new divisions comprised exclusively of Legacy Operatives, most simply return to their old division afterwards. Indeed, the division they are assigned to often seems to play as much a part in their selection as their own abilities, but their loyalties are now forever altered. While a Legacy Operative brings a lot of power to a division, with their great access to Legacy Tech and an unparalleled understanding of extra-human technology, many division-mates may be wary of the fact that their erstwhile ally may no longer be completely trustworthy. Even if the division is not informed of the nature of their summons to Changsha most will notice that their companion no longer laughs at the same jokes, finds old interests tedious and often speaks and acts in ways that can only be described as 'inhuman'.

Missions & Duties
As outlined above, Legacy Operatives are often chosen because their division is engaged in work that Hyperion has interests in. Divisions engaged in industrial espionage, extra-planetary activities, or anti-UIG operations are all prime candidates to have a Legacy Operative added to their ranks. However, to represent their divided loyalties, the GM may give the Legacy Operative a set of peripheral mission-objectives in secret to represent their orders from Hyperion.

Hand the player a piece of paper with the orders on which only they are to read. Possibilities might include
The recovery of a specific item of Xeno- or Archon-technology and returning it to Changsha.
Delivering a message, warning or assassination to a specific individual.
Destroying some important piece of data.

Regardless of whether this order contradicts those given by the Mission Officer the Ai-Jinn will not risk angering Hyperion by punishing its servants for carrying out its commands and so there is little chance of formal reprimand, though they may find themselves denied bonuses or otherwise persecuted.

Uniform & Equipment
Legacy Operatives disdain the flashy fashion statements and gang colours that are so prevalent among the Ai-Jinn, the importance of such things much diminishes in their eyes after witnessing the inside of Changsha. Most simply wear the standard-issue corporate business suit or whatever is most appropriate at the time. Whatever their attire, though, Legacy Operatives will almost invariably be carrying several items of Legacy Tech.

MEMBERSHIP BENEFITS
The alterations to their thought patterns made by Hyperion give Legacy Operatives an insight into the workings of alien technologies, and Legacy Tech in particular, that no others can match. Processes and principles that seem alien or counter-intuitive to the human mind are almost instinctively understood by them. Legacy Operatives are able to work on or repair Legacy Tech with no penalty and halve all penalties when working on Archon tech or unfamiliar Xenotech.

Access points
Legacy Agents gain access points to use Legacy Pattern Technology (page 60). You gain a number of Access Points equal to double your Rank. When you requisition an item you lose the appropriate number of Access Points. These are recovered when the item is returned. If you lose or destroy the item the points recover at a rate of 1 per week.

Mental Blocks
Finally, impregnable mental blocks prevent a Legacy Operative from divulging any information relating to Legacy Technology, the Archon Hyperion or the Archon's orders to outsiders, even under torture, the influence of drugs or psychogenic control. Any attempt to coerce such information out of a Legacy Operative automatically fails.

LEGACY AGENTS IN YOUR GAME
Because having a Legacy Agent in the division is a little different from normal here are some ideas to help you integrate it into the game.

Idea 1
One member of the division is a Legacy Agent. Hand him an order to assassinate a target which the rest of the division are supposed to acquire some information from. He should kill the target before the information changes hands. The other Agents will understandably be annoyed but the corporation will likely pay them as normal.

Idea 2
The Legacy Agent needs to sabotage a computer in a facility. The rest of the division are there for support. While they fend off security forces the Legacy Agent will proceed to the server room and blow it up. The other Agents could use the opportunity to steal a load of guns and security systems while the legacy operative is engaged.

Idea 3
A target in E.I. territory must be brought in. The individual is of interest to Hyperion and is wanted alive. To make the most of it the Ai-Jinn send the full division who also have orders to take out a nearby Russian mafia cell who are refusing to come to heel. The Legacy Agent will of course be active in both operations.

THE GOALS OF HYPERION

As it is not clear to the GM what the goals of hyperion are, how is he supposed to set tasks for Legacy Agents? There are two solutions to this.

1. Until more official information becomes available simply make it up. You should be able to come up with a sinister agenda of your own.

2. Don't worry about it. Just set the Legacy Agent random tasks which will fit into the mission. The Legacy Operatives are seldom aware of Hyperion's greater plan.

TIGER PLATOONS

Asia has a history of making some of the best jungle fighters in the world and the Ai-Jinn have ensured that this tradition has continued, following in the footsteps of such groups as:

The Vietnamese Vietcong
The Malaysian Royal Ranger Regiment
The Philipine Army Scout Rangers
The Gurkhas (Nepal)
The Special Warfare Command (China)
The Singapore Army Combat Trackers
The Tamil Tigers (Sri Lanka)

THE AI-JINN TIGER PLATOON (AKA TIGER PATROLS)

These are essentially Agents but their training is orientated towards jungle warfare. Although there is not nearly as much jungle in the world as there was 500 years ago, it is still abundant enough for the Ai-Jinn to maintain a Tiger Platoon.

The Platoon consists of 25 Agents who train together and are essentially one large Division. More often they are split up either into 5 squads of 5 Agents or sometimes an individual is assigned to a standard Agent division either to expand his training or to allow the division to benefit from his jungle skills.

Tigers, as they are known, are identifiable by the following methods.

1. Their ID Chip is updated with the distinction – Tiger Platoon

---

"This place is a fuckin' shithole. Remind me why we're here again?"
"Shut your mouth Kowalski. I'll let you know when you need to know."
"C'mon major, we never signed up for this shit, that damn snake nearly…"
"I said shut your mouth lieutenant. We're supposed to be fuckin' professionals."

The five marines pushed onwards, hacking their way through walls of thorn-vines, so sharp and hard they threatened to open wounds and sever strapping.

Hours later, as the shadow of dusk descended over the jungle, Major Connor called a halt. "Marines, according to the GPS we're less than a mile from target. We're not stopping this close so get out your night vision and let's press on. Good news is that if intel is accurate, we'll be able to make a secure camp within the target zone."

"This had better be fuckin' good," muttered Kowalski. "I don't see why we can't know what the hell we're risking our lives for?"

"You wanna take a leaf outta her book." said Adams, nodding towards the lean frame of Sgt. Mendez who had taken the brief pause as an opportunity to strip-clean her rifle.

Kowalski grinned, "If she's gonna strip something it's gonna be….."

Wet chunks of tissue spattered across Adams' face. "Shit….hostiles….take cover!"

Kowalski lay broken on the floor, his skull in two pieces some three feet apart, only the shattered jawbone still hanging onto the neck by threads of muscle.

Mendez pulled a second rifle off her back, rolled backwards off the log she was seated on and dug in, scanning the trees for signs of the attacker. Adams and Connor stood back to back, slowly treading a circle, covering all angles.

"What the fuck are hostiles doing out here Major?"
"I have no idea Sergeant. Mendez, do you see anything?"

Mendez looked up from behind the fallen tree, flicking her vision into thermal she scanned the area. The red-white shapes of Adams and Connor but nothing else…wait….a flicker of…. A massive, stinking hand grabbed Mendez hard around the jaw and yanked sharply. She just registered the serrated knife sawing across her throat but it was too late.

"Mendez….do you see anything."

Then a noise like a twig snapping, somewhere to the left; both marines spun around.

"Something out there sergeant, you see it?"

"She sees nothing now, dog."

"What the…" Connor lashed backwards with an elbow, but it was to no avail, a male, 30 maybe 40 years old, dressed in blackened, muddy fatigues, sniper rifle slung over his shoulder stood behind him; he held a serrated knife millimetres from the Major's throat. Branches and foliage were sticking out of matted hair and the facial features were almost disappearing beneath layers of filth. Adams was dead on the floor, his neck broken and head mostly sawn off.

He spoke in English with a strong Chinese accent, "I know why you're here gweilo. And I know you've brought the codes, so let's go for a little walk."

2. They are commonly tattooed with tigers, normally roaring, leaping or stealthing and backed by the Chinese symbol for tiger.

3. They tend never to wear suits, being more at home in simple fatigues and normally sporting machetes and kinetic weapons which are easy to maintain in the field.

4. They tend to be muddy, unshaven and smell of the jungle.

Typical Tiger Tattoo

PLAYING TIGER PLATOON AGENTS

Tiger Platoon are extremely useful, even when not in jungle environments. They excel at making the most of a situation and are very resourceful. You may create your character as a Tiger Patrol or use a downtime action to undergo the selection process. As long as you have the prerequisites below and agree to adhere to the downtime demands you are considered to pass.

PREREQUISITES

Ai-Jinn Agent
Survival Training
Tactical Firearms 5
Close Combat 5
Stealth 5
Physical Stats (Str / End / Agi) all at 7+

BONUSES

Weapons
Tiger Patrols are required to carry a kinetic tactical firearm when on duty. They may choose one for free upon completing training. They are also required to carry machetes (treat as short swords) which again, they receive for free upon completion of training.

Jungle Armour
All armour with an AV of 2 or more owned by Tiger Patrols is patterned in a jungle camo lamina and upgraded with some basic modifications for free. Modern jungles tend to be darker than 21st century ones so the camo is more of a black / khaki mix.

Camo
This confers a +2 bonus to stealth or hiding rolls in jungle environments.

Insect Repellent
If you're in an area where insect bites may prove a problem the repellent units in the suit will reduce the chances of you being bitten. If you are bitten by an insect roll a D10, on a 1-8 you can ignore the bite. This should only normally be rolled when the insect may carry a nasty pathogen.

Cooling Materials
This is unlikely to affect your game very much but if dehydration from heat is ever an issue Tiger Armour keeps its user relatively cool and reduces sweating, thus staving off dehydration for a few days.

Jungle Warfare Specialists
Tiger Patrols excel at jungle warfare. When fighting in a jungle environment they receive an extra temporary conviction point for every Tiger present. That includes themselves, so a minimum of +1. These conviction points are lost at the end of the combat if not used.

Jungle Defences
You are adept at avoiding the perils of the jungle. For example, identifying plant toxins, finding safe food, detecting quicksand, avoiding parasites, finding suitable campsites, spotting ambushes, etc. Normally the GM should just let you avoid them but if a roll is appropriate then you should receive a +4.

This does not extend to such incidents as fighting jungle creatures or falling off cliffs.

Ghosts of the Jungle
Tigers are at home in the jungle and leave less evidence of their presence than the animals themselves. Anyone attempting to track a Tiger incurs a -10 penalty. The Tigers themselves gain +2 to all Stealth checks when in a jungle or forest environment; this stacks with their camo armour.

Kinetic Field Repair
Tigers are taught to maintain their weapons in the field. They gain the training 'Kinetic Field Repair' for free. See page 16.

Trappers
Tigers gain the Trap Building Training for free (see the Eastern Bank). If you don't have this book the GM should simply allow you to construct effective traps without making difficult rolls.

COMMITMENTS

Training
Tigers are required to maintain their skills and must therefore give up 50% of their downtime actions in order to travel to jungle environments and train with the rest of the platoon. (Round up.)

You can opt to spend 5XP to keep a downtime action; it is instead considered that you have spent a great deal of effort honing your skills outside formal training. The GM should feel free to restrict this option if the player abuses it.

Unsophisticated
Anyone who spends any amount of time in the Tiger Platoon loses their urban sophistication pretty quickly. For this reason you receive a -6 to all rolls which the GM considers require etiquette, tact or sophistication. The GM should use discretion to decide which rolls should be penalised, for example, taking tea with a Shi Yukiro Agent would require the penalty, sharing a drink with a biker gang would not.

If you are desperate to retain this aspect of your personality then the penalty can be cancelled by spending 1XP every time XP is awarded.

This represents your struggle to maintain your airs, graces and manners in spite of your rough and ready work.

Creatures of the Jungle
Tigers are almost always unshaven, smelly and covered in mud. They live extremely hectic lifestyles and if given even a modicum of free time are expected to rendezvous with their platoon and train. For this reason they seldom have time for personal grooming. This does not affect their Looking Good or Attitude skills as they generally look very intimidating but it does nothing for their ability to blend into urban environments.

Even if the Tigers are given time to clean up they seldom will, the layers of muck and heavy, earthy smells they carry around with them are highly desirable in a jungle environment. Losing them is always somewhat of a disappointment to a Tiger who will try to address the issue as soon as possible.

Typical Tiger Tattoo

CONANA

You'd swear it was food!

Our science people have found out that a Conana a day may help prevent 2 of the 7 signs of ageing in some people.*

*Some of this information may not be true.

CONANA - THE TRUCKER'S FRIEND

Conanas are a popular snack with drivers. They are purchased in small cellophane packets and have a shelf life of 30 years making them ideal stock for out-of-the-way service stations. Typically a Conana costs 1 credit and has a chewy, waxy consistancy and tastes like a sugary, banarary, minty sausage.

When a Conana has matured for around 10 years it takes on a fishy note which connoisseurs find particularly agreeable. A Conana contains 500 kcals.

Conanas are made by Multymeat!

METAHUMAN DYNASTIES

THE HUANG ZUHOU FAMILIES

Around the time pre-natal genetic engineering became widely available (circa 2090) there were many in the world who opted to tamper with the genes of their children in order to eliminate potential illnesses and defects. There were, of course, those who took this a step further and not only sought to eliminate problems but also to augment and refine the next generation that they might be better suited to their pre-determined role in life.

In the western world controls were strict and punishments severe and although a little of this gene manipulation went on, it was generally subtle or a one-off. In the east, however, the Daegu Genelab (see page 81 of the Eastern Bank), a pioneering institute with strong (but illicit) government backing opened its services to anyone with money and contacts.

This unsurprisingly was taken up by a number of privileged, wealthy, influential and aristocratic families who had strong ties with government officials. These families had, throughout East Asia's development, played a significant role and many could trace their roots back hundreds of years. Each considered itself pivotal in certain areas of industry, research or culture and felt that by genegineering their offspring, the child's affinity to certain careers could be increased, thus consolidating their positions of power.

The project initially began well. Despite its dubious moral methodology Daegu is one of the world's leading genegineering labs and produces extremely reliable, repeatable results. Families were producing children whose potential dwarfed that of their parents. When they matured and took on positions within the family business not only were they extremely competent but they seldom thought of other careers or taking off on sabbaticals. Several cases of child executives arose where 14 year olds were heading meetings or acting as trouble-shooters for the family. This was perhaps the heyday of the Metahuman Dynasties but it was not long before things started to turn sour.

The modern practise of sterilising metahumans has its roots in the Huang Zuhou families, where the results of sustained and profound gene manipulation over generations could be studied first hand.

Genegineered cells are inherently unstable and nowadays those who have them are required to be gene-cleansed every six months. For the Huang Zuhou Dynasties, however, the ruling simply does not apply. For a combination of reasons which include tradition, Ai-Jinn intervention and the corruption of the system the dynasties have been living unsterilised and without gene cleansing for over 400 years, their seed becoming ever more tainted and twisted until some would not even be recognised as human.

THE LAW

The UIG, in 2299, passed an amnesty stating that metahumans had 12 months to turn themselves in for assessment, gene-cleansing and sterilisation. This would be means-tested and any citizen who could not afford the treatment would be subsidised. To the Dynasties this was nothing short of genetic castration and the idea of losing both their hereditary advantages and ability to bear children was unthinkable. By further pledging their unending and total loyalty to the Ai-Jinn they have achieved a state of near-immunity from UIG investigation.

After an enormous legal battle the Dynasties occupy a position within a legislative grey area. The Ai-Jinn has managed to get them classified as scientific cases and not citizens. They are not considered BIOs and so may reside on the Earth but equally are not permitted to free roam. The added fact that one of the legislators high up in the Asian UIG is secretly part of the Hien Dynasty has ensured that these rather clumsy and arguably weak laws are nonetheless permitted (this officer goes by the name of Hun Lo Gen).

To surmise the Dynasty Mandate has the following guidelines:

1. A member of a Dynasty is considered to be an individual of significant genetic match to one of the following families: The Kang, The Ling Kao, The Tao, The Ang Fen or The Hien.

2. A Dynasty Member must not leave a UIG approved lab unless for transportation to a morgue or other UIG sanctioned facility. If a member is outside one of these locations they are subject to termination with no recourse for compensation or legal action.

3. Dynasty Members must always carry an ID Chip identifying them as such.

4. Dynasty Members are not citizens. They are considered the property of the Ai-Jinn Corporation and any infractions of the law they cause are considered the actions of the Ai-Jinn Corporation.

5. The UIG may at any time inspect a Dynasty holding facility to ensure its suitability and that all actions performed within said facility are legal.

Although, as noted in point 5, the UIG are able to inspect dynasty holding facilities they seldom do. The Ai-Jinn are known to be intolerant of this type of disrespect and will often take action against the inspecting officer's family and those who ordered the inspection. This alone is normally enough to deter the UIG but the added influence of officer Hun Lo Gen tends to make inspection a rarity.

It should also be noted that although holding facilities are technically labs, they are the height of opulence and the only scientific instrumentation present is generally there at the request of the families.

The Ai-Jinn have made an art out of secrecy at almost every level of their business and this, predictably, extends to their management ethos. While nominally adhering to the standard Corporate structure, a roughly pyramidal construction flowing down from an effective oligarchy of C-level executives, the Ai-Jinn also maintain a parallel hierarchy at the highest tiers: an enigmatic dynastic subculture that completely bypasses Corporate convention and harks back to three millennia of Chinese history.

The UIG remains maddeningly tight-lipped on the subject, and no Agent of this or any other Corporation has ever been formally introduced to any of the Dynasts, although contrarily – and frustratingly – their influence is often cited to outsiders as a major factor in the Corporation's business decisions. Some suggest that the Dynasts no longer survive, the sustained myth of their existence merely employed as a proxy tool in the Ai-Jinn's intra-Corporate dealings; a veil of secret understanding whose main purpose is to firmly separate the Ai-Jinn from the barbarians.

But I respectfully submit that, given that Corporation's propensity for concealment and intrigue, it is entirely possible that at least some of the Dynasts are operating actively in the field, hiding in plain sight behind the Ai-Jinn's byzantine layers of deception. In this context, it would behove our strategic planning section to accurately log, correlate, and pattern any and all anomalous events – and anecdotal evidence suggests a remarkably high preponderance of these – in every dealing our Agents have with the Ai-Jinn, whether commercial or tactical. To accurately locate the true power centres of this Corporation would lend us a significant advantage in our efforts to control its expansion.

- from The Dragon Awoken: Threat Analysis, Ai Jinn Corporation

attr: Michael Kaspillis, EI anthropologer/geopolitical analyst
[SUPRESSED 3.12.2502, /unknownadmin]
[DELETED 4.12.2502, /unknownadmin]

PLAYING DYNASTY STRAINS

It is quite feasible to play a Dynasty Member (a.k.a. Strain) but there are some key things to remember. In this section it is assumed that you want to play an Ai-Jinn Agent Dynasty Strain. If you are thinking of playing them in another way you may need to make a few common sense alterations.

ID CHIP
You will be killed immediately if you are discovered. Fortunately as an Ai-Jinn Agent you would receive your alternate ID which you can use to store all your licenses etc. Any Dynasty Strain who was an Agent would be advised to spend 99.99% of their time with the alternate ID, making it their primary character. This gives them the disadvantage that they cannot switch to a safer ID if the UIG get too close. It would be next to impossible to play a non-Ai-Jinn Dynasty Strain Agent as you could not apply for licenses or even pass selection.

APPEARANCE
Some Dynasty Strains have extremely distinctive appearances or demeanours. This can make it easy for well trained officers and Agents to identify you irrespective of what it says on your ID chip.

FITTING IN
Dynasty Strains are extremely focused and may suffer in the modern corporate arena. For example, the Kang Strain find it extremely hard to maintain conversations with normal people. This is not only awkward for the Agent; it can be tricky for the player. Though if the player is willing to take on the challenge it can be enormous fun.

METAHUMAN TRAINING
Dynasty Strains get the Metahuman Training (see The Eastern Bank) for free at character creation as they were born that way. If you don't have The Eastern Bank then just ignore this point.

NAMING
The Dynasty Strains are understandably proud of their names and do not like to hide them. If you decide to play an Agent from a Dynasty Strain then your true surname will be that of the family.

For example, if your first name is Chonara and you are of the Kang dynasty you will be Chonara Kang.

Obviously this can attract unwanted attention so many Dynasty members choose to take a different surname when on active duty, often a middle name or one belonging to an admired individual.

THE HIEN DYNASTY

Area of Expertise Politics and Manipulation
Location   Beijing War Spire, China
Family Size   223 Members

The Hien are arguably the most powerful and influential family, not only among the Huang Zuhou but in the world. They made their name as a political Dynasty that assisted in the transformation of formerly communist China into the aggressively capitalist Ai-Jinn Corporation State.

The Hien share similarities with both the Geisha and Alpha strain metahumans (see The Eastern Bank) and have by far the least stable genome out of all the Dynastic families, however, over time this has become an asset. The Hien have the unique ability to interbreed with other metahuman Dynasts without diluting the effect of the parents strain augmentations. As a result, the Hien have a great degree of sway with the other Huang Zuhou families due to their ability to refresh their gene-pools through marriage without compromising that which gives them their power within the Ai-Jinn. Indeed, there is a distinct possibility that without them the metahuman Dynasties would have long ago degenerated into inbred abominations.

Physically, all Hien are eerily attractive, with a universally mesomorphic body-type and the pale complexion of the Chinese aristocracy, often with a slight translucent and waxy appearance, to the point where their skin resembles porcelain. However, unusual cosmetic birth defects are common owing to the great extent of their ongoing genetic turmoil, albinism, melanism, and heterochromic eyes being among the most prominent examples, though there are others. Despite their unusual appearance, the Hien are among the most personable of the Dynasts, possessing an innate grasp of human communication that makes them fascinating to others.

SYSTEM

STATS

The Hien genome is notoriously unstable and there is less homogeny among their natural traits than there is among other Dynastic families.

At character creation, a Hien strain has three points with which they can increase their natural ability maximum in any of their STATS (Strength, Endurance, Agility, Reflexes, Perception, Intelligence and Presence). So, for example, they could choose to:

Increase the natural maximum for one STAT to 13
Increase the natural maxiumum of one STAT to 12 and one to 11
Increase the natural maxium of three STATS to 11

However one STAT is deficient in some way and must have its natural maximum reduced by one to 9, this may not be one of those STATS that has a bonus.

Skills

Hien must choose Attitude, Psychology and Lying & Acting as their level 8, 7 and 6 skills at character creation, in any order. However, all these skills receive +1 making their starting values 9, 8 and 7, respectively. All other points are assigned as normal.

Genetic Cascade Syndrome

When exposed to environments that can cause genetic damage, Hien lack much of the natural resistance that comes from a stable genome, resulting in massive cascade failures where their DNA strands "unzip" and recombine, causing widespread mutation, often leading to cancer and other degenerative disorders on a scale that dwarfs those experienced by even Alpha strain metahumans.

Hien must make an Endurance check on a D10 once per session, in which a roll of 10 is always considered a failure. On a failure they suffer 2D4 points of damage distributed over any number of STATS by the GM who can use a D8 on the table below if desired. This loss is permanent until medical care is sought out during a downtime week, requiring 1000¢ per point of statistic loss to be restored.

1.	Strength	2.	Endurance
3.	Agility	4.	Perception
5.	Presence	6.	Intelligence
7.	Reflexes	8.	Reroll

Social Intuition

Hien have an inborn ability to analyse the personalities of others by reading body language, observing unconscious reactions and modulations in voice-stress and possibly even a telepathic element (though this is disputed and as-of-yet unverified) and then adapting their own unconscious behaviour to take advantage of what they detect. Hien halve any penalties they suffer to all Presence based rolls, they can be disarmingly charming even when covered in blood up to the elbows and all but their worst enemies find it difficult to hate them.

Subconscious Coercion

Hien Strain gain the Training Subconscious Coercion for free. This is detailed on page 17.

The black silken robe slipped from the woman's shoulders and flowed like dark liquid to the floor. Behringer gasped, taken aback despite a lifetime filled with innumerable conquests. She was flawless; the intricate snake tattoo that wound around her naked body artfully drew his eyes to every perfect curve and hollow, emphasised the sweetly pale marble of her smooth skin.

Smiling, she took a single, graceful step towards him and then stopped. Her lovely face contorted, first in surprise and then in pain; her slender, supple hands clenched themselves into claws. Behringer's eyes widened as the skin around the woman's jawline rippled and then split; there was a meaty crackling noise as her entire jaw pushed itself outwards, taut ropes of muscle suddenly bulging behind it. Her flawless white teeth splayed outwards as the gums widened, twisting into a ragged ring of sharp ivory points and edges.

Behringer opened his mouth to scream, and then she caught his eyes with her own. The dark crimson of her irises, the first thing he'd noticed in the bar, caught and held him until everything else seemed to fade away. He became dimly aware that his mouth was hanging open, and closed it again; he sank back onto the bed.

She was gone when Behringer woke in the morning, leaving his memories hazed and cloudy; for the rest of his life, he would never be able to explain his peculiar scars.

THE KANG DYNASTY

Area of Expertise	Industrial Science & Mathematics
Location	Enlight Archology, Kazakhstan
Family Size	144 Members

The Kang family specialise in high level theoretical mathematics and science. They have been a strong influence on the Chinese technology industry since the mid 1900's and were highly pivotal in the development of the magna-rail. The Kang have always been staunch supporters of the Ai-Jinn contributing to the technology behind the cyberlin and lending their expertise to the space program.

The family themselves are fairly reclusive, unwilling to fraternise with anyone but the Ai-Jinn's direct representatives. This is for two main reasons:

Firstly their genetic predisposition to research is now so overriding that they are consumed by it. Generally speaking they do not sleep and find themselves at a loss, getting frustrated and even violent when unable to put their minds into use. You might imagine it as an eagle in a cage pulling its own feathers out.

Secondly they are so intellectually advanced that speaking with 'normals' would be like an adult trying to discuss politics with a 3 year old. The Kang can only find companionship or even decent conversation with true intellectuals (those with Intelligence of at least 9).

The family reside within the Enlight Archology in Kazakhstan. This building is a wonderful blend of Middle-Eastern influences and its multi-spired layout allows the Kang family to inhabit their own tower which is closed off from everyone with the exception of maintenance and Ai-Jinn Agents.

SYSTEM

STATS
The Kang Dynasty Strain gain an extra +2 Intelligence at character creation and have their natural ability maxium for intelligence increased to 13. The Kang are not particularly lacking in other areas so all other STATS can reach 10 as normal.

Telepathic Sensitivity
The Kang physiology has evolved at the cost of telepathy. Kang Strains may not take any telepathic skills or trainings and if any telepathics are used within 5 metres of them they take 1HP of damage per 2 levels of the power as their sensitive brains and nervous systems contort under the psion energy. (This would be in addition to any damage from a telepathic attack if the attacker were within 5 metres.)

This damage cannot be repaired by medical technology and must be healed naturally. See page 147 of the Core Rules for healing rates.

For example, a fellow Agent uses Biokinesis 8 to heal himself. His nearby Kang ally takes 4 damage. As the Kang Agent is on active duty and has Endurance 6 it will take 8 hours to heal the damage.

Skills
Kang Strains gain an extra 5 points to spend on skills at character creation which can be assigned anywhere except Telepathics. Their skills can only be increased to 10 as normal.

Kang Strain are known for their inability to interact with other humans. Their Attitude, Psychology and Lying & Acting can never exceed 3.

Sleep
Kang Strain do not sleep, they busy themselves on other tasks such as researching, reading or study. This extra learning time grants them 1 additional XP each time XP is awarded. This bonus XP should be noted separately as it can only be spent on the following skills. It *does* contribute towards Agent level though.

Arts and Culture
Assess Tech
Business
Computers and A.I.
Corp Knowledge
Mechtronics
Science

THE LING KAO DYNASTY

Area of Expertise	Traditional Martial Arts
Location	Shanghai Spire, China
Family Size	65 Members

The Ling Kao Dynasty has a long tradition in China of running martial art schools. It is said that some of their direct descendents were teaching unarmed skills before firearms were even invented.

To this day they still maintain a fierce dedication to old-world weaponry and refuse point blank to use guns. Their bodies and reflexes are honed to a physical peak and their joints are so supple and refined they can perform moves others would consider impossible.

In exchange for the Ai-Jinn's sanctuary the Ling Kao offer perhaps the best martial arts training in the world. Only the Shi Yukiro's Masters can rival their teachings and as such there are a number of new Trainings available which are exclusive to those who have been lucky enough to study under a Ling Kao or Shi Yukiro Master (see page 11).

The Ling Kao are obvious choices as Agents, they are single minded and purposeful. The size of the family is quite small however and so they are reluctant to send their kin into the firing line. Most of their debt to the Ai-Jinn is paid through the teaching school they run at the Shanghai Spire and so the lack of Ling Kao within the Agent ranks is acceptable.

For those who do choose to embark on the Agent training program the combination of genetics, training and augmentation technology can be ferocious to say the least.

SYSTEM

STATS
Ling Kao can increase both their natural Agility and Reflexes to 11.

All other STATS can be increased to 10 as normal.

Skills

Ling Kao must take Close Combat as their skill at 8. This is instantly increased to 10 for free. It must be their professional skill and they must also have their Athletics at 6 or more.

Weapon Selection

Ling Kao refuse to use ranged weapons or explosives; a combination of strict childhood conditioning and an unflinching code of conduct means a Ling Kao would rather yield to his enemies than use a ranged weapon. As a result they may not purchase points in any firearms skills.

Although the Ling Kao will not use ranged weapons or explosives they have no issues with advanced close combat weapons such as plasma, ion or nano blades. They are honourable, not stupid and realise that the modern arena requires up to date weapons.

Martial Trainings

Ling Kao have been well trained and have access to a number of special trainings. These Trainings are not all exclusive to the Ling Kao but they are unattainable for most character types.

Iaido	Page 13
Iaido Hakanai	Page 13
Advance Under Fire	Page 12
Joint Dislocation	Page 16
Strike of the Cobra	Page 15
Martial Aptitude*	Page 15

*Ling Kao gain this free at character creation

THE TAO DYNASTY

Area of Expertise	Assassination
Location	Amur Border Spire
Family Size	46 Members

The world has always needed its assassins and the Tao have performed the task admirably. Their efficient and precise methods combined with discretion and availability have ensured that they are the first port of call for anyone wishing to 'send a message'.

The Tao's geneticists have focused on modifying the body in small, subtle ways to assist the assassins in their work. Few would generally notice the Tao augmentations and as a result they are able to blend in well with society.

One of their main problems is infertility, the gene-tampering which has gone on within them has irreversibly damaged their ability to produce offspring and their success rate even with medical intervention is extremely low. As a family they only produce one or two children a year which is a little lower than the number of them who die each year. Thus the Tao family are looking at extinction within the next 50 to 100 years.

In an attempt to avoid this outcome the Tao take on dangerous or illegal jobs for companies such as E.I., Two Snakes and Gemini. The hope being that they will curry a relationship which will allow them access to prototype technologies that could help alleviate their problem. So far nothing has been developed which is of great significance but with so many medical professionals indebted to them a breakthrough is expected at any time.

SYSTEM

STATS

The Tao's natural Agility maximum is 12 instead of 10. All other STATS remain unchanged.

Skills

The Tao must take either Close Combat or Stealth as their professional skill and automatically gain +2 to it at character creation.

Upgrades

The Tao gain the following bio-upgrades as a result of their genetic modifications:

Respirocytes

The Tao have cells in their lungs which produce an oxygen/hydrogen/nitrogen mix using elements from the food they have eaten. This allows them to breathe without external air for long periods of time. They can go without a source of air for one hour for each point of Endurance they have.
Example. Endurance 8 would allow them to breathe for 8 hours.

Collapsible Joints

The Tao can voluntarily collapse some of their joints in order to escape restraints. This effectively grants them the Joint Dislocation Training for free(see page xx).

Venom Ducts

The Tao have venom ducts on the backs of their hands. These are almost invisible to the untrained eye.

-12 to spot / identify them, -6 if you are familiar with the Tao.

Once a dose of toxin has been secreted the duct takes 4 hours to refill. Remember there are 2 ducts so you can produce two doses at a time but must then wait four hours.

	Potency	Class	Cost
Tao Venom	8	A	N/A

The Tao can secrete a dose of this venom which is roughly 5ml. It is typically smeared across a blade (which takes a full action) or placed into food. The venom takes effect immediately.

The victim must pass a 'Strength + Endurance' check with a -8 penalty.

Success – The target is semi-paralysed and loses every other action and all free actions. I.e. they can only act once every two actions. The GM should decide which is the first lost action.

Failure – The target is paralysed but can still use telepathics. A toxin purge will remove all effects.

Toughened Skin

Over the years genegineers have worked at toughening the Tao's skin whilst allowing it to remain supple. Tao gain +1 AV as a result. They can still have skin altering operations such as 'Toughskin' and 'Videoskin'.

THE ANG FEN DYNASTY

Area of Expertise   Telepathics
Location   Karachi Spire
Family Size   177 Members

Bak Tae Hung Ang Fen

These monstrous beings have been the subject of so much genegineering that their entire gene-set has become corrupted. They initially began as an intelligent family of socialites, known for their intuitive personalities and engaging conversation. As time passed and understanding grew the family began to realise it was mild latent telepathics which were responsible for the predilection to social discourse. As the biology and physics of telepathy became better understood the family employed genegineers to try and augment the telepathic part of the brain (the Advani Apparatus), hopefully expanding their mild talents into a more powerful and controllable form of telepathy.

Sadly the family were effectively guinea pigs for a group of scientists who now go by the name 'The Progenitors of Zion'. These scientists were in fact instrumental in the ascension of the Comoros corporation and now occupy an important position within their ranks. They saw the Ang Fen as corrupt, materialistic groups of inbreeds whose lives could help millions become more enlightened and peaceful.

The experiments were a disaster; the link between the telepathy and psion rifts was poorly understood and the manipulation of the Advani Apparatus caused these minuscule, controlled rifts to spiral out of control. In essence it was like subjecting the patients to continual high doses of radiation. The problem was that the source of the mutation was inside the patients head and could not be removed. Their DNA was continually battered from every side and unable to repair itself. Under these conditions the bodies of those who had undergone operations began to mutate at an unprecedented rate.

It might have been wise at this point to segregate those who had been altered and limit the damage but the effect on their telepathic abilities was so amplified that the Ang Fen would not listen to sense. They employed a different army of genegineers whose task was to keep the mutations under control rather than reverse the process.

The Ang Fen, over time, learned to live with and even relish this vile combination of twisted body and potent mind. Such was their dedication that even the children were surgically altered at birth to see whether their young bodies would deal any better with the psion–mutagens.

So far no real progress has been made but a few cases of limited mutation have arisen. These individuals seem to have a resistance to the battery of psion particles and mutate at a far slower rate than their kin. These members are the ones who are normally assigned as Agents or family diplomats, the rest of them being too hideous or deformed to make social meetings.

The Ang Fen, as a family, now have very little purpose. They live in sterile isolation in the Karachi Spire, revelling in their mutagenesis. Many live in stabiliser tanks or wired up to gene-therapy units just to stop their bodies twisting and bursting. Although their telepathics are frighteningly powerful they seldom have opportunities to use them and pay their debts to the Ai-Jinn by teaching telepathic control and occasionally offering one of their psion-resistant children to the Agent Program.

SYSTEM

STATS

Ang Fen can spend 2 additional STAT points at character creation on Intelligence, Perception or Presence. You may choose two of these STATS to have their natural maximums increased to 12.

Skills

Ang Fen gain an additional 5 points to spend on telepathic skills at character creation. These skills cannot be taken above 10.

Psion-Resistance

Ang Fen are extremely resistant to psion-energy and any telepathics targeted against them can be ignored if they pass an 'Intelligence + Relevant Telepathic Power' check. The telepathic power should be the same one used against them so to resist being hit with Assault, the Ang Fen should roll 'Intelligence + Assault'. Success means the power has no effect.

Telepathic Might

The Ang Fen have much larger Advani Apparatus than normal telepaths. This allows them to make a single, concentrated effort which can have devastating effects.

They can thus take the 'Telepathic Might' training and do not have to spend a conviction point to use it.

Psion Overload

The sheer quantity of psion energy bursting into the mind of an Ang Fen can occasionally be overwhelming. Ang Fen critically fail all telepathy rolls of a double 9 and a double 10 unless it is their profession in which case it is only 10/10.

The doors hissed open behind him and, exactly as he had been instructed, Agent Wu backed carefully into the darkness of the Eurydice Pavilion, a hundred and forty-four floors up in the Karachi Spire. He took steady, measured steps backwards, stopping only when the lights came up. They revealed a sumptuous chamber, lavishly embellished with the most gorgeous decorations; but, Wu noted, there was no gold or any other metal, not even any lacquer. Nothing at all, in fact, that would permit even the slightest reflection.

As the doors slid closed again in front of him, Wu heard a loud wet slurping noise from behind, and held himself very still. As he had been warned, the voice arrived directly into his mind. It was not particularly unpleasant; the voice was soft, reassuring, warm.

"Agent Wu. Welcome. I see that you have been instructed on the proper way to approach me; your obedience honours me."
Wu inclined his head respectfully, taking great care not to look behind himself. As he did so, he saw for the first time the corpse of Agent Kao, lying on the floor just ahead and off to the side. She was identifiable by the green and gold cheongsam she'd been wearing when she and Wu had met earlier this morning; it was difficult to make out other distinguishing features, because her head appeared to have burst like an overripe peach. Fearing that the drying pools of sticky blood might provide a fleeting reflection, Wu hurriedly straightened again.

A grotesque, agitated sloshing came from behind him, seemingly closer this time, and more words dropped into his brain. "She was warned, just as you were. Such a simple thing. And I am a Dynast of the seventeenth generation; am I not entitled to my vanity?" A sigh echoed through Wu's mind. "Yet there are always those who somehow cannot resist the urge to turn around. But not you, Agent Wu. Not you. Good. Now. Let us proceed with your briefing."

PLOT IDEAS

For Ai-Jinn

1. Comoros Agents have broken into the Karachi Spire and taken two of the Ang Fen children away with them. Your division must recover them.

2. A Dynasty member needs to travel to Italy to meet with a contact. You must escort them there and ensure they are not detained or discovered by the UIG.

3. Two of the Dynasty families are feuding. Your division must act as arbiters and resolve the dispute.

4. For your less than exemplary behaviour the division are assigned as the 'staff' to attend to the domestic needs of the Ang Fen family.

5. A Kang scientist is working on a personal project which could have profound implications. He has asked for a single division to help him collect materials and data. Your division has been assigned to help him. The work will involve the theft of some rare or exotic items, possibly of alien origin.

For Non-Ai-Jinn

1. Rumours are circulating that a Hien family member will be attending a high society ball. Attend the ball, identify him/her and take a sample of their DNA. Chip checkers are not permitted in the function rooms.

2. Infiltrate one of the spire sectors in which a Dynasty strain resides and plant listening devices.

3. Find a dynasty member outside the spire and convince them to defect.

4. A Tao assassin is known to be hunting a high ranking official in your corporation. Sort out protection for the official and intercept the assassin.

5. You have learnt that a Ling Kao martial artist occasionally teaches skills to those outside the Ai-Jinn. Find her and ask what she would want in exchange for teaching your division some rare combat abilities.

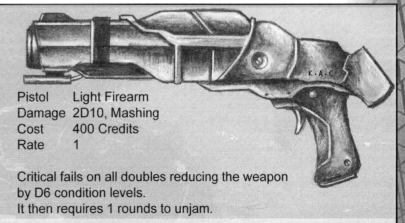

KUANG ARMS CONCERN

```
Welcome loyal purchase making.
   For your home potence we
 presenting KAC Shim 'Acending
 Gibbon' pocket hiding shotgun.
 For loving of situations where
  sneaky is first desire. Buy
    with confident and easy.
```

Pistol — Light Firearm
Damage — 2D10, Mashing
Cost — 400 Credits
Rate — 1

Critical fails on all doubles reducing the weapon by D6 condition levels.
It then requires 1 rounds to unjam.

SECTION 3

EQUIPMENT

FIREARMS

HARPOON LAUNCHER - SHIN LEE A-HAB 550 PLASMABORE EMP HARPOON LAUNCHER

A.K.A THE CAPTAIN

Special	30,000¢	300 Metres	Rate 1	EMPS Immune

The A-HAB is an emplacement weapon which must normally be mounted on a vehicle to use. It has a pivot mounting affording it a 360 degree firing arc as well as a possible elevation of +/- 45 degrees. The A-HAB is commonly used to stop large vehicles which it does with amazing ease, especially in the hands of a skilled user. In the hands of Agents and UIG it has also been used to stop rogue droids and even impair the functioning of a cyberlin.

The harpoon is attached to the launcher via a 300 metre cable. This allows it to use the power cell integrated into the launcher to deliver a massive EMP charge.

Firing the weapon
The user attacks using Perception + Support Weapons. If you hit roll 3D10+10. If you roll higher than the vehicle's AV you penetrate the vehicle armour with the harpoon. The weapon does not ignore shields.

If you penetrate the armour you deal 50 EMP damage to the vehicle.
If you don't, then you deal 5D10 EMP damage to the vehicle.

Targeting Military Vehicles – You can attempt to target the engine compartment of a vehicle. This requires you to take a -6 penalty on the attack roll but if you succeed you have an opportunity to take down military vehicles. They are considered to have an EMP of 40 against such an attack.

Man Portable A-HAB - Cost 45,000¢
Yes, a group of E.I. nukes from 'Black Thunder Division' took a standard boat mounted A-HAB, stripped it down, added handles, AG units, a lot of straps and produced a monstrous weapon with very little practical use. The A-HAB Mastodon requires Heavy Weapons 8 to fire and Strength 13 to carry. Other than that it obeys all the same rules as the standard A-HAB.

INCENDIARY RIFLE - AMS RAGEFIRE K90 INCENDIARY RIFLE (TACTICAL)

3D6+10	15,000¢	Medium Range	Rate 1	EMPS 10

The Ragefire utilises a recently developed injury mechanism which, via a beam of focused microwave energy, burns the target with such ferocity that the area struck is normally irrecoverably incinerated.
This is a ranged weapon capable of dealing Pulping Attacks. (See MoW page 132.)

It also stands a chance to randomly pulp body parts. In this case if any two of the damage dice roll a 6, then a random body part is pulped providing sufficient damage has been dealt.

The basic pulping system has been re-printed in the appendix if you do not have Machines of War. This weapon uses Energy Cells at the same rate as a heavy weapon. I.e. 1 Cell provides 3 shots.

MACHINE PISTOL - YAEGER & STANTON 'RIPJACK' AUTOPISTOL (LIGHT)

5D6	3000¢*	Medium Range	Rate 1	EMP Immune

The Ripjack autopistol is horrendously ammunition-hungry, devastatingly powerful, barks like a mad cyberwolf, is easy to conceal and has been nearly banned more often than almost any other street-level weapon. As a result, the Ai-Jinn love it. Uses SMART ammunition as a Tactical Firearm rather than a Light Firearm.

*Bulk-buy contracts with Yaeger & Stanton allow Ai-Jinn Agents to purchase Ripjacks at a 500¢ discount, for a total of 2500¢.

INDUSTRIAL WEAPONS

These weapons are all built by Tracer Li who are famous for their industrial cybernetic systems. (see Machines of War).

Legality

These weapons are not illegal and you do not need a license to use one. They may only be legally carried and used in zones denoted as 'industrial'. In commercial or domestic areas they must be stowed in UIG approved storage containers.

TRACER LI TL56 LINE CUTTER (HEAVY FIREARM)

Special	45,000¢	10 feet	Rate 1 shot per 3 rnds	EMPS 6

This weapon is a broad line plasma cutter used for chopping large pieces of metal into sections. The weapon resembles a canon but has a much heavier and more robust construction. The muzzle tapers out to just over a foot in width, although its height does not change.

When used it fires a 2 foot wide linear plasma projection up to 10 feet away. This line has tremendous severing power and can easily cut a reinforced steel joist in two with one cut. These machines are commonly used by the Ai-Jinn in wrecking yards. The weapon is held in two hands and powered by a fission cell mounted in a backpack. The cell has enough power for 20 discharges before needing to be replaced (Cost 1000¢). This is a plasma weapons and follows normal plasma weapons overheat rules.

Damage

This weapon does not deal damage is the conventional manner. Instead it ignores all AV and cuts through anything with less than 40HP automatically. You can take a penalty as on page 146 of the Core Rules to initiate a sever on a target. Needless to say, severing is automatic on any human like targets.

If you just attack in the standard manner you should roll for a random sever each time it is used.

TRACER LI STRIPPER CT05 8.8L CAUSTIC THROWER (HEAVY FIREARM)

Special	3,500¢	15 feet	Rate 1	EMPS 20

This item is used in clean-up jobs to remove layers of paint or filth from large pieces of metal; typically ship hulls, tank tracks or recyclable metals. The unit consists of a gun which is held in two hands and a backpack which contains a concentrated solution of talanic acid. When the trigger is pulled the solution is fired out in an arc. The width of the arc can be adjusted so the jet can be concentrated in a small area or sprayed over a large one.

The talanic acid compound is oxyphilic meaning it is designed not to damage pristine structural components but instead to eat away at organic and eroding areas.

Focused jet	Hits one target dealing 6D6 (Ignores 6 AV)
Arc Spray	Sprays in a 3 metre wide arc hitting all targets and dealing 2D6 (Ignores 3AV)
After effect	If you have been damaged by the spray you continue to take D6 damage a round until you are dead or the solution is neutralised by a strong alkali.

Note: If you are wearing a totally sealed, high condition (6+) suit then you take no damage from spray or jet.

Refills

The thrower takes 8.8 litres of acid which is enough for 10 uses. A refill consists of a bag of concentrate which is diluted with water. This costs 150¢.

INDUSTRIAL WEAPONS

TRACER U M44 VECTORUNE MASS DRIVER HAMMER

| 2D10+20 Dam | 9,000¢ | Close Range | Rate 1 | EMPS 18 |

This heavy piece of machinery is held in two hands by someone with strength 10+ and an artificial skeleton such as a Tracer Li or a Reaver. The hammer uses an electromagnetic mass driver to slam the impact head forward with an unprecedented level of power. It is sometimes used by emergency services to punch open stuck doors or by wrecking crews and salvagers.

System: The hammer can act as a heavy close combat weapon but does not gain a bonus based on your Strength. The weapon randomly pulps a body part (see back of book) if either of the damage dice roll a 10 and sufficient damage has been caused.

It can also be used to initiate pulping attacks at close range by taking a penalty and dealing damage as stated in the pulping rules.

No Skeleton!?
If you don't have an artificial skeleton then each time you use the hammer you take D6 points of damage which armour does not prevent.

Armour Damage
In addition each time the weapon hits a target, if they were wearing armour it loses one point of AV as the hammer smashes the plates and tears apart the weave. Very soft armour such as reinforced clothing will not be affected. The GM should request the Agent pay a relative fee to get the armour repaired.

For example, armour with AV 6 costing 1000¢ that has lost 3AV could cost around 500¢ to repair.

Ammunition
The hammer is powered by a fission cell mounted in a backpack. The cell has enough power for 100 discharges before needing to be replaced (Cost 1000¢).

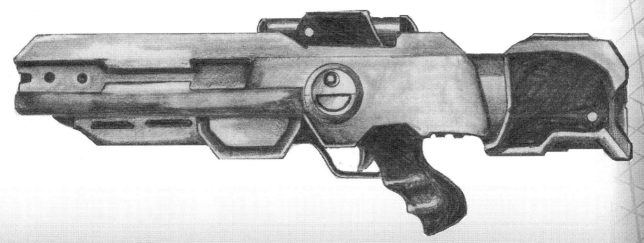

AMS Ragefire K90 Incendiary Rifle

CLOSE COMBAT

BAUSWORD - KAI LO 'TIAN SHI' BAUSWORD
| Damage D8+ Str | 600¢ | Close Range | Rate 2 | EMP Immune |

The blade of the balisword is hidden between two lengths of wood which fold out to provide the handle. This is effectively a larger version of the traditional balisong knife. Because of this the balisword has some special properties.

When folded away the weapon is very easy to conceal. It is only a few feet in length and looks like a short stick or walking cane. When in this state it can be used as a club following the normal rules. (Dam D6+Str / Rate 2)

AMMUNITION

TAIPAN DISSOLVING INJECTOR DARTS - 100¢

These darts are composed of a cellulose polysaccharide chain which, when exposed to air or moisture, begin to dissolve. The end result is that within D3 minutes of delivering their payload they have broken down into undetectable base materials; primarily carbon, hydrogen and oxygen.

The disadvantage of these darts is that they cannot be loaded into a weapon in advance as they start breaking down as soon as their vacuum sealed wraps are opened. For this reason you must spend one action opening the dart and another loading the gun immediately before firing. This wastes two actions and as such this weapon is not very useful in a fire fight. Its more common function is as a stealthy assassin's weapon.

Damage – These weapons deal one point of damage which means they require very careful aiming at totally unarmoured targets.

Note that if you have the 'Toxic Combat Training', (page 16 of MoW) then you can unwrap and load the dart as a single action. If you also have the 'Rapid Reload Training' (page 15 of MoW), then the whole process can be completed as a free action.

If you do not follow the procedure each round there is a cumulative 10% chance the dart will not fire and you end up with a dose of toxin in your weapon which will need to be cleaned out.

TAIPAN AUTO-HEALING INJECTOR DART 150¢

These function in exactly the same way as standard injector darts, (see page 44 of the Core Rules). However they contain a tiny dose of haemavine which acts to seal the entry hole made by the dart; this serves two purposes.
1.   It forces the dart out of the target.
2.   It removes any sign that the target was shot with a dart.

TAIPAN BLACK WIDOW INJECTOR DART - 200¢

The ultimate dart for clean assassinations, it combines the properties of the Auto-Healing Injector Dart and the Dissolving Injector Dart to give a completely evidence-free assassination experience.

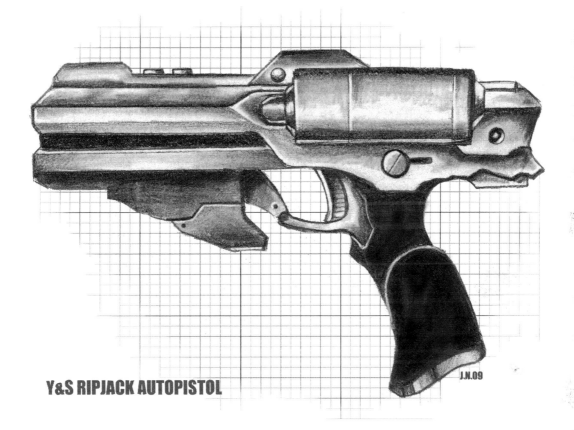

Y&S RIPJACK AUTOPISTOL

J.N.09

GUAN YU ARMOUR

member adds individual orange decals such as tiger stripes, blood spatter effects, cartoon characters, kill tallies, corporation logos etc. When inside the suit the user's voice is intentionally distorted and mechanical; this is designed to intimidate and is obviously successful as a similar system is used with the Malenbrach. Guan Yu does not confer the Voice of Authority bonus, unfortunately.

Penalties

Anyone wearing a suit gains -6 to all stealth related checks as the suit is extremely bulky and makes a lot of whining and grinding noises when in use.

By installing both of the following upgrades you can neutralise the penalty.
Adaptive Camouflage Lamina
Integrated Sound Suppression System

TRAINING - GUAN YU USE

Mechtronics 1
Access to a Guan Yu Suit.
Guan Yu Instructor

Anyone can learn to use the Guan Yu. As long as you have access to a suit to practice you can purchase this Training at the normal cost. Note that all Ai-Jinn Agents gain this Training for free at character creation. If you do not have an instructor you can still learn to use the suit but it requires another 10xp and an additional 4 weeks of downtime.
Without this training the suit is unusable.

GUAN YU HEAVY POWERED ARMOUR SYSTEM

Named after Guan Yu, an Chinese general who attained godhood, this heavy armour system has been produced in various models for over 150 years. This fact has ensured the armour is both reliable and cheap to produce, making it a favourite among Ai-Jinn Agents engaged in missions where the need for subtlety is low. The Guan Yu does not make use of Anti Grav units which is partially responsible for its low price. However, this makes it a nightmare to use and its use requires a great deal of practice. Ai-Jinn Agents are all taught to use Guan Yu in basic training and so receive the training Guan Yu Use for free.

DESCRIPTION

A full suit of Guan Yu is a fearsome sight. The armour is bulky and heavy due to the wealth of armour plating and large number of motors and power cells needed to drive the suit. A range of helmets are available most of which are intentionally feral and aggressive in appearance. Some users prefer clean, functional lines, some intimidating visors and others those with the face of a war-god or mythical beast.
The suit is normally black in colour but typically each Division

The Guan Yu! What better encapsulates the spirit of our Corporation than our armour? It is far from the most sophisticated personal defence system in the world, but sophistication and strength are two very different things; indeed, they are very nearly opposites. No, like us the strength of the Guan Yu lies not in its technical puissance but in its adaptability and its fluidity of purpose. In a way it is the corollary to the ion blades of the Shi Yukiro; for every form of attack they develop so shall our armour render us immune. The Guan Yu is not an inanimate suit of durasteel but a living creature in its own right, ever evolving to meet the challenges our foes present us with. Thus do we turn their own energy against them, for they must ever develop new strategies while we need only adapt to them, absorb them and move on. In this can be found the central tenet of our military philosophy, for when their imagination eventually and inevitably fails them we shall still remain, tempered by fires and hammers of their own making; invincible, unchallengeable, Ai-Jinn. Our victory is not an ideal, it is an inevitability.

- Dragon's Head Prasong Yao, Ai-Jinn Heavy Infantry Commander.

BASIC GUAN YU SUIT

Cost	20,000¢
AV Bonus	+6 AV
Maximum Agility	8*
Strength	+4
Stealth	-6 (This can place you in negative numbers)
Attitude Bonus	Anyone in Guan Yu gains +1 Attitude.
EMPS	The suit is immune to EMP. Any installed upgrade modules have an EMPS of 30.
Invisibility Fields	These are only half as effective as normal and so people only gain -4 to spot you, not -8.

*This applies to Trained Ai-Jinn only. Anyone not trained in the armour's use has a maximum Agility of 4. Note that this stacks with the Ai-Jinn 'Clanger' Training so the maximum Agility will increase to +10.

Power

The suit uses a fission battery which costs 500¢ and lasts about 30 days of constant use.

UPGRADE MODULES

The Guan Yu Amour Suit is a versatile piece of equipment and comes complete with five Uni-Grade ports capable of housing a range of useful additions. These upgrades vary in size, function and price but all can be installed into the suit by anyone with Mechtronics 1+ in only a few hours. Note that some modules require more than one port to install and you cannot install the same module twice unless noted.

Environmental Baffles

Cost   5,000¢
Ports   1

A re-breather system is incorporated into the armour and all gaps within the plates and mechanics are sealed. The user can breathe for 12 hours using the suit's air supply and is will not suffer from any airborne toxins. The air scrubber needs replacing after 12 hours which costs 20 credits.

Hard Ion Shield

Cost   5,500¢ for 60pt / 10,000 for 100pt.
Ports   1

An installed hard ion shield which can be activated as a free action. Because the suit is powered the ion shield immediately begins charging at the end of a combat scene at a rate of 1 HP per minute. You cannot wear a normal ion shield in the suit.

Ion Repulsion Field

Cost   15,000¢
Ports   1

This heavy upgrade creates an ion repulsion field which not only makes it harder to hit the target with any ion weapon but reduces the severing ability of such a weapon.
Ion weapon attacks suffer a -2 penalty and only ignore 5 AV.

Voice Disharmoniser

Cost   2,000¢
Ports   1

A helmet upgrade that makes the voice distortion effect of the standard Guan Yu even more effective as a tool of intimidation by adding fear-inducing subsonic cadences to the wearer's voice. Grants a further +2 bonus on Attitude rolls made to intimidate.

Psi-Shield

Cost   5,000¢
Ports   1

This upgrade can be installed multiple times. For each psi-shield installed the level of all telepathic effects directed against the suit's wearer are reduced by one; this includes your own.

ECM Field

Cost   15,000¢
Ports   2

Electronic countermeasures prevent the targeting systems used in A.I.-controlled turrets, droids and guided missiles from getting an accurate lock by electronically jamming their systems.

Attempts by automated or guided weapon systems to attack a wearer of a Guan Yu suit equipped with an ECM field suffer a -8 penalty.

EMP Shield

Cost   10,000¢
Ports   1

The user, his cybernetics and all his equipment are protected from EMP blasts. The EMPS of everything carried by the wearer is increased by 10.

Leap Pack

Cost   20,000¢
Ports   2

This sophisticated setup allows the user to leap large distances. He can jump up to 10x his Agility in metres. This requires the wearer to pass an 'Agility + Athletics' check. Failure means he has essentially catapulted himself into a hard surface and takes D6 damage per 10 metres he travelled. Armour helps against this damage. The leap function can be used once per 5 rounds as the system needs time to recharge between leaps.

Integrated Weaponry

Cost   Cost of the weapon + 1000¢ integration fee
Ports   1 per weapon

Weapons are integrated into the armour, typically on the arms but they can be added anywhere the user desires. Common upgrades include arm mounted swords, shoulder mounted tracking lasers and wrist mounted tiger claws. This upgrade must be purchased for each weapon. Integrated weapons do not have to be drawn and cannot be disarmed. They also normally have no need for clips if they use energy cells. If the player is abusing this by firing dozens of heavy plasma shots the GM should rule that the fission cell will run out early.

Anti Grav Booster Unit

Cost   12,000¢
Ports   2

The armour is streamlined and excess weight removed leaving a more athletic suit. A set of meticulously calibrated AG units are then installed into the armour taking its basic maximum Agility to 10. This means if you have the Clanger Training, it can increase to 12.

Armour Reinforcement

Cost   3,000¢
Ports   1

The suit is further reinforced with plates of durasteel. The armour becomes heavier and more solid but gains an additional +2 AV.

The Maximum Agility of the suit is reduced to 7. The suit needs to be fitted with a new movement chip to compensate for the additional weight which uses a single Uni-Grade port. This cannot be used in conjunction with the Anti Grav Booster Unit upgrade. If you have the Clanger Training you can ignore the drop in Maximum Agility.

Micro-Shock Outfitting
Cost   6,000¢
Ports   1
Micro-Shock Absorbers are installed into the lower joints of the Guan Yu suit as well as a regulator chipset which allows the shocks to react appropriately to sudden impacts. The user considers all drops 50 metres lower for the purposes of calculating damage as long as they land on their feet. This means an Agent in Guan Yu with this augmentation can jump from a 52 metre height before needing to worry about damage. Accidental falls where you don't land on your feet are treated normally.
These are often installed into an entire squad's suits so they can rapid-deploy from hover copters in urban environments.

GM note: For simplicity you can consider a typical building level is 3 metres meaning the Agent can jump out of a 17 storey window without any risk to herself.

Port Splitter
Cost   20,000¢
Ports   0
The Guan Yu design is very old and has been tried and tested for decades. For this reason alterations to the core design are tricky and disproportionally expensive. The Port Splitter can be purchased a maximum of three times and each installation gives the Guan Yu suit an extra port. This means that you can have a maximum of 8 ports on your suit.

Med-Station
Cost   6,000¢
Ports   1
The Guan Yu has a small med-station installed into it, which attaches to the user via set of needles inserted into the chest. At the beginning of each round, if the user has taken damage it heals her a maximum of 15HP even if the user is unconscious. The med-station contains enough haemavine to heal 50HP. Then a new H-Pack must be purchased which costs 1200¢. This replaces a normal medpack.

Optical Package
Cost   5,000¢
Ports   1
This integrated optical package allows the wearer to see in infra red and thermal.

Combat Talons
Cost   3,000¢
Ports   1
A set of razor-sharp, retractable durasteel talons are fitted into the suits arms. They can be extended as a reflex and do not even require a free action. They allow the use to add +5 to each unarmed close combat strike and ignore 2 points of AV. You may suffer a small GM imposed penalty if you attempt some action with the talons extended. E.g. -2 to fire tactical weapons.

The talons grant +4 to all climbing based rolls but this does not stack with other climbing aids such as palm thorns or ropes.

Adaptive Camouflage Lamina
Cost   3,000¢
Ports   1
A variant of polychromatic paint is applied to the suit and then a tough photo-electric polymer is layered over. The polymer detects the colour makeup of the ambient environment and passes the information to the paint which responds by changing its pigmentation. The end result is chameleon-like ability for the suit to change its pattern and colour based upon the environment. The lamina is also connected to a CPU inside the suit which allows the user to select from a number of presets such as desert camo, snow camo, jungle camo, Mars camo, pure black, parade colours, sentry colours, formal insignias etc.
The subject gains +3 to Stealth checks when wearing the suit.

Integrated Sound Suppression System
Cost   4,000¢
Ports   1
A modified sound suppression system allows the suit to operate silently. The system is superior to a standard Sound Absorption Field as the user is still able to hear incoming noise and he can use his smeaker and comm. devices normally.
The user gains +3 to Stealth checks when wearing the suit.

Armoured Storage
Cost   Varies
Ports   1 (This single port controls all compartments)

Armoured Storage compartments are added to various parts of the Guan Yu suit.

Size	Points	Example	Space	Cost
Small	1	Forearm Compartment	Dart / Credit Chip / Micrenade	500¢
Medium	2	Thigh Case, Chest Comp.	Pistol / Grenade / Sandwich	1000¢
Large	5	Small Backpack	Human Head / Medical Kit / Tent	2000¢
Huge	10	Large Backpack	2 Tac weapons / heavy weapon	4000¢

For every 6 points of storage your maximum Agility is reduced by 1. For example, if you have 1 medium and 2 small, you will be unaffected. If you were to add another medium space, your max agility would be reduced by 1.
You can have a maximum of 12 points of storage installed. The compartments are opened by reflex command (hence the need for a port) and are well armoured (AV 6). They do not contribute to your overall AV.

Nakamori backed up two measured paces, out of the faint pool of sulphur-yellow light trickling down from many stories above. Long seconds whispered past before the other Agent emerged from the shadows into the murky glow, and Nakamori's grip tightened on his ion katana as his eyes picked out details. The dirty ochre light slid off the harsh angles of armour plate, bolted in many layers to a recognisably human frame, rendering its proportions monstrous. Even in the semidarkness of the alley, the Shi Yukiro Agent could make out the pitting of rust and corrosion around joint seals and nano-rivet lattices, and he needed no light to smell the acrid stench of old, burned oil.

A rat skittered past Nakamori's feet, queasy luminescense glistened off a dark flow of effluent coiling down the cracked stonework to his side, but he ignored everything, fixing all of his attention on the faceplate of his opponent's suit. The narrow slit was almost opaque, betraying only a faint greenish tinge from instruments within the armoured helmet. Nakamori's eyes burned into it, seeking some contact with the Agent inside, something that might connect the two of them in the intimacy of battle.

The Ai-Jinn Agent lumbered forward with treacherous speed, actuators and pistons squalling; a thick sword stabbed clumsily up at stomach height. Nakamori took a single, precise step to the right, ion katana surging to life, and sliced through the suit's weapon just above the hilt. As it clattered to the ground the armoured Agent dropped noisily to one knee and brought up its other arm; a series of muzzle flashes seared the alley for a moment and Nakamori grunted as shrapnel spattered from the walls and a line of fire tore across his right shoulder.

Years of gruelling training as a boy had left Nakamori able to cut almost as accurately with one hand as with two. A long step took him inside his opponent's range as he hefted the ion katana; he flicked the blade on halfway through its downward arc, shut it down as soon as the same motion pulled it clear of the suit's collar armour. The green glow was instantly blanked, a dark red spattering across the inside of the suit's faceplate as the Agent collapsed.

His right arm dangling uselessly, the samurai flicked blood from the blade of his weapon and straightened. A great clanking and grinding, deafeningly loud in the narrow confines of the alley, made him look round. Four more suits now flanked him, two blocking the alley in each direction, the dark bulk of their oversized shoulderguards almost completely filling the enclosed space. Nakamori raised his weapon in his one good hand, trembling now with exertion, as the stench of burned oil rose about him like a funeral pyre.

The Jade Emperor - Oppressor Class Warship

GUAN YU DIVISION

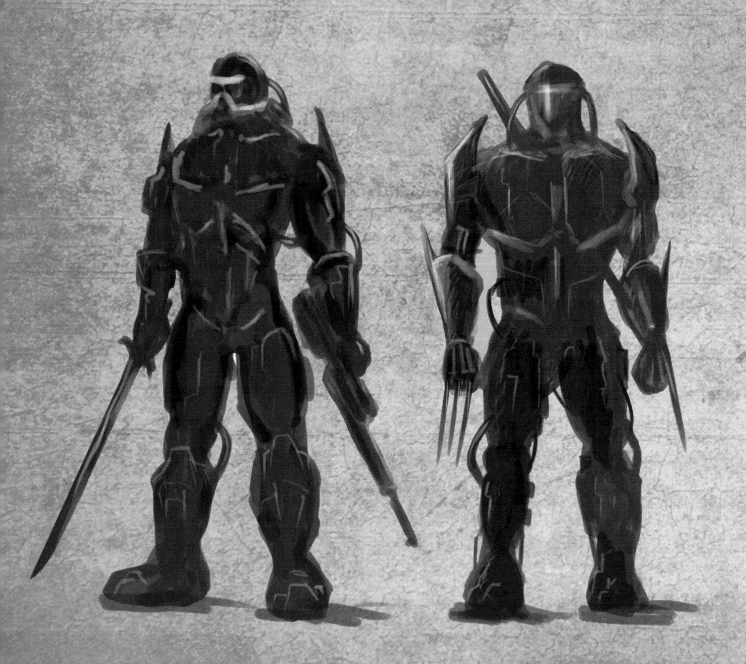

ASSAULT   CLOSE COMBAT

THE IRON OF QI

JN 09

HEAVY   SCOUT

GENERAL EQUIPMENT

POLICE LIGHTS (PORTABLE) 500¢

Typically you can only buy these items on production of a Response Driver License (page xx).

The item is a small fist sized block with clear plastic sides which when activated emits a 130db siren and blue strobing emergency lights. The power core is good for 3 years normal use. It has a reusable grip pad to attach securely to smooth surfaces but can be easily detached when necessary.

METH LAB   1500¢

This collection of trays, distillers, burners, tubes and vials is used for the creation of methamphetamine or similar shake 'n bake drugs. To use the lab you need at least Science 1 and a spare day. The process of creating the drugs is dangerous due to the toxicity of the chemicals and their volatile nature.

Making drugs in your lab

1. Acquire the chemicals; these can be purchased in general stores and over the counter at pharmacies. Enough raw materials for a day's work costs 100¢

2. Brew the drugs – this requires a 'Science + Intelligence' roll. If you fail the roll you have messed up the process and your raw materials are wasted. A critical fail means the lab explodes dealing 10D6 in a 15 metre blast radius.

3. For each point of XS you score on the roll you will make 100¢ worth of drugs. For example, if you pass your roll by 4 you will produce drugs with a street value of 400¢. You'll need to pass by 1 to cover your own costs.

Selling the meth is normally done by street dealers who can take between 10 and 50% of the cash.

VACUUM PLASMA RETROFIT   500¢

Standard plasma weapons cannot function in the vacuum of space owing to the absence of suitable gasses to convert to plasma. A plasma weapon with this upgrade has been modified to accept super-compressed hydrogen flasks to replace their atmospheric requirements when in space. The muzzle cowling also has a vaguely phallic appearance, which tends to put some people off using it outside of space.

HYDROGEN FLASKS   50¢

Allows plasma weapons to be fired in a vacuum, lasts for the same number of shots as an Energy Cell, or up to 40 rounds in the case of plasma close combat weapons. The weapon must receive the vacuum plasma retrofit (left) to make use of hydrogen flasks.

ATMOSPHERIC EQUALISER 8,000¢

This clever piece of tech is used by those interested in breaking and entering. Many modern alarm systems use shifts in atmospheric currents or pressure as part of their activation protocol. This device is an expandable frame which can be clamped onto a surface. When a hole is made into the secure area, the equaliser emits a manipulator field which ensures there is no significant shift in atmospheric pressure. It can regulate a hole up to 1 square metre.

Note that the pressure shift is generally only one stage of a good alarm system. However some crude systems, such as most car alarms are entirely based on pressure shifts.

System: Make an 'Intelligence + Crime' check to successfully place the equaliser before creating the hole.

HIGH INTEGRITY CASE (HI CASE)

Size	Example	Cost	Damage	Containment
Small	Briefcase	200¢		100
Medium	Suitcase	500¢		200
Large	1 cubic metre	1000¢		400

These are used for the transport of explosives and are resistant to internal explosions. If the explosive inside goes off the case will contain an amount of damage as stated in the Damage Containment. Any extra spills out. Damage is considered maximised for purposes of determining how much is dealt. If the case takes its Damage Containment in damage, it is destroyed.

Example – You are carrying 7 unstable grenades in a small HI Case. If something happens that might set them off such as a massive car crash, the grenades will detonate dealing 7x18=126 damage. The case will absorb 100 damage and 26 spills over onto whatever is near the case. The case is destroyed.

DATA SCRAMBLER (EMP BUTTON)   400¢

This small, button-sized device delivers a potent electromagnetic charge into any item it is attached to. The radius is only a few centimetres so it is useless as a weapon and anything with an EMPS of 2 or more is automatically immune to it.

Its normal use is for destroying electronic data such as that on computer drives. Typically the owner will attach a button to each sensitive device he owns. When a button is activated the digital data is destroyed.

Triggering the EMP Buttons.

There are two main ways to trigger the button though someone with the Jury-Rigging Training and a high mechtronics skill could try to set up different systems.

Master Button

For 200¢ a master button can be purchased which is calibrated to one or all active EMP buttons. When the master button is pressed the EMP goes off and all linked devices are scrambled. The master button is also small and usually attached to the user's belt or gun. Recalibrating the master button to activate different charges takes 15 seconds.

A.I. Link

The user requires an internal A.I. of 3 or more.
For 1000¢ a tiny piece of code is added to the A.I. and a transmitter inserted into the scalp. When the user wishes he can trigger one or all of the EMP buttons.

GRAPPLE (PERSONAL)   2,000¢

This item resembles a high-tech bracer which clamps onto the forearm. It is engineered to fit any size from a slim wrist to heavy, customised armour. A small remote neurolink is injected under the skin on the wrist when the grapple is purchased, which allows the user to control the various functions of the grapple by voluntary muscle action.

When activated a tiny, high penetration dart, connected to a 50 metre length of high-tensile cable is fired from the bracer. This dart will automatically embed itself into anything with an AV of 20 or less causing 1 point of damage. Once the dart has reached a target the cable stops unwinding and the user can reel himself in. The grapple will support a total weight of 400kg which roughly equates to:

1 heavily augmented Agent with all field kit
2 augmented Agents with field kit
3 standard Agents with some kit
4 normal humans with some kit
5 normal humans with no kit.

The dart can be directed to unhook by voluntary muscle action. The cable can also be detached in case of an emergency.

This item is repeated in Machines of War where a cybernetic version is also available.

SAT-TRACKER (UIG ONLY)   COST 8,000¢

This handheld PDA style device relays satellite and archive data to the UIG Officer giving him a digitally optimised bird's eye view of the area. He is able to view in any of the following ways, which can be mixed and matched as desired. Sat-trackers can scan anywhere in the world and have an effectively unlimited range, however certain satellite types may be at a given time, out of range meaning it is possible for a certain scan type to be temporarily unavailable. Its scanning ability can be blocked by structures, high radioactivity and sat blankets at the GM's whim.

These are commonly used in conjunction with UIG Personal Teleporters (Core Rules) and Phase Matching.

Below is a list of the common scan types available with the Sat-Tracker.

1. High resolution video, effectively viewing the area as if from a helicopter.

2. Blips – targets such as cars and people are rendered as different coloured 'circles'

3. Building Blueprint – Blueprints of the building are overlaid onto the image where available

4. Threat assessment – penetrative sensory modes allow the officer to detect cyberware and weapons. This is not accurate but will give an indication of the likelihood that the carried hardware is potentially dangerous.

5. ID Chips – This is only used in cases of extreme emergency as the UIG maintain they do not track people via their ID Chips. When this mode is active the Officer has access to all ID Chip information for every target on the Sat-Tracker. The paranoid often rely on an ID Chip Scrambler (Machines of War) to prevent this form of scanning.

6. Thermal – The Sat-Trackers show the area in terms of heat emissions.

7. Penetrative Scan – This can scan inside a building but the data is poor and only information such as '20 life forms present' or '10 vehicles present' can be determined.

Note that this item, like almost all UIG equipment, will be chip-locked and unusable by non-designated UIG.

LEGACY PATTERN TECHNOLOGY

INTRODUCTION

The Ai-Jinn has a shadowy reputation among the other Corporations for possessing access to technology of advancement and sophistication far in excess of their apparent resources. Their rivals look at the crude, smoke-belching vehicles and barking kinetic weaponry that typifies the Ai-Jinn and then shake their heads in incredulity at the otherworldly science behind the FarDrive, it looks for all the world like spear-waving savages who have learned how to build televisions.

Most suspect the invisible hand of the rogue Archons at work behind the Ai-Jinn's anachronistic advancements but ultimately no hard evidence has ever been found connecting the two, not that any is expected given the mastery of world information the Archons possess.

So far, all serious investigations into the subject have traced the source of the wonders available to the Ai-Jinn back to the mysterious 'Legacy Project'. But while the Ai-Jinn's Corporate rivals may be suspicious and envious of this 'Legacy Tech', the UIG are plainly terrified by it, especially as so much of it seems to be geared specifically to countering the gifts bestowed onto them by the remaining loyalist Archons. Worse still, many of these items are almost standard-issue among the subgroup within the Ai-Jinn known as 'The Knives' who concern themselves primarily with anti-UIG operations.

While often appearing quite ordinary at first glance, legacy pattern tech works on principles that are utterly mysterious to those used to working with common technology. Studying an item of legacy pattern tech is much like opening up your laptop and, instead of finding circuit boards, discovering that it's filled with a block of solid gel possessing variable levels of electrical resistance throughout its structure on the picometre scale. Quite simply, legacy pattern tech is incomprehensible to those not used to working with it, even engineers familiar with xenotechnology will typically be at a loss as to even describe how it functions, much less work on it. As such, characters may not reverse-engineer or make Science or Mechtronics rolls relating to legacy pattern tech items at all, including repairing or modifying them, and all Assess Tech rolls will be made at a -12 penalty; the Xenotech training (see 'Machines of War') reduces this penalty to -6.

A specific sub-sect, the Legacy Operatives, have a special capacity with regard to legacy pattern tech, see 'Ai-Jinn sub-sects' on page 32 for more details.

LEGACY-TECH ACCESS

The products of the Legacy Project are not for sale, nor are they widely distributed even within the Corporation. The combination of high production costs and the risk of such potent items falling into the hands of rivals who may, however improbably, discover the secrets of their manufacture means that they are only distributed to trusted and competent Agents.

How to Award Legacy Technology

Legacy Agents have a special system for gaining Legacy Technology as detailed on page 32. For other Agents you should offer it as a reward for partiularly important missions. As a rough guide a division could have access to Legacy Tech with an Access Point cost equal to half their combined rank.

Example, a division of 5 rank 2 Agents will have legacy tech to a value of 5 Access Points. However, this is not automatic and is only granted to those who are deserving.

LEGACY PATTERN AMOUR

PHASE BLOCK ARMOUR - ACCESS 5

Any conventional armour-type can be made of a phase-opaque material that exploits the molecular phase-matching capacity of UIG Ghost weapons (to absorb and dissipate their impact. AV derived from phase block armour is doubled versus phasing weapons. The normal AV applies to other weapons in the standard manner.

The type of armour would not change the access level very much but as an example, this level 5 item would be Heavy Combat Armour. Light Combat Armour may drop it to level 4.

LEGACY DRUGS & TOXINS

RED SHIFT - ACCESS I

Potency 10

Injected - Users of Red Shift find their ability to detect the cues most creatures, and even droids, telegraph when preparing to attack sharpened to a frighteningly precise edge, enabling them to predict the flow of combat with a degree of immediate accuracy that even prescient telepaths look at with envy.

Even the smallest sign, from a whitening of the knuckles as an enemy tightens their grip on their weapon, to a quickly-indrawn breath or whine of charging weapon capacitors, is like a flashing warning light when using Red Shift.

While under the influence of Red Shift the user is able even to dodge gunfire, the user's Initiative score in combat is automatically considered to be 1 point higher than the highest Initiative roll in the entire group, enemy and ally.

If there is more than one Red Shift user present in the combat then they must make opposed 'Perception + Observation' rolls to see who acts first. The user may also apply their Perception score as a penalty against one ranged attack made against them per round, additional ranged attacks made against them that round do not suffer this penalty. Red Shift lasts for one scene.

NEUROMEMETIC PSEUDO-VIRUS - ACCESS 3
(A.K.A - NPV, THE TEARS OF GOD)
Potency 9

Injected - The most powerful truth-serum in existance, NPV is nonetheless rarely employed unless the subject is completely expendable due to its mind-shattering effects. Occasionally though, it has been employed as a terror-weapon, leaving UIG informants as stuttering, soul-dead shells, their whole lives turned into a cavalcade of nightmares. After being injected with NPV, if the victim is posed a question they become afflicted with a form of targeted glossolalia for the next D10 minutes, during that time they will tell their interrogator everything they know about the questioned subject in rapid, mindless speech, reliving and describing everything they have experienced relating to the subject. However, once the question has been implanted it cannot be changed and, should the person injected with NPV at any time exhaust their knowledge of the subject, then they will experience nightmarish visions and sinister, distorted flashbacks as their memories are corrupted, sustaining 1 point of permanent Presence damage per minute that it continues.

Finial Kurtis sat awkwardly on the old plastic chair that they'd set up in their impromptu interrogation room and kept his eyes to the floor, visibly trying to block out the knowledge that three feet behind him Agent Ya had a Cougar trained unwaveringly at the back of his head.

Agent Jimao stifled the brief pang of pity at the sight of the pathetic little man. It wasn't hard, he had little sympathy for snitches. He took the chair on the opposite side of the table from Finny and reached inside his jacket. The man flinched slightly, but made no other move, more afraid of the present weapon in Ya's hand than the possible one Jimao might draw.

You might regret that later. Jimao thought.

He removed a small black case, about as wide as his thumb and no more than twice as long, and set it carefully on the table. Finny stared at it with a mixture of trepidation and curiosity.

"Do you know what this is?" said Jimao, opening the case and retrieving its contents - an injector filled with a clear, colourless liquid, the letters 'NPV' stamped on the side.
Finny shook his head nervously, apparently too frightened to speak. That would change, one way or another.

"Neither do I," said Jimao, holding it up to the light. "Inside it are trillions of these microscopic 'things', not quite viruses, not quite bacteria, not quite nanites, I really have no idea what they are. The scientists call it 'neuromimetic pseudo-virus', but I always thought that was a little overly wordy. Call me a romantic but I much prefer 'The Tears of God'." He paused, savouring the look of fearful confusion on Finny's face.
"But I'm getting ahead of myself, what it is is academic compared to what it does, am I right?"

Finny gave a cautious nod, as though unsure if it were a trick question or not. "Yeah, I suppose."

"Good. Well, what it does is act as the most potent truth serum known to man."

A small spark of desperate defiance welled up in Finny. "Yeah? Then why don't you quit the strongarm bollocks and use it, fucker?" he spat, like a cornered rat ready to fight with every last futile ounce of resolve left in its body.

Jimao chuckled under his breath. "For several reasons. Because, despite time being of the essence, this stuff is too valuable to waste on worms like you. Because I want to give you a chance to tell us what the UIG now know about our operations in Chengdu. But mainly because once I dose you with this, for the next few minutes you will tell me everything you told them." Jimao leaned back in his chair and put his hands behind his head, nonchalantly. "A few minutes is a long time to talk about just one thing, I wonder whether you know that much. But you see, if you don't know enough to keep the 'things' inside that vial satisfied then they'll just start looking for other things, taking your mind apart piece by piece." Jimao cracked a wide smile. "I have a lot of unpleasant memories, hardly surprising with a life like mine. What about you, Finny, do you have many unpleasant memories?"

"A few," came the furtive reply.

"Haunt you, don't they?" said Jimao, letting a ring of false but convincing compassion seep into his tone.

"Yeah," replied Finny, voice cracking as the fear and pressure started to burst his mental dams.

Jimao unthreaded his fingers and leaned across the table until they were eye-level. "And how exactly do you think you'd be, do you suppose, if those were all you had?"

The moment of truth approached.

Finny's eyes screwed up in desperation-borne hate. "Fuck you, I just passed around a bit of info and you think it gives you the right to pull this bullshit on me? Go to hell."

Agent Jimao sighed. "That's a terrible shame, Mr. Kurtis. You know I was quite impressed with your ingenuity at uncovering our legacy plant, and combined with willpower like that you could have been fit for the Agent program." He retrieved the NPV injector and flipped the cap off the lancet with his thumb.

"'Could have been', being the operative phrase, I doubt you will be much use to the Corp any more after this. Hold him down."

LEGACY PATTERN GENERAL EQUIPMENT

Q-CORE INSURGENCY COMPUTER
ACCESS 8

Appearing as a slim palmtop computer, this device is a potent data-piracy tool that incorporates, among other things, a crystalline quantum logic core that makes it faster at decryption than conventional supercomputers many hundreds of times its size. It possesses all the features of a standard hacking computer with the following additions;

1. All security systems accessed are considered to be one level lower for hacking purposes, i.e. an Elite system is considered a Secure system, a Secure system is considered a Commercial system etc. A Domestic system doesn't stand a chance, all hacking attempts made against such poorly-defended systems are automatically successful providing a critical fail isn't rolled on the hacking attempt.

2. Hacking rolls made with the computer take only 10 seconds, not 1 minute.

3. Any computer system within 10 metres can be accessed wirelessly, regardless of whether it has a WDN up-link or not.

PHASE-OSMOTIC FLUID - 'GHOSTBUSTER'
ACCESS 1

Sprayed onto a relatively porous substance such as a brick, stone or plaster wall, this greasy, colourless liquid renders the material more 'opaque' to phase matching technology, such as UIG 'Ghost' systems. Anyone attempting to use phase-matching technology to pass through a wall treated with phase-osmotic fluid is in serious danger of molecular binding.

Increase the chance of molecular binding by 45% when phasing through an obstacle that has been so treated, meaning that phase-matched attempts are made with a 50% chance of molecular binding and phasing without waiting for a perfect phase-match always results in molecular binding.

A single aerosol of phase-osmotic fluid is sufficient to cover 400 square metres.

DERESONATOR PLUG
ACCESS 2

A more convenient and covert but less effective version of the Immobiliser Shield employed by UIG marshals, this device uses the casing of a task chip. It is installed in the user's process socket where it shields them from the effects of immobiliser weapons, conferring a +8 bonus to the user's resistance roll. Unlike the UIG Immobiliser Shield there is no invasive procedure to its use and it is hard to tell it from a normal chip without installing it. A more advanced version of the Deresonator Plug (available for +1 Access point) can also include a task program, making it even harder to tell from a normal chip without first installing it and shooting oneself with an immobiliser rifle, something that understandably few are willing to go through.

MIMETIC PANOPLY - ACCESS 1 PER FORM

Using a combination of alien memory metals, piconite assembly and poorly understood variable-state material technology, these strange objects are able to take the form of several useful devices as well as returning to an innocuous 'neutral' form on command. When requisitioned, the Mimetic Panoply has a number of forms

equal to the Access Points invested in it, up to a maximum of 5. Some possible forms are listed below, though the GM may allow others, all have the 'neutral' form for free. Changing the form of a Mimetic Panoply is a free action.

Neutral - Takes the form of an object made of a shiny chrome-like metal, often an item of jewelry such as a bracelet or necklace (with chain). May also possess some small, rudimentary function, such as a working wristwatch. The size of the neutral form is dependant on the number of Access Points spent on the device, a Mimetic Panoply with only one form might be no bigger than a large signet ring, one with five could be as large as a forearm-bracer.

Binoculars - As described in the Core Rulebook (page 50).

Blade - Effect dependant on panoply size, a panoply with 1-2 forms counts as a combat knife, a panoply with 3-4 forms counts as a short sword and a panoply with 5 forms counts as a longsword. If the 'plasma emitter' form is also selected then the blade may function as a plasma weapon if the user desires but drains one second of use from the plasma emitter per combat it is used in this way.

Grapple - On command the panoply launches a grapple-spike by means of material tension, trailing behind it a textured memory-metal cable of up to 20 metres in length +10 metres for each additional form. The spike will embed itself in any material with an AV of 20 or less, causing one point of damage. It does not automatically reel but the cable's surface intelligently assists climbers, providing a +4 bonus to Athletics checks made to climb it.

Laser Pistol - As described in the Core Rulebook (page 35). May be recharged at a rate of 1 shot per 10 minutes when connected to a power supply. Standard energy cells are NOT used.

Lockpicks - As described in the Core Rulebook (page .52).

Plasma Emitter - The panoply can function as an advanced plasma cutting torch, ignoring up to 25 points of AV and lasting for 4 rounds (12 seconds). This is long enough to cut a large door sized hole in a typical steel wall. If used as a close combat weapon it ignores 25 points of AV and deals D6 damage. It may be recharged at a rate of 1 hour per turn used when connected to a power supply.

Security Bypass Device - As described in the Core Rulebook (page 52).

Self-Destruct - As a last-ditch measure the Mimetic Panoply may induce a piconite system meltdown, resulting in a plasma explosion that deals 9D10 Damage, Ignoring AV, with a 15 metre blast radius.

Toxin Filter - Stretched across the face, the panoply can act as a level 8 toxin filter.

Shield - The panoply may fold out into an armoured shield approximately 2.5 feet in diameter. This confers a +1 bonus to the wearer's AV and allows them to defend against melee attacks unarmed, if the panoply possesses 3 or more forms the AV bonus is increased to +2.

It had been a hard day at the office, it always was, and Richard Erickson, regional UIG governor for lesser southwestern Eurasia, had always been happy to accept that. Like most people he had developed coping mechanisms for dealing with daily stress, all it took was a few double bourbons and an afternoon of mind-numbing television and he was ready to deal with all the frustration, anger, pointless legalism and chilling horror that accompanied the job of a UIG official in the Eurasian corporate state. What he wasn't ready to deal with was returning home to find his wife, Eluice, unconscious in the hallway just beside the front door, as though someone had just absent-mindedly left her there on their way in. Panicked, he made a break for the living room phone without thinking about the possibility that whoever had done it was still there.

He flipped on the living room lights and immediately yelped in shock at what they illuminated. A man of mixed-Asian descent wearing a black business suit regarded him with cold eyes from the middle of the room, hands clasped behind his back.
"What the-? Who the fuck are you?" Richard stammered, his hand already going for the Raven 220 in his shoulder-holster and ripping it free.

The stranger looked unconcerned by the fact that Richard had just levelled the most powerful kinetic handgun on Earth squarely at his head, making no reaction other than to glance at it briefly.
"You have a chip scanner, do you not?" he said, almost sounding bored by the whole situation.

The cordiality of the reply caught Erikson off-guard for a moment before he unhooked the scanner from his belt and directed the scan beam at the intruder, keeping his firearm trained on him as he did. Obligingly, the stranger held out his hand to make the scan easier. A moment later and the scanner gave a readout;

Cpt. Huikai, Wu.
DOB: 14/05/2467
Corporate Agent, Ai-Jinn Mining And Macrostructure.
Logged Felonies;
6 counts, Industrial Theft
8 counts, Breaking And Entering
21 counts, Justifiable Homicide

All things considered, a relatively clean slate for an Agent.

"Look, I haven't had any dealings with Ai-Jinn business, I swear," he said, groping at a perceived lifeline.

The Agent tilted his head slightly, like a bird, a strangely mechanical motion.

"This does not concern my... employer," he said in a papery monotone.

Richard stopped in confusion a moment. "Then why-?" he began but was cut off impatiently by the Agent.
"The unpurged images of day recede; the Emperor's drunken soldiery are abed; night resonance recedes, night walkers' song after great cathedral gong; a starlit or a moonlit dome disdains all that man is, all mere complexities, the fury and the mire of human veins." he said, intoning the words as if reading from some internal script.

"What was that?"

"A poem, part of one anyway, by Yeats, I believe," the Agent replied, turning to leave.

"What? You came here, broke into my house and assaulted my wife just to read me a fucking poem?" Richard said, incredulously.

"Yes," said the Agent, barely pausing.

"Why? What the hell is it even supposed to mean!?" Richard cried aloud, anger and fear ready to push him over the edge.
The Agent sighed, shoulders drooping as though asked some stupidly trivial question.

"To answer the second part of your question; because one of the Three who were once of the Nine willed it. As for the 'why'? I do not know and probably never will, but you will, one day you will know what those words mean and then you shall act upon them. Or perhaps you shall not, in either case you will no longer be of interest to the one who sent me."

And then he was gone, vanishing into the night as silently as a ghost.

The med teams arrived quickly after Erikson called, one of the few benefits of working in Eurasia, and soon informed him that Eluice was in no danger as they loaded her onto the ambulance. He called in every spare CRO squad to search the area but they found no trace of the Agent. The forensics team found nothing either, but that hadn't surprised him, atrophic DNA covers a multitude of sins, after all. The fact that the chip scanner hadn't logged the scan, on the other hand, surprised him a great deal, it was UIG-issue and meant to be impossible to tamper with.

Except, he later qualified, by an Archon.

VOIDSEAL
Don't take chances. - A.X.E

LEGACY PATTERN WEAPONS

MINIATURISED LASER AGGRESSOR - 'GEMGUN' (LIGHT FIREARM)

1-6D10 Damage	Access Points 4	Long Range	Rate 1	EMPS 15

Though small enough to fit into an item of jewelry, this device is in fact a laser projector packing the firepower of a heavy weapon, making it an excellent assassination tool or surprise weapon. The weapon has six charges, each doing D10 damage, the user may fire off all the charges at once for a single 6D10 blast or stagger it over several shots as desired. Spent charges restore themselves at a rate of 1 per four hours without needing a direct power feed. If mounted on a ring or bracelet it is used with the Light Firearms skill, otherwise use Athletics for such items as pendants or lapel-pin mounts.

They are considered laser weapons and automatically calibrate to targeted shields after 1 round of aiming. Furthermore, due to their alien mechanisms and use of esoteric power-sources, Gemguns are not identifiable by any conventional scanner technology, including the more commonly used Archon-tech scanners.

ION-TRANSPARENT LONGSWORD (TACTICAL CLOSE COMBAT)

D8 + Strength	Access Points 6	Close Combat	Rate 2	EMP Immune

Made from a strange matte-gray metal, these weapons boast not only a fantastically sharp edge, allowing them to ignore 4 points of AV, but have the strange property of bypassing ion shields as though they didn't exist, allowing users to attack ion wall generators through the field and rendering UIG close-form ion shields, such as those found in Erabite armour, completely worthless.

Note that ion-transparent weapons do not shut down or even deplete the HP of ion shields they come into contact with, they just pass right through them without disruption. The stats for the longsword above are only one example of ion-transparent weapons; any solid metal weapon, even shurikens and other thrown weapons, can be made ion-transparent. The access point cost remains the same.

GRAVIPLASMIC PISTOL (LIGHT FIREARM)

3D10 Damage	Access Points 6	Medium Range	Rate 2	EMPS 11

This weapon uses a form of vapourised neutronium stored in a mass-negating internal containment node as its plasmic medium, as opposed to the helium used in common plasma weapons. Graviplasma shots follow all the same rules for ordinary plasma weapons but deal more damage due to the awesome concussive effect.

For purposes of determining damage type, graviplasma damage is considered both plasma and kinetic damage. After 30 shots the internal neutronium supply is exhausted and a new pistol must be requisitioned.

DECONSTRUCTION RIFLE (LEGACY PATTERN AX9 CARMANIC FLUX RIFLE) (TACTICAL FIREARM)

2D10 Damage	Access Points 8	Long Range	Rate 1	EMPS 5

This highly advanced weapon delivers an orb-state nano-shell which explodes upon impact generating a sphere of highly aggressive, corrosive nanites which attempt to dissolve anything within 1 metre of the impact point.

Anything within the area of effect takes 2D10 damage which ignores all non-nanite AV*. If the target was damaged then it continues to take D10 damage a round for the next 10 rounds which also ignores non-nanite AV.

*Nanite based armour such as naninuium body pates IS effective against all damage dealt by this weapon.

This weapon uses nanite clusters as ammunition which cost 100¢ and provide 3 shots.

Using a Tazer or EMP attack on the affected target will instantly halt all nanite activity. However you may require the target to make a science related roll to know this.

LEGACY PATTERN WEAPONS

AI-JINN FARLABS DEATHKNELL ENTROPY GRENADE

Special (see below)	Access Points	3	Support Weapons	Rate 1	EMPS 7

Entropy grenades use FarDrive-derived technology to create an undifferentiated subspace reaction, a spherical explosion of dull, grey un-light with properties similar to the energy-manipulating field created by telepaths. The field causes all energy within the 6-metre blast radius to be evenly distributed throughout its area, with the net result of disrupting all thermodynamic processes occurring within it, including life. Those killed by the entropic wake simply fall over dead, without any apparent wounds or injuries anywhere on their bodies.

When using an Entropy Grenade roll 2D8 to determine the effect on all targets within the blast radius, detailed below;

Target	Effect
Living Being*	If roll exceeds Endurance score, reduced to 0HP.
Droid	If roll exceeds Endurance score, droid fails and must be repaired.
Equipment/Cybernetics*	If roll exceeds Condition, equipment fails and must be repaired.
Vehicles (Van-size or smaller)	If roll exceeds Condition, vehicle stalls and must be repaired.

If the target is protected by a shield, whether Hard Ion or Telepathic, they suffer no risk of the above effects but the HP of their shield is instantly halved, regardless of how strong it previously was. Note that this only effects shields that have an appreciable part fitting within the blast radius of the grenade, trying to halve the shield of a cyberlin with a handheld entropy weapon is neither going to work or go well for you.

* In cases where a living target possesses Endurance-augmenting cybernetics, consider the living target to be affected first, thus retaining any cybernetic bonus or penalty to Endurance even if the cybernetic augmentation in question would be rendered nonfunctional by the grenade.

> WARNING: Class 7 UDS reaction technology is employed in this device. Testing on UDSRT is not yet complete. Neither the Ai-Jinn Corporation or its affiliates thereof are responsible for any consequence of improper use, including but not limited to: death, dismemberment, permanent physiological re-ordering, irreparable damage to cybernetics and/or materiel, spontaneous quantum events, spontaneous cosmic events, time dilation, time distortion, resonance cascades, miniature black hole chains, the end of the world, the end of the universe, the beginning of (a) new universe(s), irritation of the skin and headaches. Keep out of reach of children.

ANTIPSION SYNAPTIC SHIV (LIGHT CLOSE COMBAT)

Special (see below)	Access Points	3	Close Combat	Rate 3	EMPS 18

This weapon appears to be a bladeless knife grip until activated, as a free action, when it projects a translucent blade of contained antipsions from the emitter. Antipsion radiation induces extreme neural shock resulting in brain death if the blade is properly applied, as such these weapons are generally used as an assassination tool as they leave no forensically identifiable signs of violent death on the body.
If used in combat, not in conjunction with the Assassinate Training, this weapon deals 1 point of Intelligence damage per hit that recovers at a rate of 1 per day, subjects reduced to zero Intelligence die. The synaptic shiv ignores AV but is blocked by close-form shields. This weapon has no effect on creatures or objects which lack an Intelligence score and is likewise useless against AI.

GRAVITY GLOVE

Special	Access Points 4 for a pair	Close Combat	Rate (as attack)	EMPS 15

The Gravity Glove is made of fine, matte black material and laced with tiny filaments of dull metal. It uses a nanoscale amplified grav-driver to create massive inertia in impossibly short distances allowing the user to punch with a far greater strength than he normally could.
When a pair is worn he adds +5 to his strength when striking in unarmed close combat.
Donning the gloves takes 3 seconds but there is seldom reason to take them off. They do not affect day to day tasks.

UIG COUNTER CRIMINAL TECHNOLOGY
(GHOST TECH)

'Ghost' Solid State Phase Matching Technology

The 'Ghost' system is an Archon based phasing technology that allows the user to pass through solid matter. The system uses the principle that there is space within the structure of molecules and providing the user and his target are phased correctly a 'gate' can be created through a solid object which the user can pass through.

The system is far from tried and tested and if the phasing is not perfect, disaster can result. For those brave enough to use it, Ghost Technology offers a unique advantage that will make any lawbreaker think twice.

System: The 'Ghost' unit looks much like a PDA and is carried in a belt case. When the Officer wishes to use it, the Ghost is pointed at a target and a door-shape 2x3 metres is projected onto the surface. (This indicates the area to be phased). The Ghost unit then begins to phase match the user and the target.

Depending on the substance, there is a varying chance for the phasing to be complete. This is listed below. The GM should roll each round. When he rolls below or equal to the Phasing Percentage, the user and target are phased and the user can walk through the solid unhindered. Walking through before this time increases the chance of molecular binding.

PHASE MATCHING CHANCE

Example	Chance
Light Wood, plasterboard, cloth	80%
Moderate Stone, metal, high density polymer	50%
Heavy Durasteel, superdense polymer	20%

Molecular Binding

Phasing is process requiring extreme accuracy, when the spaces within the user and target's molecules are not aligned perfectly sub-atomic particles can 'catch' on each other and bind forming different atoms and molecules. This is known as molecular binding.

Whenever 'Ghost' technology is used there is a 5% chance of Molecular binding occurring. This is increased to 55% if the user does not wait for a perfect phase match. If molecular binding does occur the GM should roll on the table opposite to determine the results.

MOLECULAR BINDING

D10	Result
1	No effect, the molecular binding is slight and has no tangible effect.
2-3	Peripheral Binding occurs on the small parts of the body, this manifests as lumpy, unidentifiable nodules forming on the users body which can be removed with surgery. D10 such lumps appear, each dealing 1 damage. This ignores armour.
4-7	Significant Binding causes the users body to be heavily damaged. Several lacerations, burns and alien tumours manifest. The user takes 2D10 damage, ignoring armour. The wounds are profound and unnatural and must be excised during surgery.
8-9	This has the same effect as Significant Binding (above) but in addition D10 randomly determined pieces of equipment are irretrievable ruined. This can include armour, cybernetics, weapons, etc.
10	Total Binding – The user is killed as they are merged with the target on an atomic level. The user ceases to exist in any retrievable form and all of their equipment is destroyed. There may be some barely identifiable shapes in the target solid which indicates that someone tried to phase through it.

Note that all Ghost Technology will be chip-locked so that non-UIG cannot use it.

PHASING WEAPONS

Phasing weapons utilise the same 'Solid State Phase Matching Technology' as found in 'Ghost Technology'. The wounds inflicted by the weapons are a result of Molecular Binding and are particularly aggressive and hard to heal. For this reason Phasing Weapons are often used against Agents as it is practically impossible to heal in the field, forcing Agents to think seriously before engaging UIG detachments with access to Phase Weapons.

HEALING DAMAGE FROM MOLECULAR BINDING (MB)

This only applies to wounds caused by Molecular Binding, if you also take another wound from a laser rifle, this can be healed normally. You should note the Molecular Binding Damage separately; it's a rare form of damage so this should not provide any book-keeping problems.

Automated Healing Aids

When damaged by Molecular Binding the wounded area effectively becomes foreign matter and no longer part of the body. For this reason conventional automated medical aids are reduced in their efficiency to 10% (round down). They will heal normal damage first at a normal rate.

For example,
Agent Escobar has 13 points of normal damage and 10 points of MB damage. He uses an IV Medpack (20HP of healing).

The normal damage is completely healed instantly, there are 7 points of healing left in the pack. 10% of 7 is 0 when rounded down, so there is no affect. Escobar uses another IV Medpack, this heals 2 points of MB damage. He really needs to take more serious action.

Doctor's Aid

A Doctor is able to view the wound in the correct context and deal with the problem. The normal method is to totally remove the damaged area and allow the body to regrow. This does not count as severing limbs unless the GM decides it is appropriate. Once the area has been removed by someone with the 'Surgeon' training the damage can be healed as normal.

I can do Surgery, me!

You can, of course, attempt to hack out the affected area yourself without the Surgeon Training. This requires you to pass an 'Intelligence + Medicine' check with a -10 penalty. Success means you have removed the affected area. This method takes 2D10 minutes and deals an additional 2D4 damage to you ignoring armour. You can then heal all damage as with conventional methods.

Failure means you take another 2D6 damage (ignoring armour), waste your time and only remove D4 of the Molecular Binding damage (round down). You can keep trying though; persistence pays off, even with surgery. A critical fail means you can make no more attempts and must consult a *real* surgeon.

PHASE PISTOL ARCHON PATTERN PM90 GHOST PISTOL

D10 Damage | 7,000¢ | Medium Range | Rate 2 | EMPS 13

The Phase Pistol is a small but disconcerting firearm which utilises the principle of molecular binding to deal severe wounds to a target which are extremely difficult to heal. This weapon is often used as an economical deterrent because many Agents are unwilling to engage guards armed with Ghost Weapons.

PHASING PROJECTILE SNIPER RIFLE - ARCHON PATTERN PPR-21 NIGHT WRAITH SNIPER RIFLE

4D8 Damage | 45,000¢ | Long Range | Rate 1 | EMPS 8

This experimental firearm uses a long range, high penetration Ghost Unit to rapidly phase match a single projectile to any matter obstructing its path. The projectile will pass through a maximum of 2 metres of matter before the phase matching becomes impossible and the projectile becomes solid.

What this means in simple terms is that the bullet will fire through walls (up to 2 meters of walls in total).
The bullet has a sensor which will immediately stop it phase matching if it comes within 50cm of bioelectricity. This is what allows the bullet to strike a living organism. Both shields and armour are effective against this attack. Any doubles rolled when using the weapon mean the phasing is flawed and the bullet stops at the first solid surface. The rifle scope allows you to see though solid matter but only in blurred thermal patterns so you need to be sure of what you are targetting.

This weapon does not use SMART ammo, instead bullets are purchased separately for 100¢ each.

PHASE RIFLE - ARCHON PATTERN PM250 GHOST RIFLE

2D8 Damage | 14,000¢ | Medium Range | Rate 2 | EMPS 13

The Phase Rifle delivers a sizable attack and is commonly deployed to squads known to be engaging Agents and other quarry likely to use regenerating technology. Their lightweight construction and fearsome Molecular Binding capability make them an ideal backup weapon.

PHASE GRENADE

3D6 Damage | 500¢ | Support Weapons | Rate 1 | EMPS 13

The Phase Grenade is ideal when used as the opening attack against groups of adversaries utilising regenerating technologies. It counts as a 3 metre blast weapon, which deals Molecular Binding damage.

CYBERNETICS

ASTRONAUTIC CYBES

These cybernetics were designed by Voidseal, a sub-division of Amalgamated Xenological Enterprises (AXE), primarily for space environments although many Agents have found terrestrial uses for them.

VOIDSEAL TS-80 BRONCHIAL BAFFLES

Installation	Complex, 10 Hours
Cost	7,000¢
Prerequisite	I.C.E.

Micromechanical valves and pressure-regulators are installed throughout the patient's lungs and cardiovascular system, these work in tandem with the patient's I.C.E. implants to attain pressure-equilibrium with their environment.

A person with bronchial baffles is immune to explosive decompression, be it via exposure to deep space or deep-sea diving related incidents.

This confers no ability to breathe without air.

VOIDSEAL RX500 RESPIRATORY RESERVES

Installation	Complex, 10 Hours
Cost	20,000¢
Prerequisite	I.C.E.

Respiratory reserves provide a fail-safe mechanism if exposed to low-oxygen conditions by allowing the implanted individual to conduct anaerobic respiration.
The enhancement has enough power to allow a person to survive without oxygen for up to 10 hours on a full charge. The enhancement also includes a power port in the base of the spine from which the enhancement can be recharged, this takes 10 minutes.

VOIDSEAL ISQII BIOTHERMAL REGULATORS

Installation	Complex, 5 Hours
Cost	5,000¢
Prerequisite	I.C.E.

The addition of morphic insulation to the skin and pulmonary system allows the body to regulate its temperature with greater speed and intensity as well as shielding it from excessive heat and cold. A person with this enhancement could walk across arctic tundra in a t-shirt or stroll across Death Valley without feeling exceptionally uncomfortable. The regulators provide an AV of 6 against damage resulting from extremes of environmental temperature. This does not protect from flame, cryo or temperature based attacks.

VOIDSEAL 2500PQL DERMAL RADIATION SHIELDING

Installation	Simple, 2 Hours
Cost	25,000¢

Several new layers of bioengineered skin incorporating metallic and electrochemical elements are added to the patient along with respiratory and genetic enhancements that further protect them from harmful radiation. These enhancements provide protection from up to 80 Gy of ionising radiation, roughly equivalent to that of a neutron bomb.

Naturally, this will also provide some protection from directed radiation weaponry such as the UIG Seraphim, though the extreme focus of such armaments makes it less effective than it is against ambient radiation, providing a +6 bonus to resist such weapons. This enhancement is popular with paranoid space pilots who don't trust their ship's shielding to protect them from multiple trips through the Van Allen radiation belt.

OTHER CYBERNETICS

LIBERTY BLACK DIGITEYES SCOUT HAND

Installation	Complex, 4 Hours
Cost	7,000¢

The patient's hand is severed and replaced with a new one which can be detached and used as a small scout droid. The hand is either controlled via an Anascan Inner Vision GUI (See Machines of War) or a PDA / computer.

The droid can be controlled at a range of up to 4 kilometres.

Scout Hand
HP 3
AV 0
Speed 10
Defence 1

When using the droid the player should roll 'Perception + Stealth' to control it. The GM could award a bonus for appropriate trainings etc. It has no combat abilities and if spotted will not be hard to catch and destroy, though it could be entertaining to have the player try to get his droid to safety by outrunning the enemy.

The droid has a 360 degree camera mounted on the back of the hand so it has an excellent view and incorporates a microphone to collect audio data. This data is relayed to the user in real-time so if the hand is destroyed the information is retained. The droid has basic climbing skill but cannot scale vertical surfaces.

GEMINI BIOWARE KISS OF DEATH

Installation	Simple, 1 Hour
Cost	15,000¢

The patient's lips are installed with tiny glands which, when required secrete a minute quantity of tetrodotoxin (fugu fish toxin). Anyone who kisses the patient when the toxin is on the lips has an 90% chance to take it into their system.

To prevent the patient from suffering the effects of the toxin they have a number of small anti-toxin factory cells installed into their liver which are tailored to neutralise any tetrodotoxin in their body.

The system contains a custom bio-engineered glad which creates its own tetrodotoxin, thus it never need be replenished but cannot be used more than twice per day. You cannot scrape the toxin off your lips and bottle it for other uses; the quantities are too small.

Substance	Potency	Class	Cost
Tetrododotoxin	9	A	500 per Dose

This toxin causes the diaphragm to be paralysed and the victim dies through respiratory failure.

Because the toxin starves the victim of oxygen, death is relatively slow. It is not the most reliable way to kill people, especially at range and when toxin purges are to hand.

Agents can live for 10 rounds / 30 seconds per point of Endurance. Humans can live for 5 rounds / 15 seconds per point of Endurance.

If medical aid, an antidote or a toxin purge has not been applied in this time the target dies.

Medical Aid – Another person can pass an 'Intelligence + Medicine' roll at -6 to halt the toxin but they must have access to reasonable medical supplies such as a medical toolkit.

If the patient has an unconventional respiratory system then the GM may rule they are unaffected. The toxin normally comes suspended in a carrier solution to make it usable in dart weapons etc.

REAVER DRAGON'S BREATH ORAL FLAME THROWER

Installation	Simple, 4 Hours
Cost	6,000¢

A pair of micro-jets are installed inside the target mouth along with a tiny igniter set into the back of the teeth. On the user's mental command the micro-jets spray a highly combustible liquid out of the mouth which ignites and becomes a scorching torrent of flame.

2D6 Damage   2 Metre Range   Rate 1

Anyone who takes damage from the flame Dragon's Breath is set on fire. This means you take D6 damage a round until put out. You can only be set on fire once at any one time.

A successful 'Agility + Reflexes' check will put out the fire or another person can spend a round helping and do it automatically. It ignores shields and requires refilling once every 2 uses (the user can do this); the cost for this refuel is negligible. The fuel used is paracane which is available at most stations and garages.

Note that using the Dragon's Breath fills your sinuses and mouth with smoke and steam. These gases are typically blown out of the nostrils afterwards for dramatic effect.

For God's sake, shave before you use it.

-Anonymous

ANASCAN LINEAR AUDIO SYSTEM

Installation	Simple, 2 Hours
Cost	4,000¢
Prerequisite	Anascan PSE

The users hearing can be altered to work in a narrow line rather a diffuse sphere. Switching between modes only takes a second. When in linear mode the patient loses normal hearing and anything nearby becomes a muted rumble. The area (1 cubic metre) that the user looks at is now the source of incoming audio signals.

This can be altered if desired by recalibrating the software so that you can look 10 yards left of your target etc. This can be done by a competent cyberneticist.

You can only hear sounds from inside this area.

If you have an Anascan Inner Vision GUI (See Machines of War) then you can perform the recalibration yourself on the fly.

Range
200 metres if one were listening to normal voices.
100 metres if listening to soft voices
400 metres to hear the sound of a car

NEW A.I. PROTOCOL

You can install a number of A.I. Protocols equal to your internal A.I.

VOICE STRESS ANALYSER

Prerequisite	Level 2 A.I.
	Anascan PSE
Cost	4,000¢

Your internal A.I. is able to analyse a target's speech patterns and look for signs that they are lying. You gain a +4 to your rolls when trying to determine if a statement is a lie as long as the person is speaking to you. You will typically need to engage them in conversation for at least a few minutes so the A.I. can determine their typical voice patterns.

SECTION 4

VEHICLES AND CYBERUNS

"Screw you, you can't judge me! I was a god, you understand, a fuckin' god! I pointed and mountains moved, I walked and the earth trembled. My eyes could see to the ends of the world, my voice was as loud as thunder, I was a goddamn force of nature! You have no idea how it feels, not one damn clue.

Hey, look man, I'm sorry about all that shit. Please, just get me out of here, okay? I can't go on like this, living like a... a bug. I need to see it again, I need it back. Oh, okay, no, I don't have to pilot again! Please man, just let me see it again, just let me sit in the cockpit one more time, I swear I won't immerse, I just need to... hey... hey! Where are you going!? Come back, I need to see it again... I'll kill you, you bastard! I'll kill all of you! I'll turn the whole damn world to ash! You can't keep me here, I'm a fuckin' GOD!"

- Patient 36, Agent Eustace Duval, formerly of the Western Federation Cyberlin Corps.

OVERVIEW

This information on cyberlins overrides anything written in the Corporation Core Rules.

These steel gods remain unsurpassed as the most terrifying combat machines ever built. The fact that their enormous destructive force can be surgically applied makes them a far more realistic deterrent than a nuclear bomb in the modern theatre of war. At present over five thousand cyberlins stand silently, their terrible vigil seldom broken in this era of crumbling peace.

The majority of cyberlins are built by the Shanghai Cyberlin Concern (SCC) in eastern China. The Ai-Jinn's unsurpassed ability to harness resources ensure they are the only ones who can economically produce the millions of high-end components used in the construction of a cyberlin. That is not to say that the UIG and other corporations do not dabble in the field, just that they only do so when they have a very specific requirement.

A typical cyberlin costs 20 million credits to buy direct from the Ai-Jinn; which is relatively inexpensive all things considered. However, for a corporation such as E.I. to build one from the ground up carries a price tag more in the line of 1 billion credits due to their lack of a structured, efficient and automated system. The fact that cyberlins tend to be more of a deterrent than of any practical use gives cause for the corporations to limit their spending on such things.

OPEN CONSTRUCTION POLICY

In order to secure their hold on the cyberlin market the Ai-Jinn were forced to be completely open about the technology used to make the machines function. It was also because of this open policy that it was decided to outsource some of the component manufacturing to other corporations. For example, the Shi Yukiro, or more accurately Takata, build most of the optics and targeting systems, E.I. produce the thruster units used in jump packs and the Federation create a huge variety of ordnance weapons which grace many of the more aggressive units.

Basically the open construction policy ensures that no secretive or 'black box' technology finds its way into the cyberlins so that the buyers can be certain there are no backdoors, auto-destructs or failsafes inside the great machines which may be triggered in the event of a war with the Ai-Jinn. The Federation have a similar policy with their guns and such a system is essential if world trade is to flourish. Because the technology of the generic cyberlin is no secret, rival technicians are welcome to visit the factories and observe every stage of the process. All of the computer code used to program the cyberlin's A.I. and defence systems is easily accessible and any corporation is welcome to have their Agents invigilate every stage of the process if desired.

Because it is the Ai-Jinn's sheer productive power rather than their methodology which makes them so successful, there is little reason to hide the process and if they did suspicion among customers would inevitably lead to a halt in orders.

> *Of course they can bloody well gold-plate one for me; they're just being difficult. Offer them more money.*
>
> *-attr: Gunther van Rosch, C.E.O., Eurasian Incorporated.*

NON-AI-JINN CYBERLINS

All of the major power blocks build their own cyberlins albeit in very low numbers; maybe only one or two a year in some cases. This is done for three main reasons.

1. To advance understanding of cyberlin technology and hopefully reach a stage one day where they can rival the Ai-Jinn in terms of productivity.

2. To create cyberlins which utilise proprietary technology. For example, Shi Yukiro cyberlins which utilise ion weaponry or Comoros cyberlins which utilise rift technology.

3. To build cyberlins which are 100% guaranteed to have no Ai-Jinn systems inside. Despite the open construction policy, there is still a seed of doubt that when it comes to the crunch you don't want your most valuable assets guarded by a machine built by the enemy. These 'loyal' cyberlins are typically used to guard the organisation's most important assets such as capital spires or intercontinental missile silos.

THE BIRTH OF A MONSTER

Cyberlins are built in custom facilities, most of which are owned by the Ai-Jinn. These huge yards are several square miles in size and incorporate dozens of factories which make all the generic components such as limbs, actuators, hydraulics, pneumatics, frames, motors and armour. The more specialist parts are constructed either by 3rd parties such as the Shi Yukiro, or in off-premises Ai-Jinn owned factories.

THE TIANJIN CYBERLIN YARD

In north east China, on the stormy coast of the Okhotsk Sea lies the Tianjin Factory Complex. The hundreds of square miles of squat factories, belching chimneys and cavernous warehouses can be seen through the smog only as gloomy silhouettes dotted with twinkling lights and fingers of coloured flame.

Like most such facilities, the Tianjin Cyberlin Yard is a mass of large factories and storage units built around a central 'pit', which is an enormous concrete-steel hole some hundred metres deep and broad enough to accommodate four cyberlins at any one time. The sides of the pit are festooned with access shafts, gantries, power outlets, heavy manipulators and bridges. When one of the war machines is under construction teams of engineers and droids work like ants, crawling over the massive frame of the cyberlin, bringing life to the durasteel colossus.

When completed powerful hydraulic rams work in concert with air-lifters and the cyberlin's own AG units to raise it out of the pit and into the grey, storm-ridden skies above. This iconic scene is often used by the Ai-Jinn in their promotional films and literature. The sheer scale and impact of the awe inspiring image is a potent warning to enemies and a source of renewed patriotism to loyalists.

CYBERUN PILOTING RULES

PREREQUISITES

The Cyberlin Pilot Training (page 12) – Without this the system are far to complex to even begin to understand. If the GM deems you should be able to have a go then he should apply a huge penalty to all rolls.

THE RIG

The pilot is strapped into a rig which is much like a mechanical arm chair with harness points for the limbs and head. Thus when the pilot moves, the cyberlin moves. This system allows the pilot to use most of his normal stats and skills when fighting or manoeuvring. There may be modifications to these based on the nature of the cyberlin and the way the machine is being piloted.

CYBERUN PILOTING BASICS

Initiative

This is rolled as normal, Reflexes + D10. You may gain a modifier based on your cyberlin.

Turn Order

Instead of the normal order within a round each pilot takes it in turn to activate a system. When one pilot runs out of systems the other may finish activating their remaining ones, then a new round begins. These sub turns are referred to as 'Activations'. You gain a number of activations based on the Piloting Method.

Example, Pilot A has 4 Activations and Pilot B has 2 Activations. Pilot A wins initiative.

Pilot A   Fire Weapons
Pilot B   Activate Shields
Pilot A   Fire Weapons
Pilot B   Evasive Manoeuvres
Pilot A   Fire Weapons
Pilot A   Fire Weapons

HOW MANY ACTIVATIONS DO I GET?

Activations are the currency of Cyberlin Piloting and are used to perform actions such as firing weapons or deploying defences. There are no free actions in cyberlin piloting.

Full Immersion Piloting

You are connected to the cyberlin's system via a neural jack.
Add together your Intelligence, Internal A.I. and the Cyberlin's A.I., then consult the 'Activations Chart'.

Manual Piloting

You use manual control much like driving a car.
Add together your Intelligence and the Cyberlin's A.I. then consult the 'Activations Chart'.

ACTIVATIONS CHART

Total	Activations
01-08	1
09-11	2
12-14	3
15-18	4
19-22	5
23-26	6
27-30	7
31+	8

Self Aware Cyberlins

The cyberlin controls some of what happens in the cockpit.
You gain an extra 2 Activations per round but the Cyberlin decides what to do with them. Obviously if the cyberlin is hostile to you it may simply deny you access to its systems and you would need to hack it. In this case treat the cyberlin as an Elite System.

SYSTEMS

Anything the cyberlin can do other than basic perception and simple movement are referred to as 'systems'. Some systems such as weapons or shields must be activated with 'activations'.

Example systems include

1. Arm mounted rail gun
2. Decoy flares
3. Repair Nanites
4. Hard Ion Shield

Note that a weapon with a rate of 2+ can be fired at full rate and still only counts as a single system.

Some such as armour plates do not.

STATS AND SKILLS

You use your pilot's skills to use the cyberlin and they remain unchanged unless stated in the cyberlin's description. For example, all cyberlins will replace your Strength with theirs. There is only one set of stats and skills when in a cyberlin. The two entities become one. You may receive modifiers based on the cyberlin you are piloting and its installed systems.

Which STATS and Skills to use	
Ranged Weapons	Perception + Support Weapons
Melee Attacks	Reflexes + Close Combat
Sensors	Perception + Observation
Extreme Manoeuvres	Reflexes + Pilot

MOVEMENT
The cyberlin's guidance computer means that it can ignore move and fire rules so you can travel the full move distance and activate any system.

Stealth
Only light cyberlins can use stealth and even then the GM should use common sense to determine what is reasonable.

CYBERLIN HIT LOCATIONS
You can attempt to hit certain parts of a cyberlin with your attacks. Although you could argue that a cyberlin is huge and easier to hit than a human, it is assumed you are attacking from inside armour units such as APCs, MAG Tanks or other cyberlins.

If you are firing handheld weapons then the hit location penalties could be halved.

Note that untargetted hits are always considered to hit the hull.

CYBERLIN HIT LOCATIONS

Hardpoint / Arm	-6
Hull	-0
Ordnance Weapon	-8
Locomotion	-4

By hitting these targets you are able to apply all of your damage to one area and possibly destroy it. If the part in question is reduced to 0 HP the following applies.

Hardpoint / Arm
This limb can no longer be used but the weapons on it can.

Hull
When the Hull is reduced to 0HP the cyberlin will no longer function

Weapon
Ordnance weapons are considered to have 50HP
Heavy Weapons are considered to have 25HP*.
Once reduced to 0HP the weapon no longer functions.

*Note these values are higher than listed in the Eastern Bank as cyberlin weapons are armoured.

Locomotion
Once reduced to 50% HP the cyberlins speed is also reduced by 50%. When reduced to 0HP the cyberlin cannot move.

AIMING
You can aim in a cyberlin as normal gaining +2 to hit each round you aim. You do not gain a bonus to damage however.

CYBERLIN CLOSE COMBAT
When attacking in close combat you use your Reflexes + Close Combat. Other than that nothing changes. Cyberlins have a defence based on their Close Combat as in normal close combat. You do not gain the benefit of any training you have in normal combat such as 'Advanced Disarm' or 'Gun Melee'.

Unarmed Attack
You deal damage equal to the Strength of the Hardpoint Unit.

Armed Attack
Deal damage as specified in the weapon description.

CYBERLIN DEATH
When is a cyberlin destroyed? At the end of the turn, if the cyberlin is on less than 0HP after all auto repair units have activated the cyberlin is incapacitated and its systems will all go off-line. The only fully manual system is the ejector seat which fires the driver several hundred metres in the air and allows him to drop suit / parachute to safety.

BUILDING A CYBERLIN
There are some pregenerated cyberlins in the book for you to use but you should feel free to create your own. A cyberlin must fulfill the following build guidelines.

1 Hull
1 Processor
1 Locomotory System
No more than 2 hardpoint units (arms)

Use the Cyberlin Record Sheet in the back of the book to construct your metal monster.

INSTALLING ORDNANCE WEAPONS
Size	Ordnance Per Arm
Heavy	3
Medium	2
Light	1

If you attach multiple weapons to one hardpoint they can be fired as a single system but must be directed at the same target.

For example, on the cyberlin's left hardpoint is a single ordnance weapon and 2 heavy weapons. These three weapons can be fired in one activation as long as they are directed at a single target.

INSTALLING HEAVY WEAPONS
You can install heavy weapons onto the hardpoint units of a cyberlin. For space purposes you can have three heavy weapons instead of a single ordnance weapon.

For example, with a medium sized hardpoint the following combinations are valid.

2 Ordnance weapons
1 Ordnance and 3 heavy weapons
6 heavy weapons.

REPAIRING A CYBERLIN
If systems have been damaged they must be fixed. You can use a simple system of percentages to work out the repair cost.

For example, if a cyberlin hull has lost 50% of its HP then it will cost 50% of its purchase price to repair. The GM may want to round off the numbers for you to make the maths easier. If you are doing it yourself the repair cost is halved and the GM should decide how many downtime weeks it will take.

CYBERLIN SYSTEMS

Below are listed a number of common cyberlin systems. This list is by no means exhaustive and more system may be detailed in future books.

Does it Require Activation

Where the system name is written an (A) is printed if the system requries an activation. You should write this (A) on your Cyberlin Systems Sheet to remind you that the system needs activating. (P) means the system is passive and always functioning.

How Many Systems Can I Install?

A cyberlin can have a number of systems based on its processor, not it's A.I. The A.I. is an optional extra which makes piloting easier. The cyberlin has a massive central processor which runs and synchronises all of its systems. It would be possible to place an extremely powerful processor into a basic cyberlin but it would be a waste of time. Only prototype, specialist or battle cyberlins will use the more expensive processors.

Free Systems

You receive some systems for free when you start to construct a cyberlin. These are:

Processor
Hull
Left Hardpoint
Right Hardpoint
Locomotion

The routines for controlling these elements are already built into the processor.

In addition there are some other upgrades such as armour plates which specifically note that they do not count as a systems when determining what you can install in your cyberlin.

PROCESSOR

The processor determines the number of non-essential systems (essential systems are Processor, Hull, Hardpoints and Locomotion) which can be installed into a cyberlin. The processor itself is the brain of the cyberlin and micromanages all of the system setting so that weapons fire accurately as the cyberlin is moving, shields are buffered and regulated, locomotion is smooth and recoil dampers are synchronised to ensure the cyberlin stays upright and balanced when unloading 8 cannons and being shot at simultaneously.

PROCESSORS (P)		
Processor	Systems	Cost
MX5 Slave	5	500,000¢
Microflux T8	6	650,000¢
MX8 Autoxor	7	850,000¢
Datanetica FG90	8	1 Million¢
Saracen J2000	9	1.3 Million¢
Illian Ghost V2.2	10	1.8 Million¢
Cyrebrum MP8	11	2.0 Million¢
Takata R50 DX	12	2.5 Million¢

HULL

The hull acts as the main structural frame for the cyberlin. It houses the power unit, cockpit and optional systems such as shield generators, auto repair stations and numerous other sub-mechtronics.

Note that the armour value for the hull applies to all systems on the cyberlin as it determines the basic level of armour installed across the entire machine. This is included in the hull's cost.

HULLS (P)					
Standard Hulls	HP	Grade	Cost (¢)	AV	END*
SSC Dominator C10	1000	Heavy	15 Million	25	100
SCC Arbiter	700	Medium	10 Million	20	75
SCC Rogue H5	500	Light	6 Million	15	50

*Defines the Cyberlins Endurance STAT
A heavy hull MUST be mounted on a heavy locomotory system and hardpoints.

Painting Hulls

You can apply a custom paint job to the hull for following cost. Light (1000¢) Medium (2000¢) Heavy (3000¢)

A basic cyberlin has a looking good score of 5. This upgrade gives the cyberlin a Looking Good score of 8. For particularly fine custom work you can increase the score to 9 or 10 but it may cost more money.

CYBERLIN ATTITUDE

The intimidation value of a Cyberlin is based on its hull. The larger the hull the more 'Attitude' skill it has.

Light	5
Medium	7
Heavy	8

You can add or remove some points based on its duties. For example, an Atrocity class cyberlin could gain a +2. A marine reconnaissance cyberlin could have a -1.

What you use this Attitude for is up to you but scaring away enemies to save valuable ammunition is a good first choice.

MIXING COMPONENT TYPES

Due to the way Cyberlins are built components can only be matched in certain ways. What you can attach is based on the hull type you are using.

Light Hull
Up to heavy locomotors but only light hardpoints

Medium Hull
Must be medium or heavy locomotors but only medium or light hardpoints

Heavy Hull
Must have a heavy locomotor but can have any type of hardpoints.

LOCOMOTION

Each cyberlin needs a form of locomotion. The following locomotory systems can be used on all cyberlins except where noted. Locomotory systems do NOT count towards your total number of allowed systems.

AQUATIC PROPELLER (P)

This is used for cyberlins which operate in water (Aqualins).

	Light	Medium	Heavy
Cost	250,000	500,000	1 Million
Top Speed	120 mph	100 mph	80 mph
Terrain	Water	Water	Water
HP	50	100	150
Agility	8	7	6

BIPEDAL INVERSE (P)

The knee joints are reversed like a gazelle's which adds speed and agility at the cost of solidity.

	Light	Medium	Heavy
Cost	500,000	1 Million	1.5 Million
Top Speed	80 mph	70 mph	60 mph
Terrain	Moderate	Moderate	Moderate
HP	50	100	150
Agility	10	8	6

BIPEDAL STANDARD (P)

These are typical legs that most cyberlins are equipped with, they are solid and dependable but don't offer much in the way of speed.

	Light	Medium	Heavy
Cost	500,000	1 Million	1.5 Million
Top Speed	60mph	50mph	40mph
Terrain	Moderate	Moderate	Moderate
HP	100	200	300
Agility	8	6	5

OCTOPEDAL (P)

The chassis has 8 legs which allow it to move at great speed over even the most challenging terrain. This system can only be fitted to light cyberlins. If you DO want to fit it to medium and heavy cyberlins then it should only be used for rare, prototype, alien or experimental cyberlins

	Light	Medium	Heavy
Cost	1.5 Million	2 Million	2.5 Million
Top Speed	110 mph	90 mph	80 mph
Terrain	Rough	Rough	Rough
HP	75	120	200
Agility	9	8	7

QUADRUPEDAL (P)

The chassis has 4 legs which allow it to move over the most difficult of terrain but at a low speed.

	Light	Medium	Heavy
Cost	1 Million	1.5 Million	2 Million
Top Speed	50 mph	40 mph	30 mph
Terrain	Rough	Rough	Rough
HP	100	200	300
Agility	7	6	5

TRACKS (P)

A set of heavy tank tracks which offer great stability but a greatly reduced Agility. The cyberlin is also extremely hard to knock down.

	Light	Medium	Heavy
Cost	500,000	1 Million	1.5 Million
Top Speed	80 mph	70 mph	60 mph
Terrain	Moderate	Moderate	Moderate
HP	50	100	150
Agility	6	5	4

ANTI-GRAVITY HOVER (P)

The hover chassis is not normally available on medium and heavy cyberlins. If you DO want to fit it to medium and heavy cyberlins then it should only be used for rare, prototype, alien or experimental cyberlins

	Light	Medium	Heavy
Cost	1 Million	10 Million	30 Million
Top Speed	100 mph	85 mph	70 mph
Terrain*	All	All	All
HP	50	100	150
Agility	10	8	6

*The cyberlin can travel over water.

PRIMARY HARDPOINT UNITS (ARMS)

Each cyberlin can attach 2 upper hardpoint units. These attach to the sides of the hull much like arms. Although a cyberlin normally has 2 arms, it is not compulsory and they do not both have to be of the same type.

When a hardpoint is reduced to 0 HP it cannot be used. The weapons attached to it CAN still be used.

Hardpoint units DO require activation.

MANIPULATOR (A) (RATE I)
This acts much like a human arm and allows the cyberlin to hold tool or pick up objects. You cannot wield a weapon two-handed in a cyberlin as there is not enough flexibility.

	Light	Medium	Heavy
Cost	250,000	500,000	1 Million
Strength	50	75	100
HP	25	50	100

Possessing a manipulator allows a cyberlin to make close combat attacks and wield close combat weapons (both at rate 1). One ordnance weapons can be mounted on a manipulator.

CONVERGENT ARTILLERY CANNON (A)

Damage 40D10 + 100
Cost   2 Million
Range   Long
Rate   One shot per 2 rounds
EMP   Immune
HP   150

This represents the heaviest ground-mobile weapon in common use at the current time and can only be fitted to heavy cyberlins.

The entire arm is a single convergent artillery cannon of unrivaled power. Weapons can be attached to this arm as normal. The C.A.C is 45.88 metres in length. This counts as a hardpoint so it does not contribute to your max. no. of systems.

ROCKBREAKER (A)
This hardpoint attachment is normally used by slave class miner cyberlins but can be used by mêlée based battle class as well.

	Light	Medium	Heavy
Cost	250,000¢	500,000¢	1 Million
Strength	50	75	100
HP	50	75	150

Possessing a rockbreaker allows a cyberlin to make close combat attacks.

Special Attack - Gravity Nexus
The Rockbreaker has a powerful grav-engine which allows it to land earth-shattering blows. This allows the cyberlin to double its strength when attacking with this hardpoint.

It needs 4 rounds to recharge.

WEAPON MOUNTINGS (P)
If you wish you can essentially skip hardpoints and attach the weapons directly to the hull. This upgrade does not count as a system and is simply an internal bridging unit.

	Light	Medium	Heavy
Cost	100,000	200,000	300,000

It has no hit points and cannot be destroyed.

ORDNANCE WEAPONS

Ordnance Weapons are the staple ranged attack form of cyberlins. For reference these weapons have are heavily armoured and have 50hp. (AV will be the same as the Hull).

You can attach a maximum of two to each hardpoint unit. Note that if you attach two ordnance weapons to one hardpoint they can be fired as a single system but must be directed at the same target. These systems DO require activation.

PAN LEE TSUNAMI K8 HEAVY ASSAULT CANNON (A)

Damage - Special
50,000¢
Medium Range
Rate 1
EMP Immune

Dimensions   7.0 Metres in length, 300mm dia barrel

This weapon is not generally used to attack heavy armour due to the lack of penetration. More commonly it is utilised for suppressing large numbers of ground troops by deluging them in thousands of rounds of ammunition.

Damage
The weapon is sprayed over an area of roughly 50x50 metres. Everything in that area receives 4D10 damage.

If targetting an enemy cyberlin shield it will reduce it by 500hp

PAN LEE HURRICANE ORDNANCE PLASMA (A)

15D10+15 Damage
100,000¢
Long Range
Rate 1
EMP Immune

Dimensions   7.5 Metres in Length, 600mm dia barrel

The armour penetrating power of the Hurricane makes it ideal for counter-armour attacks such as cyberlin-cyberlin combat or assaults on tank divisions etc.

PAN LEE SIRROCO TYPE 09 RAIL CANNON (A)

15D10+30 Damage
150,000¢
Long Range
Rate 1
EMP Immune

Dimensions   10.0 Metres in Length, 400mm dia Barrel

The king of counter-cyberlin weaponry, the Type 09 can punch a hole through even the toughest opponent. However, there is one major drawback, the projectile itself is fairly small so whenever fired there is a 10% chance it passes through a non-essential part of the mech and effectively deals no damage.

If you hit an enemy cyberlin roll an additional D10, on a roll of 10 the attack has no effect, even if you hit. This is not the case when attacking non-cyberlin targets.

The Type 09 can be fired through walls by firing at -4 and ignores 25 points of AV.

PAN LEE TYPHOON LX88 SNIPER CANNON (A)

15D10+10 Damage
200,000¢
Extra Long Range (3 Miles)
Rate 1 shot every 2 rounds.
EMP Immune

Dimensions   13.0 Metres in Length, 400mm dia Barrel

This is one of the largest arm-mounted ordnance weapons currently available. Although the typhoon can only fire every other round it can deliver a shot up to 3 miles away.

For every mile past the first you should apply a -4 penalty.

Each round you aim with the sniper cannon you gain a +4 to hit but no bonus to damage.

CYBERUN MELEE WEAPON (A)

Light   50,000¢   +30 Damage
Medium 75,000¢   +50 Damage
Heavy 100,000¢   +75 Damage

This weapon is held in a manipulator and adds to the cyberlin's close combat damage. It can take any form such as a wrecking ball, sword or axe.

The price of the weapon can be tripled in order to make it a plasma weapon which ignores 25 points of armour value or x10 to make it an Ion weapon which ignores 75 points of AV.

Ion weapons are only available to Shi Yukiro cyberlins.

PAN LEE TORNADO GUIDED MISSILE ARRAY (A)

9D10 Damage per Warhead
100,000¢
Long Range
Rate Special
EMPS 50

Dimensions   5 Metres in Length, 16 x 300mm dia Barrels

The Tornado is a shoulder mounted missile array which holds up to sixteen guided warheads. The user can opt to fire between one and sixteen missiles at a time but they must all be directed at the same target if being fired in the same round.

Each missile counts as a separate attack for armour purposes.

Missiles must be purchased separately; the price above refers to the launcher unit.

A heavy guided missile costs 1,000¢

Procedure

Lock-On - Locking on counts as an Activation

Roll Perception + Support Weapons, success indicates lock-on is achieved. Faillure wastes the activation.

Penalties
Lock on Disruptor   -6
You are in a complex manoeuvre such as jumping   -2
Opponent is in evasive manoeuvres such as jumping -2

Once lock-on is achieved you can use your next Activation to fire the missiles; no roll is needed. Unless the opponent deploys countermeasures you will hit with all missiles.

PAN LEE TEMPEST X5 AM ORDNANCE LASER (A)

15D8+15 Damage
100,000¢
Long Range
Rate 1
EMP Immune

Dimensions   7.1 Metres in Length, 300mm dia barrel

An essential weapon for counter-armour* cyberlins. These weapons come fitted with AM (auto modulators) which means the weapon will automatically penetrate all standard shields. If the target is using a shield frequency scrambler then you roll a D10, on 1-3 the cyberlin's A.I. predicts the shield's frequency pattern and the laser ignores the target's shields.

*Armour in this instance refers to other heavy vehicles, not defensive armour plates.

KNOX DEADLEAF ML9000 HEAVY MINE LAYER (A)

30D10 Damage per Mine
100,000¢ for the Layer, Mines are 1000¢ each.
Capacity (Light 30 mines) (Medium 45 mines) (Heavy 60 Mines)
Range Medium
Rate 3
EMP Immune

Dimensions   2.0 Metres in Length, 1000mm dia Barrel

The Deadleaf uses a pneumatic launcher to fire up to 3 mines in an arc in front or behind the cyberlin. The mines land approximately 200 metres away from the launcher and contain sophisticated sensors which ensure the mines are not triggered by friendly units.
Mines are naturally coated in a basic scanner blocker and so require a Mine Sweeper Sensor to detect.

Stepping on Mines
If you have not detected a mine then there is a chance you'll step on it. Each round you are in the rough vicinity of the mine (200m) and moving, roll a D100. There is a cumulative 5% chance you will stand on it.

Effect
The entire force of the mine is directed at the locomotory module of the cyberlin and it ignores shields.

SHIELDS, DEFENCE AND REPAIR

Cyberlins utilise hard ion shields in the same way as other vehicles. It should be noted however that if an Agent were to physically climb onto a cyberlin and attach an explosive to its leg this would bypass the shield. For practical purposes you can assume the shield is surrounding the cyberlin at a distance of 2 feet.

ARMOUR PLATING (P)

Cost   100,000¢ per plate

These massive sheets of laminate durasteel are bolted onto the Cyberlin to provide additional ablative armour. You must state where the plating is located and it provides an extra 100 HP for that location. Once the cyberlins Agility has reached 0 it cannot move. You must attach plates as evenly as possible over the structure or it will throw off the balance of the machine; i.e. you should not just attach 4 plates to 1 leg.

Depending on the size of the cyberlin they are attached to they will reduce its speed and Agility.

Cyberlin Size	Agility Reduction	Speed Reduction
Light	-1 per plate	-10 MPH per plate
Medium	-1 per 2 plates	-5 MPH per plate
Heavy	-1 per 3 plates	-2 MPH per plate

Armour does not count towards your total number of systems

COVERT SHIELD (P)

All Sizes   300,000¢

The cyberlin's shield is no longer visible. This upgrade is seldom used but can occasionally be employed to make an opponent believe the cyberlin is vulnerable and make a mistake.

This does not count towards your total number of systems.

AUTO REPAIR SYSTEMS (A)

Basic	50HP per round	1 Million ¢
Advanced	100HP per round	3 Million ¢
Elite	150HP per round	5 Million ¢

The system takes an Activation to turn on, after which nanite colonies dotted around the cyberlin dispense nanite repair drones to fix the cyberlin's failing systems. They heal an amount of damage to the machine as stated above each round and will continue to function until the cyberlin is repaired or they expire.

You can decide which areas the nanites repair. E.g Hardpoints, locomotary systems etc.
You can only install one of these systems at a time.

They can function for a total of 10 rounds but can be manually turned off using an activation. Refilling a unit costs 10% of its purchase price.

They repair at the END of a round.

SHIELD REGENERATOR (A)

All Sizes   500,000¢

This powerful hypercharger allows the hard ion shields of a cyberlin to be regenerated at a rapid rate.
Each round the shields regenerate 10% of their total.

Example, your cyberlin has a 1000HP shield, each round it will regenerate 100HP irrespective of the current total. It will even regenerate shields which are totally depleted.

STANDARD HARD ION SHIELD (A)

Cost   1000¢ per HP

The cyberlin is fitted with a number of shield generators which work in the same way as standard hard ion shields. They function as a single shield.

Maximum		
	Light	700 HP
	Medium	1,000 HP
	Heavy	1,500 HP

This does not count towards your total number of systems.

SENSORY

Cyberlins can be fitted with a range of sensory and targetting upgrades. The most popular are noted below.

SCOUT ARRAY (P)

All Sizes   1 Million¢

Prerequisite - Sensory Array

The basic sensor array is heavily upgraded granting the cyberlin greater sensory resolution.
The cyberlin's perception is based on the pilot's perception. This increases that value by 2.

MINE SWEEPER (A)

All Sizes   200,000¢

This upgrade to the cyberlin's sensors allows you to spend an Activation to search for mines. Simply roll 'Perception + Observation'. Each point of XS detects one mine starting with those closest to you.

FLARE LAUNCHER (A)

All Sizes   50,000¢

Fires powerful flares into the air which illuminate the whole battle area. The flare lasts 10 rounds and each replacement flare costs 100¢. The launcher can hold 10 flares at a time.

SENSORY ARRAY (A) (P)

All Sizes   500,000¢

The cyberlin is equipped with broad-spectrum sensor arrays that can be used to scan for a wide range of phenomena such as;

Sources of Electricity or Radiation
Chemicals & Pathogens
Lifesigns
Vehicles
Buildings

The sweep is conducted in a 90-degree arc from the cyberlin out to a range of 5 miles and will notify you of anything unusual. In order to search for unusual specific items you must use an Activation. For example, if you are looking for a particular vehicle or person.

If the GM deems it tricky to find then he may request a 'Perception + Observation' roll. For example, attempting to ascertain if a ground troop is carrying a specific weapon or if a tank is broken or simply has all its systems turned off.

PREDICTIVE TARGETING LOCK (A)

All Sizes   1 Million¢
Prerequisite   Cyberlin A.I. of 1+

By activating this system the cyberlin brings a number of A.I. controlled targeting units into effect which take into account the movements of you, your enemy and external physical forces. This grants a +4 to hit with your next ranged system. This includes acquiring a lock-on.

ENVIRONMENTAL SEALS (P)

Light   1 Million Credits
Medium   1.5 Million Credits
Heavy   2 Million Credits

The unit is totally sealed and waterproofed allowing it to go underwater without a problem. It is also fitted with aerators which provide air to any system which may require it for their function. In addition any airborne toxins cannot enter the cockpit.

AUGMENTED VISION SUITE (P)

All Sizes   300,000¢

A range of optical technologies allow perfect vision even at night and through smoke or rain.

COUNTERMEASURES

Countermeasures are used to reduce the chance that a guided lock-on style attack will hit your cyberlin.

LOCK-ON DISRUPTOR (P)

All Sizes   200,000¢

This technology produces carefully calibrated energy fields around the cyberlin which make it very hard for an enemy unit's software to lock onto you.

Anyone using A.I. assisted lock-on gains a -6 penalty.

SHIELD FREQUENCY SCRAMBLER (P)

All Sizes   300,000¢

This installs a scrambling technology which limits an auto modulating (AM) laser's ability to bypass a shield. If you are shot at by an AM laser weapon the attacker should roll a D10. On a 1-3 the attack ignores your shields but on a 4-10 does not.

ELECTRONIC COUNTERMEASURES (ECM) (A)

Basic   200,000¢
Advanced   500,000¢
Elite   1 Million¢

A complete system of decoy units and guidance disruptors serve to reduce the likelihood that guided weapons will strike your cyberlin.

System

At the start of a round you can use an Activation to prime the ECM. If you are attacked with a guided system during that round they will activate automatically.

They will remain online until used at which point you will need to spend an activation to re-prime them but are only effective against one volley before repriming is needed.

ECM	Roll Needed *	Max Number of Counters**
Basic	1-2	3
Advanced	1-5	5
Elite	1-7	8

*Roll below this number on 1D10 to counter each incoming attack
**You can only counter this number of incoming attacks per round.

Example

You have an advanced ECM. Your opponent opens up at you with 7 guided missiles. You can only neutralise up to 5 so you roll 5D10. Each one that comes up with a 5 or lower has neutralised a missile.

EXTREME MOVEMENT

These upgrades influence the more advanced movement of the cyberlin such as its ability to jump or fall.

JUMP UNIT (A)

Light   500,000¢
Medium   1 Million¢

Using a jump unit a cyberlin can launch itself into the air for short periods of time. The jump pack contains enough fuel for 5 rounds in the air. Each round, the cyberlin can travel 200 metres by using the jump pack so it could traverse a distance of 1km in 15 seconds if it used all its fuel at once. Only light and medium cyberlins can use Jump Units.

GRAVITY RAMS (A)

Light   100,000¢
Medium   200,000¢
Heavy   300,000¢

Using high-powered antigravity units, the cyberlin's personal gravitational reference can be momentarily rendered a fraction of its normal value. This is usually used to drop cyberlins into combat arenas from aircraft but requires perfect timing from the pilot or A.I.

On the round that Gravity Ram systems are activated the cyberlin takes no damage from any fall, no matter how high. After use they require D10 rounds to recharge.

SALVAGING

Its not unreasonable for the division to scavenge some of these items and use them for their own creative purposes. Perhaps mounting an ordnance weapon or some gravity rams on their vehicle.

The GM should ultimately oversee the salvaging process but some useful skills would include:

1. The Jury Rigging Training
2. A high Mechtroincs skill
3. The Cyberlin Pilot Training
4. The Ai-Jinn Mechanic Training (Machines of War)

EXTRAS

These do not count towards your total number of systems)

CYBERLIN A.I.

Cyberlins start with no A.I. You can increase it one level by spending 100,000 credits per level to a maximum of level 10 for 1 million credits. Adding a personality is free when you spend this much on a high-end war A.I.

STANDARD EJECTOR SEAT (A) OR (P)

This is included in the cockpit and comes free whenever you purchase a hull. The ejector seat fires by default when your hull reaches 0HP. You can turn this setting off in which case you must use an activation to fire the seat. If for some reason you cannot perform this activation then you will most likely die in the burning carcass of the machine.

THE SCC

The Shanghai Cyberlin Concern is the largest manufacturer of Cyberlins in the world. The SCC is a subsidiary of the Ai-Jinn and as a result are able to draw on their vast resources to ensure they remain unrivalled in their ability to produce cost effective, high performance mechs.

Location: SCC has several factory units situated across South East Asia, each of these manufactures sub-components which are assembled into the key parts of a cyberlin. These are then shipped to the central assembly plant in Tianjin where the final macrostruction is completed.

I CAN'T AFFORD A FLIPPIN' CYBERLIN!

No, most likely you'll never be able to buy one. The prices are here for completeness and in case the GM feels like running a scenario where you may be able to build one yourself.

The most likely situation that will allow you to build a cyberlin is if you are a highly skilled cyberlin pilot and the corporation has asked you to design one for a purpose. Perhaps your division has been placed in charge of an important facility and you have been granted permission to construct a cyberlin to guard it and a budget.

Still, it's nice to be able to plan one or if the game gets really high level then maybe one day you *will* be able to construct your own looming steel beast to guard your collection of gold plated guns and stolen ion katanas.

THE SCALE AND SPEED OF CYBERLIN COMBAT

You may have noticed that cyberlin combat works on a massive scale and a fight between two cyberlins is not as punchy and quick as it might be between two Agents. You should therefore bear the following in mind.

1. Have something for the other Agents to do during the combat. Maybe they could be fighting ground troops or contributing to the effort in tanks. Perhaps they could have some heavy support weapons to help erode the cyberlin's defences.

2. Cyberlin battles are rare and not a staple of the game so if it takes a long time to enact the titanic war it should not slow your game down on any significant scale.

CAN MY AGENT FIGHT A CYBERLIN

YES! He can indeed. All the numbers are in place for you to engage a cyberlin in close combat. It should be a simple task to determine how to take on a cyberlin in close combat. The cyberlin has a Defence, AV, HP and appropriate skills. A high level division may well be able to take down a light scout cyberlin without too many problems. To take down a battle class cyberlin single handed may require a little more dedication.

SAMPLE CYBERLINS

The sample cyberlins listed in the Antagonists section at the back of the book are standard mass-produced models used across the world and as such do not have the same cost as if they were custom built.

They are considered to be piloted by a skilled individual. If you wish to change the pilot you will need to change some of the STATS (Ref, Per, Int and Pres) and all of the Skills.

Scout Class Cyberun - The Eye of Horus on Patrol Duty at Tianjin

CURSED REGRESSION. A BODY OF STEEL, BUT FRAIL FLESH AT THE HEART. WITHOUT THE FLESH, THE MACHINE FAILS. WEAKNESS. ANATHEMA. DO NOT VENERATE THEM.

-ATTR: LEVIATHAN, CHIMERA PROPHET OF THE CULT OF MACHINA

The meeting in Tianjin had already dragged on an hour past its scheduled time, but Shuyan Cheng was nothing if not practiced in procrastination. Effortlessly she deflected or manoeuvred around the increasingly terse questions of the Federation rep and the more superficially polite enquiries of the Shi Yukiro zaibatsu; she bore the lascivious stares and double-entendres of the EI negotiator with long-accustomed ease. The Comoros ambassador sat quietly, betraying no hurry or impatience; waiting, reflected Cheng, was something Comoros were well schooled in.

Finally, just as it seemed as though the Federation rep was about to lose his temper and leave, a discrete chime sounded in Cheng's inner ear. Standing, she moved slightly around the conference table, so that her back was to the vast picture window on the north side; with the office at ground level, the only view it currently afforded was of a gentle bluff spanning a long stretch of featureless coastline, storm winds and driving rain pelting at the armoured glass. "Very well, gentlemen," she said, voice tinged with just the right hint of resignation. "We can offer you the mineral rights to TY-322 at a 20% margin, since that appears to be the stumbling block here; rights to be renegotiated on a five-year basis. I trust that meets with your approval?" A concession, of course, that Cheng had been ready to make since the beginning; but petty negotiations were not the real purpose of the meeting here.

The Federation rep surged to his feet. "Well, it's about damn time, Cheng. Why in hell we've had to spend the last three hours going back and forth on this I don't know. I've got to get over to Changi before midnight and it's going to be –"

The man's words were cut short by a titanic rumbling that shook the small office and dragged all eyes over to the window. A wave crashed against the distant shoreline, sending a curtain of spray up into the gunmetal skies, and then a towering, gleaming form was rising up from behind the bluff, the pounding rain hammering off its massive metal shoulders in a hazy aura. The bluff itself obscured the edge of the cyberlin yard, creating the impression that the monster was pushing forth from the earth itself.

Though several kilometres distant, the scale of the colossus was sufficient to allow them to make out details, particularly the massive black cylinder of the artillery cannon. The cyberlin flexed and twisted as the pilot ran brand-new systems through startup checks; the eerie, penetrating whine of the gigantic actuators cut through the even the noise of the storm. The giant cannon swung down, locked into place, and fired a test round; there was a percussive noise so loud it was painful even through glass and at this distance, and a hilltop off to the east simply vanished in a short-lived pall of dirty red flame and a great billowing of dust.

"Ah yes, the Tianjin Cyberlin Yard; they have just completed work on our latest-model Lu Bu battle-class project," commented Cheng, brightly but redundantly. All four of the Corporation reps were already staring fixedly at the behemoth as it pivoted and twisted under storm-lashed skies. And, Cheng knew, all four would go home, and report to their superiors, who would report to their superiors; and so on until the orders began to roll in, as they always did, and the fear began to ripple through the Corporations, as it always did. Both outcomes, she reflected, would earn her a bonus. Cheng allowed herself the briefest of smiles; behind her, the storm continued to rage beneath the birthing cries of the newborn metal god.

VEHICLES

> "It's 106 miles to Chicago.
> We've got a full tank of gas, half a pack of cigarettes,
> it's dark and we're wearing sunglasses.
> Hit it."
>
> - The Blues Brothers

THE TAI-LAN AUTOMOTIVE CONCERN

Tai-Lan are the Ai-Jinn's main domestic vehicle manufacturer and have facilities all over the East. They produce mass market cars for budget conscious customers but are also contracted to build the Ai-Jinn's Agent issue vehicles. These often have augmentations such as armour, A.I. vectors or gun mountings.

DA ZHAN MIUTARY AUTOMETRICS

An Ai-Jinn subsidiary that produces the bulk of the Ai-Jinn's war machines such as P-tanks, armoured cars, submarines, armed hovercopters and anything else besides cyberlins, which are the sole province of the Shanghai Cyberlin Concern. Their vehicles are among the most reliable in the world and disdain technical frippery in return for sheer ruggedness and the ability to cope in almost any environment. Da Zhan also have a frighteningly fast production rate, a fact that nearly turned the course of the Corporate War to Ai-Jinn's side more than once.

KALARI

Kalari dominate the more exotic end of the automotive market and specialise in high-end luxury cars and performance vehicles. Kalari are sufficiently rare that when one is seen heads generally turn and the price tag lets everyone know the driver has money to spare.

AI-JINN AGENTS
BUYING AI-JINN VEHICLES

As an Ai-Jinn Agent you naturally receive a favourable rate when purchasing Ai-Jinn-built vehicles. Typically you receive a discount of 5% per level of Rank.

Example, you are a Rank 5 Agent and want to buy a Sabrehawk bike (12,000 credits). You will recieve a 25% discount resulting in a total cost of 9,000 credits.

CIVILIAN VEHICLES

TAI-LAN PINKO
8,000¢

Currently the most popular car in Asia, the Pinko was an overnight success when it launched in 2188. Its compact bubble-like chassis is able to seat 5 with room to spare and the micro-jet engine allows a surprisingly large amount of boot space. The car comes in a range of pastel shades with white vinyl seats and a clean, simple dashboard.

Vehicle Statistics

HP	30
AV	3
MPH	90
DM	+1

Compulsory Safety System (CSS) - The Pinko's popularity made is an obvious choice for the UIG Compulsory Safety System (CSS) which ensures a driver follows a simple set of checks before she sets off. The UIG subsidise the production of the Pinko on the understanding that each is shipped with the CSS. Before the Pinko will move the vehicle's computer walks the driver and any passengers through a series of safety procedures and will not move until all of them are met.

This requires a number of minutes to carry out equal to 5 minus your XS on an 'Intelligence + Drive' roll (Miniumum 1 minute). Bypassing the Pinko's CSS requires a hacking roll versus a SECURE system, with a total penalty of -8 due to the proprietary nature of the CSS software.

TAI-LAN TLS 1800 SABREHAWK SPORTSBIKE
12,000¢

The Sabrehawk is the latest in a long line of high performance sports bikes from Tai-Lan. It features a range of cutting edge design features to make it the lightest, quickest and most responsive vehicle in its class.

Vehicle Statistics

HP	20
AV	2
MPH	280
DM	+3

The Sabrehawk can be fitted with a nitro for 1,000¢ which increases the top speed to 330mph for 9 seconds (3 rounds). During this time the Driving Modifier (DM) is reduced to 0. This nitro can be used once per 10 mins.

TAI-LAN ZX5000 WARRIOR OFF-ROAD DIRT BIKE
10,000¢

The Warrior uses a classic aprosine alloy chassis but has a number of modification made which allow it to take the kind of beating you'd expect in a heavy off-road environment. The panels are durasteel-laminated and the wheels are reinforced with kethelin polymer to resist deformation.

Vehicle Statistics

HP	30
AV	5
MPH	200
DM	+2

The Warrior can be fitted with weapon mountings on the side, front and rear for a price of 150¢ per mounting. The firing mechanisms are linked to customisable buttons on the dash. If you fit more than 2 tactical weapons the driving modifier should be decreased by 1.

TAI-LAN BISON 4.0 EXTENDED 4X4 SUV PICKUP
35,000¢

This monster SUV is commonly used by Agents (usually Ai-Jinn) or insecure males who want to make it appear that they might be Agents. Either way, the Bison is a tough, uncompromising vehicle built to a high standard and easily customisable (-10% to all upgrade costs). The Bison is extremely long and can seat five in the crew compartment even though it has a large pick-up style bay in the back. For an additional 1,000¢ a hard cover can be purchased to cover the pick-up bay. (500¢ for a cloth cover)

Vehicle Statistics

HP	90
AV	4
MPH	200
DM	+1

Note: The Off Road Vehicle in the Core Rules is mispriced and should cost 30,000¢.

TAI-LAN 'COMANCHERO' FAMILY MIDSIZE CONTINENTAL
15,000¢

A spacious and practical family car, widely bought in the open cities but also a popular purchase for spire and archology citizens. It features large-legroom seating arrangements, a high-capacity boot spacious enough to fit a whole set of camping equipment with a baby stroller on top and full air-conditioning with radiation and particulate matter scrubbers for those long family road-trips through contaminated areas. The Comanchero has developed a number of colourful nicknames, none of which are supported by Tai-Lan, among them being 'The Emasculator', 'The Comanchero Family Midlife Crisis', and 'The Sexual-Identity Assassin'.

Vehicle Statistics

HP	45
AV	3
MPH	180
DM	+0

Atmosphere Controls - The Comanchero's air-conditioning systems function as a level 8 toxin filter versus atmospheric toxins providing the windows are wound up.

TAI-LAN 'WILDCAT'
35,000¢/45,000¢

A good, all-purpose ATV (all terrain vehicle) from the Tai-Lan Automotive Concern, the Wildcat comes in two different models; Civilian and Military. The Civilian version of the Wildcat is favoured by non-spire-dwelling middle class people wanting to pick the kids up from school and look good doing it, the Military version comes in handy when trucking teams of strike-Agents across blasted wasteland. The two uses are not entirely diametric opposites.

Vehicle Statistics (Civilian/Military)

HP	50/75
AV	1/3
MPH	150
DM	+1/+2

All Terrain - Penalties for driving over rough terrain are reduced by 2 when driving this vehicle.

HONG KONG AUTOMETRICS 'BRONZE STALLION' LUXURY SALOON
27,000¢

A classic in its own time, the Bronze Stallion is immensely popular among gangsters and Agents alike due to an (apparently) unforseen construction quirk that made its doors strong enough to serve as bullet-shields. Reliable and with a good top speed, the Bronze Stallion makes an excellent choice of getaway or pursuit vehicle; it is also a relatively good-looking machine with clean lines and three-box saloon design. The default paint-job on all factory units is metallic bronze, but can be changed for an extra 500¢ surcharge.

Vehicle Statistics

HP	45 (Special)
AV	3 (Special)
MPH	220
DM	+1

Bulletproof Doors - The doors on a Bronze Stallion can be used as cover, incurring a -6 penalty on shots made against them. Each door is capable of sustaining 30HP of damage with an AV of 6. Attacks made against the passengers from the sides also incur a -4 penalty even if the passenger is not making an active attempt to use cover unless the shot is called versus the head or upper torso, with the usual penalties.

TAI-LAN 'DAO BO' SPORTS SUPER-ROADSTER
72,000¢

Due to extortionate UIG levies resulting from its apparently unsafe design, the Dao Bo never became a widely-sold vehicle. More's the pity, because the Dao Bo is a work of art. Incorporating a powerful ten-chamber nanofactured ion-stream engine with orbital steel cowling and a chassis / control system designed as a collaborative work by no less than three 'Archimedes'-class A.I.'s, the Dao Bo is one of the most precise and maneuverable fast cars ever made. This vehicle is also marketed as the 'Storm Blade' outside of Chinese-speaking territory.

Vehicle Statistics

HP	30
AV	1
MPH	270
DM	+3

TAI-LAN 'IMPERIAL LOTUS' EXCELSIOR LANDYACHT
47,000¢

Vary rarely seen in usage by anyone who's not a UIG or corporate official, the Imperial Lotus is designed to impress, being one of the largest cars available on the market. Typically chauffeur-driven, the Imperial Lotus features a spacious passenger carriage and real all-walnut interior furnishing; the upholstery is synthetic leather as standard but can be upgraded to the real thing at an additional cost of 4,500¢. The vehicle is neither particularly fast or manoeuvrable but it is the height of comfort and is made with an armoured chassis, bulletproof windows and other security measures as standard to protect whatever VIP is currently riding it.

Vehicle Statistics

HP	80
AV	5
MPH	160
DM	-1

Fully Armoured - Attacks against the vehicle's occupants suffer a -6 penalty and the vehicle's AV is added to the occupant's own for the sake of calculating damage, on a failed attack the vehicle takes the damage instead of the occupant.

Help Alarm - The vehicle is fitted with a high-amperage tracer beacon that can be activated by the driver or passengers at any time as a free action to immediately send a request for assistance to whoever the signal is directed at, typically the UIG and the passenger's Corporation.

TAI-LAN MUNGO 5.5 PEPE TRANSPORT VAN
26,000¢

The Mungo has long stood as the benchmark for light haulage. Its robust construction and ample storage space combine with light handling and a comfortable ride to make a very acceptable package. The UIG use them, the corporations use them, the public use them; the Mungo is without doubt the world's favourite van. The model detailed here (the Pepé) features an integrated snack machine in the dash and run-flat tyres as standard; essential for making those long distance journeys on time. The front seat can accommodate 3 people and the max load is 14 cubic metres (3000kg).

For an additional fee of 1000¢-4000¢ a customised storage unit can be installed into the back. This allows the user to set the van up for the type of work needed. An electrician might have dozens of small boxes, a carpenter may have a system to store sheets of board and tools and a caterer a stabilised refrigeration unit.

Those designed for Agent use often have a few additional seats in the back, weapon racks, locking restraint bars and wipe clean surfaces.

Vehicle Statistics

HP	60
AV	4
MPH	140
DM	+1

TAI-LAN PEON
11,000¢

The Peon is churned out in the thousands and is the van for those who need a transportation vehicle but cannot afford the more customisable and spacious Mungo. The van is a simple, no-frills affair which comes in a range of basic colours with few optional extras.
Despite its low cost and smaller size, the Peon is still a valuable asset for many small businesses and in true Ai-Jinn style it is reliable and solidly constructed. The Peon can seat two adults in the front seats and can hold 6 cubic metres of load (1200kg).

Vehicle Statistics

HP	50
AV	4
MPH	100
DM	-1

TAI-LAN DREAM MAKER 104 MOPED
2,000¢

The Dream Maker 104 is a sedate entry into the world of motorised vehicles. Able to accelerate to 50mph in only 10 seconds this racy little number is high on every trend-setter's wish list.

The Dream Maker comes in a variety of pastel shades as well as hot-pink, lime-green and cream-white. Buckle up and don't forget a helmet.

Vehicle Statistics

HP	18
AV	1
MPH	50
DM	+1

MILITARY VEHICLES

TAI-LAN THUNDERBUS X3000 HEAVY TRANSPORT
50,000¢

This large articulated lorry is commonly used by companies for freight haulage where magna-rail or shuttle is either impractical or too expensive. The Ai-Jinn corporation also occassionally allocate them to their divisions to use as a mobile headquarters. The cab is detachable from the trailer and the capacity of the trailer is 120 cubic metres so you can easily set up drug labs, interrogation suites, workshops etc.

Vehicle Statistics

HP	200
AV	4
MPH	120
DM	-3

THE KALARI 5000 GT
320,000¢

One of the most desirable sports cars currently in production, the Kalari GT is a two seater which can technically fit another two in the back, though in considerable discomfort. The vehicle itself, with its fierce sculpted lines, organic air-intakes and styled lights, looks more like a weapon than a car.

Vehicle Statistics

HP	35
AV	3
MPH	280
DM	+3

KALARI NX2000
40,000¢

A popular car with street racers, the NX2000 is a 4 wheel drive saloon car with a highly tuned engine and brutally hard-edged looks. It features the latest aerodynamic and handling technologies to keep the car glued to the road around even the most severe corners, with little skill. In addition to its good looks and excellent handling the NX2000 is based on a modular construction pattern allowing it to be easily customised. (Costs for customisations made to the NX2000 are reduced by 20%.

Vehicle Statistics

HP	40
AV	4
MPH	230
DM	+2

DA ZHAN MK.IV ARMOURED PERSONNEL CARRIER
450,000¢

The current standard for Ai-Jinn military deployment. Like all Da Zhan products the Mark Four emphasises ruggedness and durability over speed and is designed to serve as a mobile waypoint fortress as much as a means to quickly get troops into combat, in keeping with the Ai-Jinn's style of 'take-and-hold' warfare. Since the end of open hostilities between the corporations, the Mark Four has seen more use deploying Agents into urban warzones where it has served admirably.

Vehicle Statistics

HP	150
AV	20
Shield	100
MPH	70
DM	-1

Weapons

2 Pintle-Mounted Machine Guns, 90-degree firing arc on each side.
1 Turreted Rocket Launcher, 360-degree firing arc.

The Mettle of Da Zhan - Da Zhan vehicles are made with simple, tried-and-tested methods using high-quality components and are designed to be able to tolerate a great degree of structural misalignment before they will fail entirely. As such, Da Zhan vehicles do not lose a condition level when repaired unless the repair roll was a critical failure (pg.31 of the Core Rulebook).

Hermetic Sealing - The vehicle is completely shielded from the outside environment, with internal air-recyclers, electro-reactive radiation shielding and triple-layered atmospheric seals. The driver and passengers are immune to atmospheric toxins and other bio-hazards outside the vehicle for as long as it remains sealed.

DA ZHAN 'BLUE EMPEROR' LEAW-TANK
850,000¢

Designed to be the bane of enemy armour, the Blue Emperor incorporates a potent ordnance railgun mounting as its primary weapon. The Blue Emperor is a sniper-tank, destroying the target from well outside its field of fire and then retreating before an effective counter-attack can be mounted. In battle they are sent out ahead of the main force to neutralise enemy vehicles and ensure that when the Ai-Jinn army arrives it not only has mechanised superiority, but mechanised dominance.

Vehicle Statistics

HP	250
AV	15
Shield	150
MPH	80
DM	-1

Weapons

1 'Sirroco' Turreted Ordnance Rail Cannon*, 90-degree firing arc at the front.
1 Machine Gun, 360-degree firing arc.

The Mettle of Da Zhan - Da Zhan vehicles are made with simple, tried-and-tested methods using high-quality components and are designed to be able to tolerate a great degree of structural misalignment before they will fail entirely. As such, Da Zhan vehicles do not lose a condition level when repaired unless the repair roll was a critical failure (pg.31 of the Core Rulebook).

Hermetic Sealing - The vehicles is completely shielded from the outside environment, with internal air-recyclers, electro-reactive radiation shielding and triple-layered atmospheric seals. The driver and passengers are immune to atmospheric toxins and other bio-hazards outside the vehicle for as long as it remains sealed.

Stealth Modifications - In addition to a morphic camouflage layer, the Blue Emperor's tread-plates are specially shaped so as not to kick up very much dust when driving over arid ground, its chassis is radar- and ladar-resistant and its twin-stage ion turbine engine is near silent-running. All rolls made to detect the Blue Emperor outside of immediate visual range suffer a -4/20% penalty.

DA ZHAN 7-SERIES 'BLACK TURTLE' ARMOURED PATROL VEHICLE
400,000¢
Designed for quick response and policing within captured urban territory, the Black Turtle armoured car sports a primarily antipersonnel-geared weapon payload and somewhat less armour than is the standard for Da Zhan products. Black Turtle units have seen more use than most other armour since the end of the Corporate Wars simply becuase of the fact that they are still useful in dispersing rioters and assaulting urban strongholds.

Vehicle Statistics
HP   200
AV   15
Shield 50
MPH   100
DM   -1

Weapons
1 Turreted RPG Launcher, 360-degree firing arc. Typically loaded with knockout gas, flash-bang or riot grenades.
2 Pintle-Mounted Machine Guns, 90-degree firing arc on each side.
1 Ramming shield (see below)

The Mettle of Da Zhan - See Above

Hermetic Sealing - See Above

Ramming Shield - Designed for smashing down barricades, the vehicle is equipped with a durasteel ramming shield that allows it to ignore up to 5 points of the rammed target's armour and also protects the vehicle from taking damage when ramming, provided the AV of the rammed target is under 20.

DA ZHAN 'ROLLING THUNDER' MOBILE FORTRESS
1.5 MILLION ¢
The Rolling Thunder lives up to its classification of a 'Mobile Fortress' at nearly thirty metres in length and sporting 325mm layered ceramic-durasteel armour that make it utterly invulnerable to most infantry armaments even before its massively powerful 'Aegis'-class hard ion shield is taken into account. The Rolling Thunder is designed to be a massive show of power, it's impregnable hull bristling with an apocalyptic arsenal of missile-arrays and heavy weapons able to dish out damage on a level that makes it a threat even to cyberlins.

Vehicle Statistics
HP   600
AV   30
Shield 500
MPH   30
DM   -3

Weapons
4 'Black Hurricane' Missile Arrays loaded with Heavy Missiles, 270-degree forward firing arc. Each array houses 10 missiles.

1 'Hurricane' Turreted Ordnance Plasma*, 90-degree forward firing arc.

6 Pintle-Mounted Sub-Machine Plasmas, 90-degree firing arc, three each side.

2 Knox Deadleaf Minelayer*

The Mettle of Da Zhan - See Opposite Column

Hermetic Sealing - See Opposite Column

Regenerative Shield - The vehicle's shield recovers lost points at a rate of 10 per round as long as the engine remains active.

MCP (Mobile Command Point) - The Rolling Thunder contains a carrier bay for up to 20 armed and equipped soldiers and a war-room outfitted with hacking computer terminals with full wireless WDN access, a command screen that can synchronise with communicators and smeakers for continuous realtime contact with allies, a SatBlanket and a coffee machine.

*These ordnance weapons can be found on page 77.

DA ZHAN MARK VII RED TALON SUBMERSIBLE P-TANK
300,000¢

The Pressurised-Tank is a small, utilitarian fighting vehicle which seats only one driver.

As this is such a mainstay of the Ai-Jinn Military it is featured in the Antagonists section at the back of the book (page 160).

MAG TANKS

MAG Tanks require the Cyberlin Piloting Training (page xx)

MAG (Mobile Armoured Gunnery) Tanks are commonly used in environments where the locomotary system of a conventional tank makes it unsuitable. MAG Tanks use a multipod design (typically 6 or 8 legs) to allow them to clamber over a range of terrain types which are normally tricky to navigate. The hull is normally extremely well armoured and mounted on a platform suspended between or above the legs.

There are a range of MAG Tank designs, each created for a specific function although all share the following features.

Anti-Immobilisation System
MAG Tanks can function with only 3 legs although their speed is reduced to half.

All Terrain Mobility
MAG Tanks can cross all reasonable terrain with no issues. They cannot climb sheer surfaces more than 10 feet high unless equipped with anti-grav engines.

DA ZHAN BLACK WIDOW URBAN ASSAULT MAG TANK
I MILLION c

Vehicle Statistics
HP 150
AV 15
Shield 150
MPH 40
DM -1

Weapons
Twin linked 'Hellstorm' missile array. This fires a pair of medium rockets (6D10) at a single target. The missile bay can hold 8 rockets giving a total of 4 attacks.
1 turreted rail gun mounted on the top of the hull.
2 grenade launchers loaded with a range of grenades; typically smoke, heavy frag and heavy incendiary.
1 Undermounted M50 Machine Gun which can fire forwards or backwards so that it will not damage the legs.

Each round the pilot can fire 2 of the weapon system as well as driving the vehicle.

The Mettle of Da Zhan - SeeOpposite Page

Hermetic Sealing - See Opposite Page

UIG DESERT SCORPION SNIPER MAG TANK
I MILLIONc

Vehicle Statistics
HP 250
AV 20
Shield 200
MPH 80
DM +1

The Desert Scorpion is a shining black MAG Tank with 8 legs and an emphasis on speed and ranged combat. It's commonly used in large open areas such as deserts or plains where its immense top speed means that if it spots you and you don't have a fast vehicle, you are going to be in big trouble very soon. They are always piloted by professionals so their attack values are noted below.

Weapons
2 x Forward Mounted Sniper Cannons
AT 30, Dam 2D12+30, Ignores 10 AV, Rate 2, Range 3 miles.

The Scorpion must line itself up to use these, which the driver can do as a free action.
These are aimed by the on-board A.I. and are considered to always have aimed for three rounds. (This is taken into account with the AT above). Each can be fired at a separate target if desired.

Every mile after the first, the cannons receive -5 to hit so at 3 miles they fire with an AT of only 20.

2 Turreted Rail Guns
AT 18, Dam 6D10, Ignores 15AV, Rate 1, X-Ray Scope

Electro Defences – Anyone engaging the tank in close combat receives a 4D10 electric shock which knocks them back from the tank and ignores AV.

Smoke Dispenser - The Scorpion can send plumes of smoke into the air creating a cloud 30 metres in diameter. Thermal will help to spot it but most thermal units only work up to a few hundred metres. Although the rail guns are limited to around a mile, the sniper cannons function at a distance of 3 miles.

A.I. Co-pilot - The level 7 A.I. co-pilot ensures that all weapons can be fired each round by helping the pilot with a range of tasks.

Hermetic Sealing - See Opposite Page

See page 93 for an illustration of a MAG Tank.

MAG TANKS IN YOUR GAME

Mag Tanks make great enemies for divisions of high level Agents and can be used as 'monsters'. They can be a very convenient encounter for an advanced division as the Mag Tank has high armour, HP and shields but only a few attacks. You could consider it much like adventurers fighting a small dragon in a traditional fantasy setting. The tanks are quite mobile and can chase the Agents across urban terrain, smashing down buildings and scuttling over ruins with ease. If the players are really advanced you can always have them attacked by a battalion of Mag Tanks.
There is a great cinematic feeling when a player takes on a tank in close combat and wins.

VEHICLE UPGRADES

There are additional vehicle upgrades on page 56 of the Core Rules.

Underlighting   50¢
A series of lights are installed along the underside of the vehicle giving the classic under-chassis illumination you expect from a street racing car.

In-Car TV   100¢
A small 10 inch screen is fitted into the vehicle allowing the passengers to watch their favourite programs on the move. Larger screens can be fitted with the price rising by 20¢ per inch. By doubling the price your screens can be made waterproof and scratch resistant so they are suitable for attaching to the outside of the car.

Custom Paint Job

Bike	**500¢**
Car	**1000¢**
Van	**1500¢**
Lorry	**3000¢**
Mag Tank	**5000¢**

Nothing says 'made' like a custom paint job, from from candy apple green to flaming skulls.

Custom Upholstery   4000¢
The interior of the vehicle is decked out with a custom, real leather re-work.

SonicAir Thunder Horn   300¢
This ear-splitting piece of horn technology has an adjustable output to vary your horn volume from a subtle whisper to a glass-shattering siren. You can program the horn with up to 30 audio files from a computer, allowing it to play your favourite music at completely unacceptable levels.

Thief Lock   1000¢ (Illegal)
If someone tries to steal your car the engine immobilises and the doors lock sealing the thief into the car and filling it with poisonous gas (Potency 4) which will kill a normal human in 30 seconds.

You then receive a phone message informing you of the incident.

It is even equipped with a small task A.I. that taunts the thief while they're dying with phrases such as "You're never going to get out, it's utterly pointless. You shouldn't have been such a delinquent little shit, should you?"

Gear Stick Ornamentation
The standard head of the gear stick is replaced with something more befitting your ride. Examples include

Silver Skull	300¢
8 Ball	100¢

Wooden Dragon's Head	500¢
Modern sculpted metal	75¢
Giant semiprecious stone	1,000¢
Giant precious stone	100,000¢
Gun grip	100¢
Phallic Lookalike	75¢

High Capacity Fuel Tank 400¢
This doubles the size of the existing fuel tank.

Smugglers Compartment
This is a compartment built into the vehicle which is difficult to find with a cursory search. Anyone manually checking the car takes a -8 / -40% penalty to find the compartment. You can augment these spaces with crystal weave (see the Eastern Bank page 40), this costs triple the normal cost.

Vehicle	Size	Cost
Motorbike	Pistol / Fist	500¢
Car	Rifle / Head	1000¢
Van	Heavy Weapon	1500¢
Lorry	Human Body	2000¢

Sports Exhaust   200¢
This ensures your car puts out a better exhaust note and uses its fuel even more efficiently. This increases the top speed of the car by 5mph

Bullet Proof Glass

Moderate amount of glass (car)	300¢
Large amount of glass (bus)	1000¢

In vehicles which have a significant amount of glass such as cars and buses, the glass can be installed to give a +1 bonus to the vehicles AV.

Personalised License Plates
Complete the look with a license plate which says something about you.

Obscure, only the owner would understand	300¢
(E.I. Agent John Moore has **EI AJM1**)	
Distincive, its obvious you have style and cash	2,000¢
(E.I. Agent John Moore has **JM 1**)	
Famous, perhaps a single word or famous date	20,000¢
(E.I. Agent John Moore has **JONNY**)	
One of a kind, this plate screams wealth	1 Million ¢
(E.I. Agent John Moore has **E I**)	

Modern registration plates are made up of between 2 and 7 alphanumerics with spaces and are purchased directly from the UIG.

VEHICLES AND FUEL

Modern vehicles use a fuel called Paracane, a clean burning, bio-sourced, combustible alternative to petrol or diesel. Paracane is suitable for all vehicles.

Modern engines work with a similar principle to 21st century ones, though obviously much more efficiently. For this reason a good mechanic is still worth his weight in gold when it comes to repairing and modifying vehicles.

FUEL COSTS:

Paracane is a cheap fuel and service stations still dot the endless highways, manned by reluctant, string-vest wearing oiks. A litre costs around one credit and will take you roughly the following distances

Vehicle	MPL	Typical Fuel Tank Size
Motorbike	150 miles per litre	5 Litres
Car	100 miles per litre	10 Litres
Van	70 miles per litre	15 Litres
Lorry	50 miles per litre	30 Litres

Because of the combustibility and efficiency of paracane, fuel tanks are generally quite small.

The costs are very low generally speaking so calculating fuels costs is not really necessary.

Example, travelling 1000 miles in a car would cost 10 credits

DOES IT EXPLODE?

Of course it does, what kind of action game would be complete without exploding cars, barrels and fuel stations?

Steel Dragon XC90 Mag Tank

SECTION 5

AI-JINN BUSINESS & MANAGEMENT

MANAGEMENT

The management structure of the Ai-Jinn is a fairly simple affair. The CEO makes the executive decisions which ultimately dictate the Ai-Jinn's development. These orders are passed down the ranks until they reach someone who can execute the required plan. This is a fairly common practice for most corporations.

One of the key differences with the Ai-Jinn is the level of deniability which is incorporated into the command structure. In the Western Federation your commanding officer (to the extent of his power) takes all responsibility for the actions of the division, both legally and within the Corporation. The Ai-Jinn do the opposite and anyone who is apprehended by the UIG for criminal behaviour is expected to sacrifice themselves for the good of the Corporation.

For example, if one member of a division engaged in illegal activities is caught he may well confess to a larger or non-existent crime if he believes it may prevent his fellow Agents from getting caught. The Ai-Jinn corporation are not blind to this level of loyalty and will throw all of their legal power behind the accused individual to get him acquitted. If he does end up in jail or under threat of depersonalisation then they will do everything they can to free him or make his time in prison as easy as possible.

Yuan Quingzhao - CEO of the Ai-Jinn

The corporation has been known to spend millions of credits to free a single rank 1 Agent. They believe (with good reason) that for an Agent to know he has the unequivocal support of a multi-billion credit corporation is the best form of loyalty enforcement possible. The subsequent sense of camaraderie, trust and duty give the Ai-Jinn the strongest inter and intra division bonds seen within a modern corporation.

RANK 10 - THE CEO

The current head of the Ai-Jinn is Yuan Qingzhao, a woman of great tenacity and at present the only female acting as a CEO within the five major Corporations. She has been in command since the death of her predecessor Jing Lei, who was murdered in his bed by Clan Hitori in 2401.

The death of Jing Lei is still considered to be the epitome of a perfectly executed assassination. Not only was no security triggered but all three backups of Lei's psyche matrix were simultaneously destroyed. One was under lockdown in the Shanghai Spire, one was on Lunas Colony and one was held by an unnamed division who were on active duty in Odessa; this illustrates the planning and influence the Shi Yukiro needed to exert in order to complete this assassination.

At the time of Lei's death Qingzhao was Shadow CEO and Kuan-Yin Liang was the Dragon's Head. Both were rank 9 and eligible to be elevated to the position of CEO. A great deal of discussion and debate ensued but it was essential a new leader be chosen swiftly before the other Corporations took advantage.

The voting council, also known as the Pa Hsien (or the 8 immortals), decided that in the current political climate a war-monger (as Kuan-Yin Liang was) was not the best person to have in charge of the Corporation. Instead Yuan Qingzhao was selected to direct the Ai-Jinn, which she has been doing for the past century with great success. As a token of respect to the Dragon's Head she gave him carte blanche to compile a plan which would avenge the death of the former CEO.

Appearance

Qingzhao is of Chinese birth and appears to be around 30 years old with clean, hard features, short black hair and no obvious cybernetic upgrades. She spends a great deal of her time practising martial arts, primarily muay thai but given her life span of over 220 years it would be safe to say there are few disciplines she is not proficient in. If encountered in her private quarters she will normally be wearing traditional clothes associated with the art she has been practicing or a more universal black combats and vest.

When she leaves her chambers Yuan tends to wear a traditional Chinese cheongsam (tight fitting patterned dress) with her hair pinned up with hair sticks (similar to chopsticks but with beads hanging from the ends).

Attitude

Yuan has remained surprisingly level headed and modest considering her position of power. She is more than happy to speak to junior Agents if time permits and although curt, she does not generate the sense of unease and trepidation that someone such as Gunther Van Rosch does. She believes whole-heartedly in the Ai-Jinn's commitment to one another as individuals and sees building relationships with the troops to be sowing seeds of strength and allegiance. After all, how can you expect someone to die for you if you will not even meet with them?

Goals

Yuan's corporate policy is at present one of expansion. It is not the time for war and with the other Corporations building structures as fast as they can the Ai-Jinn are making a killing. Few corporations build their own structures these days, preferring to focus on their areas of speciality. Likewise the Ai-Jinn don't build their own weapons or manufacture their own medicines.

The Ai-Jinn's space projects still go ahead unchallenged. The other corporations strive relentlessly to uncover the FarDrive's secrets or build their own from scratch but it seems futile. It is widely believed that although the Ai-Jinn were able to create a basic FarDrive based on the hulk they recovered, it was not until the intervention of a rogue Archon that the technology was refined to a state where it could be economically and reliably manufactured. It still frustrates the UIG that the allied Archons refuse to impart the FarDrive's design to them despite the fact that the Ai-Jinn are cruising around the cosmos in their own fleet of craft.

Yuan has continued to sanction the creation of more mining bases, factories and trial colonies, convinced that it's only a matter of time until the other corporations get their hands on the drive. When that happens she intends to be several steps ahead in the race to colonise and exploit space.

Qingzhao's other main area of interest is the consolidation of organised crime cells. Although the Ai-Jinn claim to have around 50% to 60% of organised criminals on their payroll, that leaves a significant portion of them running free, or worse, working for the enemy. Her current initiative is to place competent divisions in charge of a single old city apiece, these Agents establish a firm hold on part of the city and gradually take over or eliminate anyone who will not play by the Ai-Jinn's rules. This method has been successful in many of the East Asian cities but has met with limited results in Federation, Comoros and E.I. territory.

Security

Since the death of Jing Lei security has been increased significantly. The CEO is now based in the Amur Border Spire (see the Eastern Bank) and copies of the psyche matrix are secreted in various locations around the world by the hattamoto-yakko reducing the risk anyone will divulge their locations. The CEO is always accompanied by the hattamoto-yakko wherever she goes. They taste her food, guard her car, pat down her appointments etc. She also uses a battery of stealth and reactive ion fields to prevent ranged assassination.

Although originally not a proponent of excessive cybernetics, the death of Jing Lei and her promotion to CEO gave Yuan cause to rethink. She now boasts a wealth of custom built, top of the range cyberware giving her not only exceptional physical abilities but allowing her to survive a concerted attack from a range of powerful weaponry.

RANK 9 - DRAGON'S HEAD (MILITARY COMMANDER)

The Dragon's Head is an extremely important position within the ranks of the Ai-Jinn. He has authority over all of the Corporation's military operations including the development of new war technology, deployment of defensive measures and the creation of contingency plans in the event of war. Although he can be overruled by the CEO, the only other way for him to be countermanded is by 2 or more opposed votes from the voting council.

The current Dragon's Head is Kuan-Yin Liang. He has been a long standing Agent of the Ai-Jinn, working his way up the ranks by demonstrating exceptional command and strategy. Although he was not active during the Corporate Wars, Liang has since made countless tactical decisions and policy shifts which the have seen the Ai-Jinn through some tricky times.

As an individual Liang is stoic and unflappable. He never speaks without considering what he is about to say and has little time for fun or recreation. Most of the time he can be found at his desk, analysing intelligence reports for any signs of opportunity or weakness within the Ai-Jinn's rivals. He tends to be irate when disturbed and only drags himself away to practice the martial arts (as demanded from all Ai-Jinn) and for occasional benders of drinking and gambling with his old Division. If anybody wanted to speak to the Dragon's Head in an informal manner these alcohol fuelled marathons would be the best time to catch him. During

Agent Kuan-Yin Liang, Dragon's Head of the Ai-Jinn

such times he tends be carefree, generous and seems to exude a sense of camaraderie. Evidence perhaps, that he remembers vividly his days of skulking through the Old Cities, rifle in hand, hunting the Shi Yukiro like the snakes they are.

RANK 9 - SHADOW CEO

The Shadow CEO's main responsibility is to act as an advisor, confidant and executive to the CEO. While the CEO herself will ultimately decide the direction of the Corporation, it is the Shadow CEO who will help her think through the ideas and look for potential holes. When the plans have been finalised the Shadow CEO will then allocate the various aspects of the plan to lower ranks leaving the CEO free to postulate future schemes.

The CEO's directives are considered by the voting council and four votes against the proposal will halt it and force a rethink. This does not often happen however, not because the CEO's ideas are flawless but due to the simple fact that anyone openly opposing the CEO is taking a risky political stance. The Shadow CEO will arbitrate with the voting council, making sure they understand exactly what the CEO's intentions are and that the ideas are not dismissed due to misinterpretation.

The Shadow CEO's other duties involve the promotion of Agents above rank 5. From ranks 1 to 4 the system generally takes care of itself and division mission officer's deal with the administration. When an Agent is about to become rank 6, however, she reaches a point where she can start to have a serious effect on the machinations of the corporation as a whole.

For this reason the Ai-Jinn begin to closely monitor any Agent who has passed rank 5 and occasionally bring them in for interviews or set them special tasks to assess their loyalty. It is ultimately down to the Shadow CEO to decide whether an Agent will ascend to rank 6 or 7.

Any Agent ascending to rank 8, 9 or 10 must be stringently checked and assessed by all existing Agents of Rank 8+. The Ai-Jinn are extremely careful not to let anyone into the upper echelons of the Corporation who is not 100% trustworthy.

The current Shadow CEO is Huan-Jae Kwon, a Korean woman of impeccable character who has been the right arm of the CEO Qingzhao since her ascension to head of the Ai-Jinn. Huan-Jae is extremely serious in all of her duties and does not share Qingzhao's ideas of bonding with the troops. She keeps them at a healthy distance believing they should fear and respect her. She maintains that affiliation with the Ai-Jinn is reward enough and that if an Agent keeps to the philosophies of the Corporation he will, in time, reap all the rewards he deserves.

In keeping with her clinical and efficient persona Huan-Jae dresses in a sombre, if well tailored black suit jacket and skirt. Her black hair is pulled back tight and she appears around 25 years old though her true age is closer to 120. Huan-Jae lives an extremely regimented life which you could set a watch by, her only vices being traditional oriental arts such as calligraphy and embroidery. She remains single, having been used by men in the past and now seeing such coupling as a sign of weakness.

Anyone lucky enough to reach rank 5 had best be careful as they will have attracted the scrutiny of Huan-Jae. Even though they may not realise it, it is probable their actions are being closely monitored and any sign of disloyalty could result in a severe and sudden career plateau.

RANK 8 - UIG POLICY ADVISOR AND HIS DIVISION. (THE SWORD AND THE FIVE KNIVES)

The Ai-Jinn's institutionalised hatred of the UIG is no secret. This extends to the point of them having a department dedicated to its dissolution who are often equipped with Legacy Pattern Technology. The detail is made up of 6 Agents, typically a Rank 8 and five Rank 7s. The Rank 8 acts as a kind of mission officer known as the Sword who takes the comments and instructions of his superiors and formulates plans which are executed by his specialist division (the Five Knives). He is of course able to commandeer other divisions as he needs them but they are seldom as suited as his own tailor-made team.

The missions undertaken by the Five Knives are invariably highly illegal and subtlety is a far more important weapon than martial prowess. Although the Division occasionally perform assassinations or terrorist attacks they tend to work in a way that does not give the UIG cause to retaliate.

A typical assignment would be to corrupt a UIG Official or steal the plans of a new anti-Agent weapon. These missions, if performed correctly are extremely hard to identify and even harder to track back to the culprit.

Agent Jan Tao – The Sword
The current Sword is Jan Tao, an Agent whose list of grievances with the UIG go back several decades. Members of his family, both blood and criminal, have fallen to the uncompromising hand of the UIG.

Jan Tao - The Sword of the Ai-Jinn

Tao himself was born into extreme poverty in Gun Nai, an isolated provincial town which had been left untouched by the corporation and the UIG for decades.

Tao was 14 years old when Malenbrach in drop ships arrived at the village and demanded it be cleared in preparation for the construction of a new administration facility. Although the UIG made provision for each family to be re-housed in the nearby old city of Yumen the results were disastrous. Not only were the villagers separated into different parts of the city, breaking up their community, they were housed in near-slum conditions and having no concept of city living or criminal culture were immediately the target of opportunistic street gangs.

Many of the villagers were robbed, raped, beaten and murdered over the following weeks and despite repeated requests the UIG did nothing to resolve the situation. Tao's family were the victims of one such attack. His mother was ravished and his father killed trying to defend her. Tao himself knifed one of the attackers to death but was beaten into a coma for his trouble. It was only when his mother approached the local Triad begging for help that things improved. The marauding gang was killed to a man and the Triad arranged for Tao's medical costs to be taken care of on the understanding he and his mother would work for the Triad when everything had stabilised. Although Tao was put to work pushing drugs and his mother employed in a bordello, they were both safe, well fed and rewarded for their work with money and clean accommodation.

In time Tao was invited to join the Triad as a full member and his mother was able to cease her unsavoury work. He showed tremendous initiative in several areas of work but displayed the most enthusiasm for anti-UIG activities. Although he worked within the Triad's operating boundaries he was able to create a disproportionate amount of trouble for the lawmen. It was no surprise that he was approached by the Ai-Jinn and offered a place in the Agent Training Programme.

During his time as a field Agent he achieved notoriety as a pioneer in anti-UIG warfare. He was personally responsible for making the Legacy Project (page 32) what it is today and is known to have killed over 200 officers and destroyed more than 2 billion credits worth of UIG assets. Despite these achievements, he has never been docked a single rank point and to this day continues to infuriate the UIG with his schemes.

> *Death to the corrupt oppressors! Take arms against the UIG!*
> *Sì!*
>
> *Death to the machineries of power! Attack from all places without pause!*
> *Sì!*
>
> *Death from the shadows! Leave no trace!*
> *Sì!*
>
> *Death before betrayal! Uphold loyalty to our brothers!*
> *Sì!*
>
> *Death without quarter! Never forget! Never forgive!*
> *Sì! Sì! Sì!*
>
> *-Rallying cry of the Sword and the Five Knives*

RANK 8 - THE VOTING COUNCIL (THE 8 IMMORTALS)

This is a group of eight Rank 8 Agents, named after the wise immortals of Chinese myth, who act as a voice of reason and safeguard for the corporation as a whole. They have the power to force a rethink on any decision made as long as 4 members agree. Even the CEO herself can have her orders countermanded by the council.

The number 8 holds great significance in Chinese mythology and it is no coincidence that there are 8 members, each of rank 8. Their identities are not common knowledge and they do not spend all their time festering in a boardroom, picking over fine details. Each member is a competent Agent in their own right and may also hold other positions; for example, the Sword (above) could also be a council member.

When a matter of significance has been decided by the CEO or her advisors it is relayed to each of the council members, normally face to face but sometimes by a secure communication if necessary.

Ideally the council will meet up to discuss the proposition at the first available instance but failing that, a member's decision can be sent in on a secure transmission. Normally a simple yes/no is sufficient making it quite a difficult system to corrupt.

Elevation to council status is earned by impeccable loyalty, consistent good judgement and broad political understanding.

RANK 7 & 8 - REGIONAL GOVERNORS

These men and women are the governors of the four Ai-Jinn provinces. There are actually five chairmen as one is assigned to Shi Yukiro territory, which the Ai-Jinn consider to be rightfully theirs. More is written about this in the section on Provinces on page 99.

The chairmen are elected by firstly being recommended by their peers and if this recommendation is taken seriously then the CEO, Shadow CEO and Voting Council will make an assessment.

The position holds considerable power but like-wise great responsibility. Each province must be productive and fulfil its role in the betterment of the Ai-Jinn in terms of productivity, political strength and national defence. If a province begins to show signs of declining in any way the governor must immediately make a full report, which if unsatisfactory will result in his immediate replacement.

Each governor is free to deal with any problems and implement expansions in his own way as long as he is following the overall directives set forth by the CEO.

Each Governor is detailed with the respective Province. These start on page 99

THE FIVE GOVERNORS

Agent May Lin Chow - Governor of the Western Province
Qhinlong - The Azure Dragon

Agent Simon Yo - Governor of the Northern Province
Zulong - The Vermillion Dragon

Agent Jan Tsai – Governor of the Central Province
Huanglong – The Yellow Dragon

Agent Samantha Yeung – Governor of the Southern Province
Bailong – The White Dragon

Agent Yasuhiro Kotabe – Governor of the Eastern Province
Xuanlong – The Black Dragon

Dream no small dreams for they have no power to move the hearts of men. - Goeth

Since the inception of the very first corporations more than a millennia previously, arguably the single most crucial factor in their success or failure has been people; those key individuals whose specific personal qualities drive them to succeed against their competitors. The methods by which corporations ensure that they retain the services of such individuals has, therefore, always been a defining feature of their corporate culture. And this remains true today, even though the vast size, power, and influence of the Five otherwise renders them almost incomparable to their forebears of a thousand years previously.

To examine the ways in which the Corporations engender loyalty, therefore, is a singularly revealing exercise. The Shi Yukiro, as might be expected, taps into age-old traditions of consensus-based obedience to the Corporation as overarching social group. The Western Federation plays off insularity, isolationism, and quasi-Puritanical values to convince its key assets that life is better in Federation territory than elsewhere. Comoros employs a similar theme of righteousness, matched with an ethos designed to skillfully exploit the feelings of disenfranchisement that many of its component geographical groups have historically been prone to. Eurasian Incorporated simply woos its most valued Agents with outrageously vast bribes, usually rather transparently euphemized as 'performance bonuses' or, on occasion, stationery expense claims.

But it is the Ai-Jinn, whose best Agents are typically those who have already defected from other organizations and quite frequently rival Corporations, which has perforce elevated the assurance and preservation of loyalty into an art form. One side of this is its familial structure; the organization has blended the family-group ethos of countless petty and major crime syndicates spanning the last six centuries with various Confucian tenets of filial piety, and the resulting bonds are in almost all cases formidably strong. The other is the punishment of those few who are tempted to stray so far from the fold that the Ai-Jinn decide they cannot be retrieved. Exemplary punishment of traitors is by no means a new concept; the challenge, for the Ai-Jinn, is to find new and relevant ways to command attention amidst a populace long desensitized to violence and horror. To this end, it is rumoured that fully a quarter of the Corporation's R&D assets are entirely dedicated to discovering novel, graphic, and above all memorable means of executing traitors; if the stories are to be believed, the blood- and oil-smeared laboratories below the ACF in Beijing ring almost ceaselessly with screams as these hard-working career scientists tirelessly pursue their goal.

- from The Rise of The Corporation-States
attr: Dr. Edmond Treval

THE FIVE PROVINCES

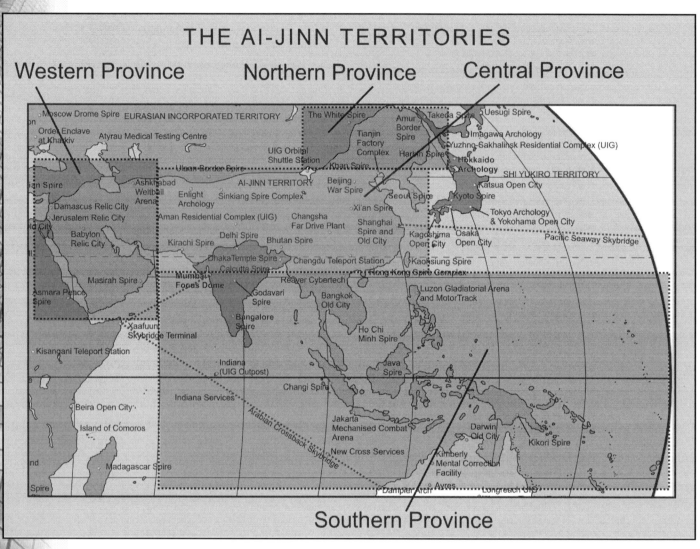

THE AI-JINN TERRITORIES

Western Province · Northern Province · Central Province

Southern Province

Moscow Drome Spire · EURASIAN INCORPORATED TERRITORY · The White Spire · Amur Border Spire · Takeda Spire · Uesugi Spire
Order Enclave at Kharkiv · Atyrau Medical Testing Centre · Tianjin Factory Complex · Imagawa Archology · Yuzhno-Sakhalinsk Residential Complex (UIG)
UIG Orbital Shuttle Station · Harbin Spire · Hokkaido Archology
Ulaan Border Spire · Khan Spire · SHI YUKIRO TERRITORY
...an Spire · Ashkhabad Weltball Arena · Enlight Archology · Sinkiang Spire Complex · AI-JINN TERRITORY · Beijing War Spire · Seoul Spire · Katsua Open City · Kyoto Spire
Damascus Relic City · Xi'an Spire · Tokyo Archology & Yokohama Open City
Jerusalem Relic City · Aman Residential Complex (UIG) · Changsha Far Drive Plant · Shanghai Spire and Old City · Kagoshima Open City · Osaka Open City · Pacific Seaway Skybridge
...ic City · Babylon Relic City · Delhi Spire · Bhutan Spire
Kirachi Spire · Dhaka Temple Spire · Chengdu Teleport Station · Kaohsiung Spire
Calcutta Spire · Hong Kong Spire Complex
Masirah Spire · Mumbai Focus Dome · Reaver Cybertech · Luzon Gladiatorial Arena and MotorTrack
Godavari Spire · Bangkok Old City
Asmara Peace Spire · Bangalore Spire · Ho Chi Minh Spire
Xaafuun Skybridge Terminal
Kisangani Teleport Station · Indiana (UIG Outpost) · Java Spire
Changi Spire · Arabian Crossback Skybridge
Indiana Services
Beira Open City · Jakarta Mechanised Combat Arena · Darwin Old City · Kikori Spire
Island of Comoros · New Cross Services · Kimberly Mental Correction Facility
...nd · Madagascar Spire · Ayres · Dampier Arch · Longreach UIG
Spire

The Ai-Jinn's territory is vast so it assigns a governor to each province. These provinces are defined as follows:

Western Province
Northern Province
Central Province
Southern Province

Note that the Japanese islands are sometimes known as the 'Eastern Province' by the Ai-Jinn, illustrating the fact that they believe these are a rightful part of Ai-Jinn territory and will one day be reclaimed.

Although each of the provinces is a dynamic and highly varied area which requires careful political, economic and military control, each one has a very different character. This influences the way in which the Ai-Jinn operate in the region and, of course, the operations of their allies and enemies.

THE WESTERN PROVINCE

(The Bottle Neck, The Crucible, The Promised Land, Ping Heng)

This region is also known as the Holy Land due to it having the largest Order of the Faith concentration in the world and its obvious links to religious beliefs. It has many similar issues to the Eastern Bank but does not have the classification of a Capital Code Zone. There are four main reasons for this:

1. The Comoros Corporation does not use Janissaries to ignite the fires of conflict within this region as they do in the Eastern Bank. Moreover, they work closely with the Order to maintain peace.

2. The Order of the True Faith has a relative stranglehold on this area and they are extremely good at maintaining the peace. For this reason the UIG don't need to apply much in the way of

additional pressure.

3. The Western Province tends to be quite a 'spiritual' place and the inhabitants are, for the most part, less commercial than most. For this reason it's quite low on E.I.'s list of places to deluge with capitalist goods and services and they tend to stay out of the area.

4. The Ai-Jinn's objectives within the Western Province focus on spying and subversion. The area is festooned with Order Enclaves which the Ai-Jinn have been forced to permit over the last few centuries as concessions to the people, to comply with UIG law and by way of apologies for acts of aggression. They cannot just charge in and reclaim these enclaves and neither would they want to. Rather they seek to insert their Agents in and around the area, watching for signs of weakness and sowing seeds of dissent and corruption in the hope of shaking the foundations of the Faith.

THE BARIKA KEBE ALLIANCE

A significant problem is the 'alliance' between the Order and Comoros in this region. Although there are no official treaties and both groups don't always see eye to eye, their unity provides strength. Whilst they are not fighting one another they are learning, growing and ultimately becoming less assailable. The idea of two of the most potent groups of telepaths working together is a terrifying prospect, not just for the Ai-Jinn but for all of the other Corporations.

The alliance is mainly due to two individuals.

The first is Sister Anisiah Barika, a formidable woman who holds the rank of Prelate within the Order and has jurisdiction over all the enclaves within the Middle East. The second is Mr. Camora Kébé, a rank 7 Comoros Agent entrusted with all political decisions made in North East Africa.

That two individuals with such similar goals should have been forced into close proximity is fortunate for both the Order and Comoros. From their first meeting it was apparent great things would happen and for the last 45 years the area has become more and more stable until it is one of the safest places to live in the world.

Sadly this union has not been repeated anywhere else in the world and although Comoros and the Order bear a mutual respect for one another, should either Anisiah or Camora die, the alliance would likely crumble within days.

THE BARIKA KEBE INITIATIVE (BKI)

To counter this powerful alliance Governor May Lin Chow (opposite) has put together a scheme entitled the Barika Kébé Initiative. This audacious plan unites the Federation, the Shi Yukiro, the Ai-Jinn and E.I. with the single purpose of ending the Comoros-Order alliance.

Initially the project was met with suspicion by the non-Ai-Jinn members but over time it has been considered a necessary evil and each corporation has one or two Agents deployed in the Masirah Spire to be a part of the scheme. This small cooperative effort seems to have no bearing on any other aspects of corporate policy and the Ai-Jinn still try and rip the hearts from the Shi Yukiro on sight but nonetheless, this small non-UIG enforced initiative is a small sign that the warring factions can act in harmony, even if

they are only doing so in order to destroy something peaceful.

RUNNING BKI GAMES

Such missions give you an excellent opportunity to allow the players to pick any corporation they want to play (except Comoros) and go on missions without them being UIG monitored or approved. There is no reason the division cannot be made up of two Shi Yukiro and two Federation Agents and so all kinds of interesting combinations can arise.

Although Governor Chow is technically in charge of BKI operations, she is not foolish enough to dictate everything that should be done. She would rather work in co-operation with Agents and come up with a plan together which will make the most use of everyone's talents.

If she does have to deal with dissent from non-Ai-Jinn Agents she will likely contact the Agents' superiors. Each Agent has been assigned here for the benefit of the corporation and antagonising Chow is definitely not going to help anyone.

BKI MISSIONS

Ultimately the assassination of Barika or Kébé would more than likely end the alliance. However, this has proved impossible as they tend to be well secured deep within Comoros and Order strongholds. In light of this May Lin concocts a range of missions which serve to destabilise the fragile alliance without revealing her nature or being too overt. Some examples are given below.

1. Assume the identities of Comoros Agents and attack Order assets
2. Take on Order identities and travel to nearby Comoros cities. Spread damning propaganda about the Comoros Corporation.
3. Assassinate some of Barika's close co-workers and make it look like Kébé's doing. This could also be done the other way around.
4. Steal secrets from one half of the alliance and plant them on the other half.
5. Rally extremists who are opposed to the alliance and equip them with armaments so that they can form a rebellious faction.

> When the blameless and the righteous die, the very gods for vengeance cry.
>
> Vlad Taltos

AGENT MAY LIN CHOW

GOVERNOR OF THE WESTERN PROVINCE

QHINLONG - THE AZURE DRAGON

May Lin has an unrivalled knack for both diplomacy and deceit and earnestly promises to work with Comoros and the Order to maintain the state of peace which exists in the Middle East. Her real work however, lies in organising cross-corporation divisions with the sole purpose of wrecking the beautiful harmony so many have worked to create.

So far her work has only met with partial success. She has done an incredible job of uniting the Corporations against Comoros and the Order, but as regards making any real progress towards ending the alliance, has fallen woefully short.

She is kept in power only because so far she has managed to convince both Comoros and the Order of her good intentions whilst quietly hacking away at their foundations but unless she shows some positive results in the next few years she will be looking for another job. Continually fighting for her position has made May Lin an extremely edgy woman who can become ferociously angry when things do not go to plan.

THE NORTHERN PROVINCE

This is the smallest of the provinces but as a significant part of it is within the Eastern Bank, the Capital Code Zone* plays an important part in the way Governor Yo handles things. The region is sandwiched between E.I. and Shi Yukiro territory and so Yo certainly has his plate full ensuring the area remains both stable and uncompromised.

Welcome to the lands of hatred, my friends. Perhaps you think this a figure of speech; please understand I am not given to such flourishes. Here, the land crawls with our enemies and they hate you; and they are everywhere, under every rock and behind every wretched tree. Here, the law is swift and brutal and it hates you; it watches you for the slightest misstep, that it might reach out and crush you in the name of justice. Here, the land itself hates you, and will rise up against you; it will poison the careless, freeze the unprepared, consume the foolhardy. And here, should you falter in your vigilance against our enemies, the law, or the land, you will feel the brunt of my hatred, over many days. And then you will find that all the hatred that this place teems with is as a spring breeze next to the hatred I can bring to bear on the incompetent.

*attr: Agent Simon Yo, Governor of the Northern Province
Welcome address to Agents*

For those without the Eastern Bank Supplement, Capital Code Zones are areas of political instability where the UIG run a police state regime and all rank point loss is multiplied by 5 in an attempt to reduce crime.

Aside from the legislative nightmare which is the Capital Code Zone, the Northern Province has a serious issue with the People's Free Army of Ayan (PFAA). This group of freedom fighters is a remnant left behind after the corporate wars. Their cities destroyed, their families killed and their purpose lost, hundreds of men and women banded together for security, comfort and to create a unified front against the corporate oppression.

Many years ago there was a massive Ai-Jinn military base at the city of Ayan, it was also a gathering point for mercenary soldiers hunting for work. The end result was that Ayan was packed full of high value assets and was a tempting target for one of the Ai-Jinn's many enemies.

The crucial point and one that would cost the Ai-Jinn dearly was when they intercepted a signal from a Eurasian air base that an air strike was about to be made upon Ayan. More important than the information itself was the fact that Ai-Jinn intelligence had both intercepted and decoded the signal. Rather than warn the Ayan people and mercenaries and let E.I. know this, they evacuated their most valuable assets and let the strike go ahead. Hundreds of thousands died in the bombing but the Ai-Jinn easily justified the loss to themselves and went on to make several decisive attacks against E.I. using their new information, the tragic loss of life just another atrocity to add to the Ai-Jinn's remarkable and shameful record.

Those left behind were understandably furious and bitter and their hatred formed the roots of the People's Free Army of Ayan. Because of the high contingent of mercenaries, bounty hunters and even ex-Agents who founded the army, the PFAA has a surprising level of competence.

THE PEOPLE'S FREE ARMY OF AYAN
The PFAA are driven by vengeance. Mercenaries are not a soft lot and understand that in a war, almost anything is justifiable but the total obliteration of Ayan was a step too far. Now they make their home in the polluted, twisted jungles far to the north of the province, planning and executing attacks against the Ai-Jinn and its assets.

Generations of hatred and murderous training have been concentrated over the years into what is arguably the most effective guerrilla army on the planet. Although you can draw parallels between the American Underground and the PFAA in that both are a thorn in the side of their respective corporations, their methods and reasoning differ considerably. Whereas the Underground are essentially a political movement who would cease their activities if the Federation changed their policies, the PFAA will never rest until they see the Ai-Jinn ground to dust and the ashes launched into the sun.

SUPPORT
The PFAA have a surprising pool of resources, not only do they receive considerable donations from the Shi Yukiro and Eurasian Inc, they also have representatives within the civilised cities who work to raise awareness of the PFAA's work and garner public support. This is not always successful and these individuals often find themselves beheaded or gutted and left in the street as a potent reminder of what happens to those who oppose the Ai-Jinn.

There are enough wealthy individuals and organisations around the world who either sympathise with the PFAA or resent the Ai-Jinn enough to keep the funds coming in. The Western Federation are happy to sell armaments to anyone who can pay which ensure the People's Army are not just an enthusiastic resistance movement but a serious threat to the stability of the Ai-Jinn.

METHODS
The primary operational method of the PFAA is sabotage. The Ai-Jinn rely so heavily on their industrial plants that when they go down, even for a short time, the loss can be calculated in millions. Bearing in mind the PFAA has access to all manner of guided missile systems and heavy ordnance, the Ai-Jinn are understandably fearful and ensure that countermeasures are installed into all of their important facilities.

BASE OF OPERATIONS

The PFAA are based in a series of bunkers and encampments dotted around the Shenyu jungle. The bunkers are deep underground protected by SatBlankets making it very hard for the Ai-Jinn to detect and destroy them. The encampments are mobile and are moved every few weeks to reduce the chance of their locations being determined.

The Ai-Jinn occasionally run air-sweeps in an attempt to find and bomb these nests of unrest but the anti-aircraft missile batteries hidden within the jungle give rise to high casualty rates and so these exercises are not common. A more reliable method of finding their bases is to HALO* drop platoons of jungle-trained Agents into a suspected PFAA area. The platoon will then covertly move onto the enemy postion, often at night, kill everyone and destroy all assets.

*High altitude, low opening.

THE SHENYU JUNGLES

At the northern tip of the province are the Shenyu Jungles, a vile result of the heavy pollution given off by the Ai-Jinn's immense factory complexes. The jungles cover an area of roughly 40,000 square miles and are notable as being one of the most polluted regions on the planet outside France, Australia or the Freestates. Conditions in Shenyu are pretty terrible but the PFAA and their families have been living there for many generations and have built up a certain tolerance to the toxins.

Although they are described as jungles the term is not really accurate in an ecological sense. For a start, it's extremely cold and much of the ground is permafrost. A haze of mist and smog drifts between the trees which, although densely packed, are blackened from the pollution and often brittle and stunted. In a relatively short time their leaves have become leathery and small which seems to allow them to cope with the pollutants better but as a result they are less than a tenth as efficient as a normal leaf, explaining the generally poor condition and reduced size of the trees that bear them.

JUNGLE HAZARDS

The jungle is a dangerous place at the best of times and the pollution only serves to make things worse. Anyone who visits may suffer from any of the following problems.

Shortness of breath

Unless you wear a level 7 toxin filter or better you will find breathing difficult.

-1 Endurance while in Shenyu due to the pollution.

Tissue Repair

Not only do wounds heal slower in this environment, you also stand a high chance of infection from the airborne pollutants.

Heal rates are halved in Shenyu, this does not effect medical healing such as Medpacks or the work of a Field Surgeon.

When you are healed roll a D10, if you get equal or above your Endurance you contract a disease known as Shenyu Fever.

Shenyu Fever (Level 9 Toxin)

This takes about 6 hours to incubate, after which you lose 1 point of Strength, Endurance and Agility and 5 HP each day the disease goes untreated. The victim dies when they reach Endurance 0.

The disease can be cured by a toxin purge or using Biokinesis 9.

SHRIKE TREES

The shrike trees which grow in Shenyu is covered in microscopic spines which break off when brushed past. Unless you are wearing armour which covers every part of you, there is a chance you can be stung by the tree. Toughskin does not make you immune, the needles are so fine and sharp they simply pierce it.

System: When moving through an area containing shrike trees roll 'Agility + Stealth'.

You gain +4 to this roll if you have the Survival Training.
You gain +4 to this roll for wearing a whole suit of armour

If you fail you are stung and the potent poison enters your system.

Shrike Poison (Level 7 Toxin)

Roll to determine where the poison manifests. Although it may have entered via the cheek or hand, the thorn tip travels around the blood for a few minutes until it breaks down and the poison is released into a random area. This area is paralysed for D4 hours.

The poison has sadly seldom been tapped to use as a combat toxin. It only has a shelf life of around one day when removed from the tree. It is rumoured a few gifted individuals have worked out how to store it for around a week but at present the only viable way to use it is to have a shrike tree in your flat and tap the poison just before use.

SHRIKE POISON		
1	Head	Head Paralysed You are rendered unconscious.
2	Right Arm	Body part totally paralysed Treat as though severed.
3	Left Arm	Body part totally paralysed Treat as though severed
4	Left Leg	Body part totally paralysed Treat as though severed
5	Right Leg	Body part totally paralysed Treat as though severed
6	Upper Torso	Both arms totally paralysed Treat as though severed
7	Lower Torso	Both legs totally paralysed. Treat as though severed
8	Affects two areas roll twice, re-rolling any 8s. .	

QUICKSAND

Anyone stepping into quicksand can make a 'Reflexes + Athletics' check with a -6 penalty to quickly grab onto something and pull themselves out. Failure means they start to sink at a rate of 1 foot per round. In 5 rounds they will be submerged and start to suffer the effects of drowning as on page 148 of the core rules.

Each round the victim can try the check again but a further -3 penalty is added every time. If allies are present with some rope or a branch they can pull you free without a problem.

TRAPS

There are numerous traps laid through out the jungle, normally in places where assaulting Ai-Jinn troops would pass. A range of traps can be found in the Eastern Bank supplement. If you don't have it then the GM should just make some up. Typical examples would include pit traps, sprung branch traps and mines.

JIGGERS

All manner of nasty creatures live in the jungle, some burrow under your skin, some drill into your eyes and lay eggs, others just bite you and leave behind disease. The GM can feel free to make up some effects but below are some examples:

Gat Flies – These hang around in areas of still waters. If you pass near roll a D10. The creatures can get through tiny cracks in armour so only a sealed suit will keep them away.

When you roll the D10, if you get higher or equal to your AV you have been bitten. You are infected with Shenyu Fever as on the previous page.

Petris Worms / Tree Worms – These nasty creatures live in trees and randomly drop onto the heads of warm blooded creatures. They then wait in the hair or clothes until the victim stops moving, generally because they are sleeping. At this time they migrate towards the eyes where they tunnel in, lay their eggs and die.

This results in increasingly blurred vision for the next week. (Cumulative -1 to sight based tasks each day to a maximum of -4).

In a week the eggs hatch and the eye is effectively blinded. The hundreds of tiny worms then burrow out, destroying the eye and causing immense pain. They travel through the hole in the back of the eye socket and enter the circulatory system where they feed on blood and grow.

This gives the victim an intense fever (-3 to Strength, Agility, Reflexes and Endurance) until the worms pass out of the system.

When they are mature after 2D4 days they breach out through the skin and drop to the floor where they find a tree to climb and begin the process again.

The disease can be cured with a toxin purge but the eye is considered ruined. Cybernetic eyes cannot be affected.

Tiger Patrols
Note that Ai-Jinn Tiger Patrols can be considered to know all these facts about the Shenyu jungle due to their training.

AGENT SIMON YO
GOVERNOR OF THE NORTHERN PROVINCE
ZULONG - THE VERMILLION DRAGON

Agent Yo has the unenviable task of ensuring his Agents maintain a low profile within this Capital Code Zone. On top of this he has the added burden of suppressing PFAA attacks on Ai-Jinn assets whilst trying to wipe them out for good by attacking their base of operations. The Ai-Jinn are not unsympathetic to his problems and two of the five Tiger Platoons are assigned permanently to his contingent of divisions.

Yo is extremely intolerant of Agents who risk attracting the attention of the UIG without good reason. Any Agents taking a happy-go-lucky attitude to work will meet with severe disciplinary action and could have licenses suspended or weapon choices restricted.

This policy does have an upside though as Yo is more willing than most to spend a significant portion of his budget training Agents and equipping them with equipment suited to the job. If the player's division is working on missions which Yo is ultimately overseeing they may be entitled to a few freebies. Although the Agents may not meet Yo himself, the GM should feel free to award some of the following improvements by giving the Agents a week of downtime and then either allocating them something from the list below or making something appropriate up.

1. Intensive Stealth Training
Your skills in Stealth are improved. +4 XP to be put towards increasing your Stealth skill.

2. Legal Awareness Training
You are taught more details of the law to help avoid ugly UIG confrontations. +4 XP to be put towards Corp. Knowledge

3. Division Legal Aid
To help reduce rank point loss a lawyer is assigned to the division. See The Eastern Bank for more information on lawyers.

4. Silenced Weapons
All kinetics weapons are silenced, even heavy ones.

5. Invisibility Fields
Each division member is given an invisibility field.

6. Evade Surveillance
You gain the 'Evade Surveillance' Training (The Eastern Bank) providing you have the prerequisites.

7. Area Knowledge
You gain the 'Eastern Bank Knowledge' Training (The Eastern Bank) providing you have the prerequisites.

8. Weapon Upgrades
Your primary weapon is increased by two condition levels or you gain 2000¢ to spend on weapon upgrades. A selection of weapon upgrades can be found in Machines of War.

9. Contacts
You are put in contact with some important people, gain 8 points of contacts. No more than 5 points allocated to any single one.

10. Urban Acclimatisation
You are educated in the ways of the street, you gain +4XP to be put towards increasing 'Street Culture'.

THE CENTRAL PROVINCE

The Central Province has the highest concentration of Ai-Jinn assets including numerous spires, factories and research facilities. It is perhaps the most important province and is central to the functioning of the Ai-Jinn as a whole. Agent Jan Tsai has governed the Central Province for the past 76 years with a surprisingly low level of serious incidents. He has a large contingent of Agent divisions at his disposal who are assigned to the various assets around the province.

Although the eastern-most sector of the Central Province is located in the Capital Code Zone of the Eastern Bank, Tsai does not make such a big deal of it as his colleagues. His concerns tend to centre around maintaining the stability of the province as a whole. Tsai ensures that seasoned mission officers oversee capital code missions and only sends extremely experienced Agents to the Eastern Bank zone and lets them work as they see fit. As a consequence these Agents are generally well rewarded for their work with free training, advanced equipment, more pay, improved accommodation and a healthy dose of cushy missions such as tours of duty on the Xing Gong Orbital (see page 139).

UNDERGROUND TAKEOVERS

Because there are so many Ai-Jinn assets in the Central Province, there are a lot of divisions working with the general duty of 'policing'; basically there to keep an eye on things and offer a guiding hand rather than do the corporation's direct bidding. This can take many forms but one of the most common is a resident division who are given a single asset within an old city such as a small casino, brothel or gun store, and told to slowly take over the city by dominating the underground.

Such a division should have a decent grasp of criminal organisations, rival faction methodology and street culture. From the moment they are assigned they will need to become familiar with the city and determine who runs what. If there are any gangs loyal to the Ai-Jinn these will be utilised and any who are not will be identified and either brought to heel or eliminated.

Steadily the division will increase its power base, recruiting gang members, running protection rackets, eliminating competition and intimidating rivals until they can be considered to have the city in a vice-like grip. Once this state is reached it is merely a case of fending off newcomers. This is normally made easier by the Ai-Jinn assigning a few junior divisions to the area so that they can learn the ropes under the guidance of experienced Agents in a relatively safe environment.

ADDING UNDERGROUND TAKEOVERS TO YOUR GAME.

This can be an excellent campaign arc for an Ai-Jinn division. You'll need to make sure that the division is fairly competent and versed in street culture and crime. You can start by picking an old city which is slipping away from Ai-Jinn control; you could just pick one by looking at an atlas; for example, Tongshan. Then just decide on an asset which Agents start with; for example, a nightclub which is doing very badly. The Agents are given the money to buy the business outright, they can then establish a centre of operations there.

You can leave the game fairly freeform, perhaps asking the players a few days before the game what basic plans they have, then you can arrange a few encounters based around what they want to do. Some examples of what such a campaign could include are listed below:

Searching for good help (it *is* hard to find).

Setting up security for the business.

Killing off or taking over the competition.

Dealing with the UIG when they come to investigate the legitimacy of your business.

Setting up illegal businesses which operate within the main business, e.g. pushing drugs from your nightclub.

Dealing with existing gangs and mobsters who don't take kindly to your presence.

Building a successful business in order to generate money to buy extra legitimate operations. You can use the Business rules in the Eastern Bank or make it up yourself.

Run a protection racket to generate additional revenue.

Take care of the clients who may have problems they want solved.

Control the local UIG, maybe you can bribe or intimidate the officers.

Look after the staff. You may need to prevent your prostitutes being beaten up, your drug pushers arrested, your bouncers attacked and your managers threatened.

Identifying legitimate clients and rooting out spies or UIG undercover officers.

Gain influence in legitimate companies without giving them cause to get the UIG involved.

As the game progresses the division may need to leave the city now and again to acquire resources, perform assassinations, attend meetings or in the line of unrelated duty. This allows the Agents a change of scene from the gritty streets.

Since the Lan Nai division has moved into Gan Ho Old City the crime rate has fallen to an all time low. Before you praise the work of Feng Lun and his Agents, I would ask you to look at these productivity figures on Gan Ho for the 2488-2489 fiscal year.

You'll notice they show a worrying decline. We have since learnt that Agent Lun has taken a somewhat 'Federation' approach in his duties and massacred any gang which did not offer its unequivocal fealty.

Rather than discipline Agent Lun I suggest we promote him, increase his budget and send him to Tokyo where his obvious skills may be better realised.

attr; - Agent Jan Tsai - Governor of the Central Province

AGENT JAN TSAI
GOVERNOR OF THE CENTRAL PROVINCE
HUANGLONG - THE YELLOW DRAGON

Agent Tsai could be thought of as laid back but this would be a mistake. His calm, apparently relaxed demeanour is more a product of absolute control and a calm, rather than lax attitude. Tsai is a skilled delegator and his province is so hectic he has become adept at selecting the very best staff for the job and putting a great deal of faith in their work. Instead of overseeing dozens of plans he asks for honest status reports from Mission Officers (MO) and helps them overcome problems they are having. If a division has made an absolute hash of a mission, instead of getting mad and docking rank points Tsai will talk with the commanding MO and use his wealth of experience to try and work out a solution.

If, upon examination, there is blame to be laid then Tsai will take action but his attitude of understanding and resolution has always received better results than simply demoting anyone who makes a mistake. This policy not only ensures that Tsai is always kept up to date in an honest and frank manner, it means his Agents learn and develop rather than being constantly held back on mundane duty. The respect he commands also spurs his Agents on to do their best for him, more concerned about letting him down than any punishment he might administer.

THE SOUTHERN PROVINCE

This province is characterised by a mass of islands which are home to an incongruous mix of wealthy citizens and bands of roving pirates. The Ai-Jinn have taken significant steps to clean these areas and ensure there are active weather satellites keeping much of the region as a perpetual sunny haven. They have even re-established large colonies of flora and fauna which have taken to the environment well and although young in ecological terms, the environment is very reminiscent of a tropical paradise, if a little tamer and not so diverse.

The citizens who dwell in these islands are typically very rich and have moved here to take advantage of some of the most pleasant and least polluted island and coastal real estate available. Unfortunately this makes rich pickings for the gangs of pirates known as Cai Qian who scour the southern seas looking for wealthy citizens partying on their yachts or lounging at their beachfront properties.

Although described as islands, many of the landmasses are still huge and provide a variety of environments ranging from the magnificent Java Spire to the slums of Jakarta and the eclectic neon jungle that is Old Bangkok. Although most of the region is heavily policed by Ai-Jinn soldiers and Agents there is an enormous amount of space that simply does not get the attention it needs. It's these neglected regions in which the Cai Qian make port.

THE CAI QIAN

The Cai Qian are noted here instead of in the organised crime section as they are neither very organised, or under the control of the Ai-Jinn. They are also indigenous to the southern province and seldom found elsewhere.

The name Cai Qian refers to a long dead pirate lord active in the Qing Dynasty who commanded a fleet of around 1,000 warships and 20,000 pirates.

The Cai Qian currently claims to have around 14,000 members who are divided into a number of clans. Each clan has a leader and each leader ultimately pays respect to the current lord of the Cai Qian. This structure is universally approved by all clans who acknowledge that it has worked well for hundreds of years and, even in times of crackdown, has allowed the Cai Qian to survive.

CAI QIAN STRUCTURE

Chinese	Approximate Translation
Hai Ba	Sea Lord / Sea Tyrant

Current leader of the Cai Qian

Can Ren	The Bloodied / The Merciless

One of twelve council members who are elected from the 12 most powerful clans.

Shuai	Commander

Head of a clan

Ji Zhang	Captain

The captain on a pirate vessel

Zhong Wei	Lieutenant

A sub-commander on a pirate vessel

Hai Dao	Pirate

A common pirate

Yu	Fish

An initiate who is in the process of proving himself worthy to join the Cai Qian

Each clan comprises around 500 pirates manning somewhere around 50 boats. Some boats are small skiffs with only a few men on board, others are great warships equipped with anti-grav drives which can take over 100 crew.

Some sample clans include

The Guandao
The Dragon Typhoon
The Thundering Storm
The Sharks
The Scourge of Lin Shi Men
The Bloodied Sails
The Skulls of the South Seas
The Jakarta Rats

THE CAI QIAN CODE

Although all Cai Qian ultimately report to the Hai Ba, they are not required to have all their activities authorised. Their only binding code is as laid out opposite and breaches of this code invariably end in death unless there are extenuating circumstances.

THE CAI QIAN CODE

One half of the ship's takings shall be given to the clan.

One tenth of the clan's takings shall be given to the Hai Ba

A Cai Qian will never disclose information about the Cai Qian to non-members

All disagreements are to be settled in full view of other Cai Qian. If such actions result in a death then so be it.

Cai Qian do not steal from or harm other Cai Qian unless it is a public settlement as above.

Cai Qian are for life.

Although this code is fairly crude it has served the pirates well for many years.

The code states nothing about obeying orders and enforcement of discipline within the Cai Qian normally takes the form of beatings, lashings, keel hauling, imprisonment, disfigurement, restriction of privileges, removal of wealth and occasionally death.

CAI QIAN METHOD

Although the boats used by the pirates tend to look like ramshackle piles of junk, they often hide powerful engines and sophisticated sensory equipment, both vital for the location of quarry and the evasion of the law. Before attacks are made, the boats tend to hang around in isolated bays or in sea caves waiting for their scanners to pick up a likely target. When the word is given the ships emerge from their various hiding positions and move in on the target. There will often be 3 or 4 ships used to take down a typical target, some used to cut off avenues of retreat and others to attack the vessel.

The target is normally disabled using a heavy EMP harpoon (see page 47) and then boarded using ropes, extendable gangways, personal grapples or acrobatics. The victims can seldom withstand such an attack and are usually slaughtered but sometimes kept as slaves. The captured boat is then either scuttled, used for spares, sold to black market buyers or occasionally added to the fleet.

CAI QIAN AND THE AI-JINN

The Cai Qian are one of the few bands of criminals the Ai-Jinn do not have much control over. Their methods are so brutal and uncontrolled that the effect they have on the Southern Province is almost all negative. The Ai-Jinn do not want their wealthiest citizens robbed and murdered and whereas the Yakuza or Triads are fairly discreet organisations whose activities tend to be limited to the old cities and targetting other criminals or the poor, the Cai Qian spread fear among the upper echelons of Ai-Jinn society. For this reason the Corporation cannot allow the pirates to operate unchecked.

One might wonder why the Ai-Jinn have not crushed the Cai Qian outright already and there are two main reasons.

Firstly the Ai-Jinn have made a massive dent in the Cai Qian over

the last century. They originally numbered around 40,000 at their prime, the current figure of 14,000 illustrates that the Ai-Jinn have made significant inroads into the pirates' numbers but as their ranks dwindle they become more wary and harder to track down. The pirates now use much smaller fleets than they did and make extensive use of SatBlankets to hide their presence. They have also changed their attack patterns, which makes the location of their next strike hard to predict. If the Ai-Jinn are having a crackdown then the pirates will lie low or perhaps start attacking coastal properties instead of boats. Their evasiveness and knowledge of Ai-Jinn methodology keep the pirates one step ahead. It should also be noted that the Cai Qian are not afraid to use terrorist tactics to get their way and have no scruples about bombing passenger liners in order to create diversions or to show the corporation they are serious.

Secondly the Ai-Jinn would quite like to take over the Cai Qian rather than destroy it. A fleet of mercenary pirates at their beck and call could provide no end of uses and if they could be redeployed to target Shi Yukiro or E.I. assets then they would make an excellent addition to the personnel roster. The Ai-Jinn have been known to dispatch the odd division now and again to assassinate the Hai Ba or bring down the council but so far to no avail. Infiltration seems to be the most likely method of finding out enough about the Cai Qian to engineer some kind of mutiny and bring the dogs to heel.

CAI QIAN STYLE

The pirates have a mix of styles but are normally dressed in a combination of loose-fitting clothing and salvaged armour. They are mostly of oriental extraction, although there are a smattering from the rest of the world. Almost all seem to wear their hair long, usually braided or tied back.

As regards combat, the Cai Qian use anything that works but all are adept at close combat which is vital for boarding guarded ships. A leaning towards dual weapon use (Close Combat and Light / Tactical Firearms) is very common and makes them effective at close and long range.

Cybernetics are not a common upgrade as the pirates don't tend to have large amounts of ready cash or access to skilled cyberneticists. Nonetheless, some Cai Qian are upgraded with the usual array of armoured plates, cybernetic legs and body spaces. The most common non-weapon item carried, which even the poorer pirates strive to acquire, is a personal grapple (page 59), (cybernetic or wrist mounted) which aids considerably in boarding enemy ships. See the Grapple Hook Combat on page 12.

AGENT SAMANTHA YEUNG

GOVERNOR OF THE SOUTHERN PROVINCE

BAILONG - THE WHITE DRAGON. A.K.A THE RED BITCH

The Governor of the Southern Province is Samantha Yeung, a former pirate who went under the name of the 'Red Bitch' in her more anarchic days. After running with the Cai Qian for 15 years and reaching the position of Ji Zhang (captain) she came to find the life unfulfilling and ultimately pointless. No matter how many yachts she burnt and how many privileged families she killed, there seemed no end in sight; it would just go on until she died.

The night she was brutally raped by members of a rival clan finalised her decision to leave the Cai Qian and, although she had no idea of what to do instead, she immediately left on a skiff for Bangkok. In very little time she ended up in a bust up with some local Triads where both her attitude and martial prowess were noted by the group's leader, Agent Kim Sach Tai, who offered Yeung the opportunity to try out for the Agent Training program rather than be slaughtered on the streets.

Yeung never looked back, she retook her old birth name (although she is still known as the Red Bitch by many) and began to work her way up a far more promising career path.

Yeung's current posting after 60 years of service is as Governor of the entire Southern Province. Her intimate knowledge of the way the Cai Qian work is a considerable asset to the Ai-Jinn and UIG forces sent to dispatch the nest of pirates. The Agent divisions under her control serve a variety of functions from guarding VIPs and wealthy individuals to Cai Qian infiltration and overt search and destroy missions.

Agents working in the Southern Province are of course expected to carry out all the normal duties you would expect and despite the presence of the Cai Qian, all manner of unrelated incidents constantly demand a division's attention.

Yeung is very demanding of her Agents and after being a Cai Qian captain for so many years has some fierce and innovative ideas of punishment. One famous incident saw an Agent have his synaptic modulation turn off, be nailed to a board and left in the searing tropical heat for 3 days following an off hand remark about her relationship with another female Agent. On the plus side, she demands all her Agents are competent pilots and as soon as they are assigned to her province she gives them a few weeks off to attend piloting courses. This is done to ensure they can travel about the thousands of South Sea Islands without the need for recruited pilots.

PILOTING

System: If posted to the Southern Province for more than a few missions each Agent gains 5 XP to increase their piloting skill.

Any spare XP can be saved but can only be spent on piloting at a later date. If you already have piloting 10 then instead you receive 2 weeks of downtime.

THE EASTERN PROVINCE

The Eastern Province isn't noted on any maps and doesn't have any defined boundaries. The term refers to the islands of Japan currently held (wrongfully in the opinion of the Ai-Jinn) by the Shi Yukiro. Although the Ai-Jinn as a whole have their sights on consolidation and development of existing territories as opposed to expansion, the Eastern Province is always viewed with greedy, covetous eyes.

THE FIFTH LAND

It should be noted that old-school Ai-Jinn do not even call the Shi Yukiro territory 'Japan' instead referring to it as 'The Eastern Province', 'Di Wu Tu' (The Fifth Land), 'Xin Zhong Guo' (New China)'.

Those who currently dwell there are known as 'Zu Hu (Tenants), Ni Yi (Invaders) or Trespassers'.

The Shi Yukiro take particular offense to these terms and are likely to react strongly if they are used in their presence.

Current operations to seize the Eastern Province from the Shi Yukiro are sadly still in their infancy as the Eastern Bank Capital Code Legislation has made operating in this region extremely risky. Instead of out and out attacks against Shi Yukiro assets, the Ai-Jinn wages a war of attrition, sending their Agents in to subtly disrupt affairs in an attempt to destabilise the Shi Yukiro Corporation as a whole. The ever present problem is whether they send in seasoned Agents who will be sorely missed but are more likely to succeed or use newer Agents, who lack experience but are also more expendable.

So far the Ai-Jinn have met with no real success and although they have made some inroads into damaging the Shi Yukiro, the reciprocal attacks by their hated enemies cause as much if not more damage. Ai-Jinn territory is so huge and they have so many assets dotted about it that the Shi Yukiro seem to find it relatively easy to send in assassination or sabotage squads who, with little effort, are able to cause massive disruption to the Ai-Jinn industrial machine.

A leaning towards long term infiltration and the establishment of more Japan-based yakuza is currently underway in the hope that a more subtle, less aggressive stance will catch the Shi Yukiro off guard. At the same time this may reduce the Shi Yukiro's desire to seek continual retribution by attacking Ai-Jinn assets.

Whether this will work only time will see but the ongoing reward policy for Shi Yukiro bounty is still in force and gives all Ai-Jinn Agents a strong incentive to cause as much damage as possible to their old rivals.

SHI YUKIRO BOUNTY

Any Ai-Jinn Agent damaging the Shi Yukiro corporation when not specifically mandated by the mission will recieve rewards from the Corporation.

Act	Typical Rewards
Killing a SY Agent	His Rank x 2 in Rank Points.
Recovering SY tech	1-5 Rank Points
Destroying Assets	1-10 Rank Points.
Collect Intelligence	1-10 Rank Points

These rewards can be supplemented with cash and other benefits as the GM sees fit.

AGENT YASUHIRO KOTABE

GOVERNOR OF THE EASTERN PROVINCE
XUANLONG - THE BLACK DRAGON

Yasuhiro (Yasu) Kotabe was born in Japan to Japanese parents. They were both Agents in the Shi Yukiro corporation and Yasuhiro's path had been laid out for him at an early age.

At the age of 10 Yasu's parents both came to say goodbye. He didn't understand but when told by his teacher the next day that honour had demanded both of them commit *seppuku* (ritual suicide) it was more than he could accept. Although he dutifully continued his training until the age of 22, every waking hour Yasu seethed with a burning desire for vengeance that he knew could be best exacted with the help of the Shi Yukiro's hated enemies, the Ai-Jinn.

After diligently completing the Agent Training Program Yasu spent 17 years working with his division, establishing himself as a model Agent and waiting for the day he could cause the most harm to his parents' murderers. The division was working in the Kagoshima Spire underswell culling mutants and ensuring the reactor was safe and that all security measures were in place. Yasu was assigned the task of checking and resetting the access codes and making sure only the technicians knew the new ones. All went well and the division moved on to other work.

It was two weeks later that an Ai-Jinn saboteur division infiltrated the underswell, met up with Yasu and using a combination of force, access codes and insider information, made their way into the reactor and set it to blow.

The explosion could be heard across Asia. Kagoshima Spire was utterly destroyed and over a million people died that day in what has been the largest loss of life since the Corporate wars. This act was more than enough to convince the Ai-Jinn of Yasuhiro's sincerity and he was enlisted into their ranks immediately.

To Yasu, however, the vendetta had only just started. His every waking moment is dominated by thoughts of vengeance and the Ai-Jinn are extremely careful to ensure that although he has a position of great power, he does not have access to information which he could use against his new employers.

Anyone meeting Agent Kotabe will be overwhelmed by the vehement passion in his voice and the fervent bloodlust which seems to ooze from his every pore. He is extremely capable as a combatant having spent much of his training at the Taurus Academy under the tutelage of Master Uesugi. When not plotting the downfall of the Shi Yukiro he personally leads a division named 'Burn the Sun' specifically trained to act as a counter Shi Yukiro task force.

As the sun slowly sank beyond the horizon it threw long, graceful shadows from the ancient cherry trees, their branches still laden with blossom even though the small lawns and koi pools seemed to be scattered with drifts of pale pink petals.

Two men stood on a small wooden bridge, one draped in the heavy, red robes of the samurai, the other wearing a dark, tailored suit.

"Jeimuzu, my brother," said the samurai bowing his head, "it has been too long, your presence has been sorely missed."

"And I have missed you Kusani, but as you know duty has once again come first."

"Of course," the samurai nodded, "as it must, but I sense you are troubled my young friend. I see the weight of a decision on your shoulders."

"No fooling you," laughed Jeimuzu. "Indeed, during my work in Shanghai I've seen a lot. The Ai-Jinn have such a stranglehold over there and what's worse, its here too, everywhere you look…I guarantee. They've got their insidious fingers in everything. Does that not scare you Kusani?"

"Scare me? No. Did my lessons not sink in? Surely you know that such a disorganised rabble will never be able to threaten the Shi Yukiro. They are street thugs and little more. Look inside yourself Jeimuzu, consider our past, our present and our future. Do you really think the Ai-Jinn could ever topple us?"

Jeimuzu shook his head and turned away. "You are right master Kusani, of course you…"

With a single, almost imperceptible flash of movement the katana was drawn and sent in a graceful arc through Jeimuzu's neck, wiped clean of blood and silently replaced.

The samurai knelt and turned the head, looking into his student's lifeless eyes.

*"No…**you** are right Jeimuzu…we **are** everywhere."*

LOYALTY WITHIN THE AI-JINN

Those who ally under the banner of the Ai-Jinn are known to be the most loyal and, ironically, incorruptible employees in the world. Even the UIG envies the low levels of defections and anti-Ai-Jinn sentiment within the corporation's ranks.

Their two fold approach of iron-tight pack mentality coupled with severe punishments for traitors has meant that levels of intra-corporation crime and corruption are so low that, as a machine, the Ai-Jinn is one of the most efficient corporations, second only to the Shi Yukiro.

Employees are paid fairly and there is very little waste. The Ai-Jinn have little time for rich trappings, pay-offs, massive corporate bonuses, wild expense accounts or decadent corporate dinners, all of which were so common with many of the world's leaders throughout history.

Although not taken to the extremes espouses by Comoros, this no nonsense attitude endears the higher echelons of the corporation to its citizens and workers. Although there may be poor, starving people in many of the cities, there is a feeling that the leadership is not squandering all the public's money on luxury items and things are getting better.

This feeling that the Ai-Jinn are working for the people is a powerful tool and enemy Agents in an Ai-Jinn city may find it harder than expected to get the locals to inform on their corp.

The Agents themselves tend to share this point of view, most Ai-Jinn Agents have criminal backgrounds and their unified dislike for the UIG gives them a common bond. They know the corporation will do its best for anyone on the wrong side of the law and although this can prove a huge expense for the Ai-Jinn, they know that the gratitude and loyalty of its workforce more than makes up for the cost.

This has not always been the situation however. The Ai-Jinn are known to have committed several atrocities against its own people in the past and there are most certainly parts of the 5 territories which the Ai-Jinn treat with little or no respect. It is for this reason that many an Agent may find himself on loyalty enforcement duty,

visiting areas under Ai-Jinn control and taking whatever steps they deem necessary to ensure the population remain loyal, even if they are not happy about it.

INITIATION RITES

A large number of the Ai-Jinn's Agents are taken from the seedier areas of life or are defectors from other Corporations. This could potentially leave them open to disciplinary and loyalty issues. To address these problems the Ai-Jinn often set new divisions the task of aggressive strikes against their former associates. These strikes are not everyday sabotage runs or random assassinations, such acts would easily be tolerated by the targeted party in order to secure an insider. Rather they are acts which are designed to ensure that the defection is genuine such as the torture and murder of your ex-mission officer's family.

This practice is common to many street level gangs whose insistence on initiation rites ensures the recruit is serious in their new vocation.

Often the Ai-Jinn will also insist on some evidence of the task such as video or forensic data which is held by the corporation to dissuade the Agent from defecting or leaving. Fortunately, the Ai-Jinn genuinely are a bastion of safety and an excellent vehicle for those wishing to continue to work in the seedy world of crime.

RUNNING INITIATIONS
The GM should ideally run a series of initiation games for a new Ai-Jinn division. Not only does it enforce the characters' backgrounds and provide some great plot ideas but it also serves to distinguish the Ai-Jinn from other corporations and hammer home their criminal roots.

Below are listed some sample new Ai-Jinn Agents and how the GM could run their initiations.

Defected E.I. Cyberneticist
The defected Agent could easily be an infiltrator sent to work his way up in the echelons of the Ai-Jinn and report back from time to time. To root out such people a decisive and profound strike against the former employer is an obvious solution. For example, the defected Agent must find E.I.'s leading cyberneticist. They must then capture him and force him to work for them. His family could be taken and held hostage to ensure the quality of his work.

Motorcycle Gang Member
If the Agent is still in contact with the gang and on speaking terms then that is not really an issue; contacts are important. However, he should make the gang aware that he is no longer bound to their code of conduct and will only work with them on a mutually advantageous basis.

LOYALTY ENFORECMENT MISSIONS

These missions can be an interesting alternative to a more conventional mission and can force the players to use unusual methods.

Simply turning up at a mountain village and demanding fealty is not going to work. Whether the division use displays of power, technology, compassion or friendliness, it can make for a fun game.

This mission could involve the division aiding the gang to cement relations and put them in their debt. Obviously if the gang take the position of 'no-one leaves', then the mission could be to wipe them out.

Escaped Criminal
The issue with an escaped criminal is that he could have been released by the UIG on the assumption that he will infiltrate the Ai-Jinn. For this reason the corporation will have to be very careful and his first few missions will be fairly basic so the need for intelligence access is low. Such missions may also target UIG or civilian assets which would make it hard for the UIG to justify the infiltration.

For example, making a series of terrorist attacks against a UIG housing complex would not only serve to weed out infiltrators but may also have a secondary function; it could act as a distraction so that a more senior division could work somewhere else in the city while the UIG are otherwise occupied. This is a common tactic used in the Eastern Bank.

Yakuza Member
The yakuza are mostly under the control of the Ai-Jinn but there are clans scattered across East Asia who either remain independent or support the Shi Yukiro. Thus when a new yakuza joins the Ai-Jinn who is from an unproven clan it is wise to assess his loyalty before giving him more delicate work.

A typical mission could be for the yakuza to attack a Shi Yukiro asset. This is fairly simple and one that can be tailored to ensure an honourable Shi Yukiro would not perform it; for example, bomb a historic *samurai* graveyard.

If the mission officer simply believes the yakuza may be loyal to another clan then he could insist they bring the clan under the control of the Ai-Jinn. If the clan refuse, they die. Simple.

One of the great things about these mission types is they are very simple and straightforward. They typically involve some principal concepts of an Ai-Jinn game such as terrorist attacks, murders, kidnappings and gang takeovers. Don't feel you need to run an initiation for every Agent unless you really want to, just the ones whose past could be considered to conflict with their current position within the Ai-Jinn.

MAINTAINING LOYALTY

Once a division has been assessed over the first few telling missions and judged loyal their disposition must be carefully monitored. Ai-Jinn Agents are, by nature, often devious, tricky, two-faced and expert liars.

It's not unreasonable to assume that they may get a better offer from another Corporation, a wealthy independent criminal or the UIG who may value their insight in the criminal world. To keep an eye on their Agents the Ai-Jinn use the simplest tool available to them; the vigilance of other Agents.

Anyone who suspects disloyalty is obliged to report it. The integrity of an Ai-Jinn division is essential and so normally you might consider Agents reporting each other for disloyalty to be

dangerous and rift-generating behaviour but the management have taken a certain tack which seems to make the job of vigilance just part of everyday life.

Instead of telling tales, the act of reporting another Agent has been turned into a deed of kindness. It's your opportunity to 'save' your brother or sister before she becomes corrupted by a brutal world. Temptation is everywhere and Agents are only human (well mostly). By being watchful of your co-workers and alerting the Ai-Jinn as soon as you spot potential dissention, you could nip the problem in the bud.

If a player suspects another player then ideally the information should be passed on outside the game to avoid inter-player arguments and for maximum fun. If your group is made up of well rounded types who are good role-players let them do it whenever you like.

LOYALTY ASSESSMENT
Typically the suspected Agent will be called in for a 'little chat' with a high ranking Agent skilled in psychology and loyalty assessment. (This is normally represented by the 'There is Only Ai-Jinn' Training.)

The results of this chat determine the next course of action.

The Agent is Loyal
No further action is taken, the one who reported him is not held accountable and everything continues as it was.

Inconclusive
The rest of the Agent's division are consulted and asked to all keep an eye on him. If further suspect behaviour or comments are noted refer to 'Seeds of Disloyalty' below.

Seeds of Disloyalty
The Agent is considered to be doubting the path he is treading. He will be sent for immediate 'attitude correction' at the ACF in Beijing (page 112).

Traitor
The Agent has passed beyond redemption and will be interrogated or executed. This will be a sudden affair, the assessing Agent will give no clue he has failed and will send him on his way as normal. At some point in the next 48 hours the Agent will be targeted by one or two experienced Divisions who will take him down and bring him in. Whether he is executed immediately is a decision made by the corporation's higher ranking Agents.

AVOIDING CORRUPTION WITHIN THE SYSTEM
Agents are encouraged to report the slightest sign of dissention. For this reason the 'little chats', as they have become known, are a common occurrence and Agents stop being too concerned about them after a while. The assessors will even call in Agents who have not been reported, just to keep them on their toes and to act as control tests which can be used as comparisons in the future.

In many organisations there has long been a stigma attached to informing on your co-workers, especially if they are your superiors; this inevitably leads to corruption. Imagine a scenario where you see an ally steal a few credits from the mission officer's drawer. If you inform on him, word will almost inevitably leak back and the whole division may not trust you anymore. Moreover, if the accusation is disproved you could end up being a laughing stock and thought to be making it up. The situation worsens if you think your mission officer is crooked. You'd end up choosing sides and digging yourself into a deep, deep hole.

The Ai-Jinn system of openness allows you to report anyone without repercussions regardless of status. It's considered a kindness and more often than not the individual will be exonerated or at the most sent for attitude correction. Everyone wins in the end and the integrity of the corporation is maintained.

THE ATTITUDE CORRECTION FACILITY IN BEIJING

This large complex of low, grimy buildings 4 miles outside Old Beijing is salvation to some, nightmare to others. Originally intended to educate citizens about the potential benefits of being a part of the Ai-Jinn, its current function is to halt dissention in its tracks and enlighten those who have strayed from the path.

Anyone sent to the centre is in for a tough time; the strict regime, regular interrogations and constant surveillance can be extremely draining and if you falter you can expect to spend even more time here than you anticipated.

The interior is made up of dozens of bleak cells, patterning rooms, sensory deprivation tanks and interrogation chambers. These areas are ill-maintained and the rusty pipes and peeling walls all add to the sense of desolation and despair. This environment is psychologically crushing and is used by the staff to make life on the outside seem all the better.

There are several types of correction that occur, these are listed below.

SUBCONSCIOUS INDOCTRINATION (TAKES 1 WEEK)

This is perhaps the most serious and unlawful process which involves exposing the subject to harsh neural patterning. This can physically alter the psyche matrix of the patient over time, forcing their brain to function in a different way. This method is rarely used on Agents or employees as it entails some degree of mental retardation which lowers their overall capability.

More commonly it is used on civilians who have shown rebellious behaviour and are capable of inciting action against the Ai-Jinn such as DLA members, anti-Ai-Jinn activists and terrorists. Normally death would be the simple solution but this can often martyr the individual.

By reworking the subject's mind the Ai-Jinn can attempt to subdue them without inciting a riot. If the indoctrination is exposed, of course, even more terrible repercussions may ensue.

The indoctrinated will not knowingly act against the interests of the Ai-Jinn. They tend to be slow to respond and act a little dreamily. They will occasionally quote Ai-Jinn doctrine or lecture those around them about the Ai-Jinn being the only path to a better world.

System
Indoctrinated lose 2 points in Reflexes and their Intelligence is reduced by 4 points to a minimum of 3.

Their conviction pool cannot exceed 1 and they cannot spend conviction from special trainings such as Conviction of One. Indoctrinated will report all acts of suspected disloyalty as soon as they can and will not break any laws unless ordered to do so by an Ai-Jinn Agent.
They will follow all orders given to them by an Ai-Jinn Agent regardless of repercussions.

BEHAVIOURAL MODIFICATION

Through a series of mental exercises, propaganda exposure and continued interrogation the subject has imperfections in her attitude ironed out. The end result is a tweaking of the mind which can cause the subject to lose undesirable traits such as:

Lightheartedness with regard to Ai-Jinn business
Disrespect for Ai-Jinn authority
Criticism of Ai-Jinn policies
Unconstructive criticism of other Agents
Sympathy for non-Ai-Jinn organisations
Feelings of hopelessness and apathy

System

WILLING SUBJECT – (TAKES 1 WEEK)
If the subject is willing then the modification is automatic. They should role-play their new attitude by being extra-loyal and highly supportive of the Ai-Jinn. They are more likely to criticise anyone showing opposition to the Ai-Jinn and even exact their own judgement against them circumstances permitting. They may extol the virtues of the corporation and regularly point out that the Ai-Jinn is a most excellent organisation.

The subject's permanent conviction pool is reduced to 4 for the next two missions.

RESISTANT SUBJECT – (CAN TAKE MANY WEEKS)
Each week the target must make a 'Presence + Attitude' roll.

Each week after the first the patient gains cumulative -1 penalty on the check until they cannot resist any longer, fail the roll and succumb to the modification.

The end result is the same as 'willing subject' above. The only way to get round this is to be pulled out by a high ranking Agent or to fool the assessor.

Fooling the Assessor
Each week the subject may roll an opposed 'Presence + Lying & Acting' check against the assessor's 'Perception + Psychology' (normally around 16). The subject has a -6 penalty to this roll but conviction may be used. (The subject can add his 'Mind Telepathy' score as a bonus if he posses it.)

Success indicates they have fooled the assessor and may leave the facility even though none of the conditioning has taken.

LOSING THE CONDITIONING

It is possible to shake off the effects these forms of mental conditioning by immense acts of willpower. The subject must focus extremely hard for a number of weeks, using a considerable amount of his mental energies to slowly break through the mental shackles.

System: For the next 3 missions (not sessions) the Agent cannot use conviction as he is considered to be putting all of his extra drive into breaking the conditioning. At the end of the 3 missions he is considered to be back to normal.

A Note on Role-playing This Section

Indoctrination methods are not meant to wreck Agent concepts or make people play characters they did not want to. If you don't like it leave it out. However, these ideas are important to Ai-Jinn philosophy and method so if you don't like them you should try to use something of your own devising.

Optional Rule for Getting Players Paranoid and Hating Each Other

Yes, that's why this rule optional. If you wish you can consider all words that come out of a player's mouth to be essentially *in character.*

When a player says, "Oh sod it, kill him, he's annoying me. Actually no, better not, he is our superior officer," or something similar, you can consider that it's the dark side of his character manifesting. It's somewhat like the vibes or uncontrolled emotions he gives off and his division members will pick up on this kind of thing. You thus force the players to act in character all the time which makes them wary of every word they say.

This style of play is not to everyone's taste but can make an interesting change now and again or if you are going for that Orwellian feel.

ALLOCATING TIME

This process can take many weeks; you should consider that other division members are engaged in typical duties. You can give them a little cash to represent this. Typically 20% of their standard mission pay for each week the conditioning is going on for. Thus rank 1 Ai-Jinn Agents would get 140¢ a week. This serves as a bonus for loyal Agents.

Further to this, his Ai-Jinn superiors may demand follow-up classes which further impress upon the Agent a healthy corporate outlook. These effectively strip away the Agents future downtime by way of a punishment. 1-5 weeks is a good amount with more time being taken for more serious breaches such as insubordination or disobeying orders.

For example, Agent Johnny Ya has been extremely rude to his superior Agent Lun. Despite Agent Lun's warnings he maintained this attitude and even endangered the mission by attempting to disobey orders. Agent Lun, was fairly tolerant though and because of Johnny's track record only sent him for behavioural modification. Johnny did not resist, the process was successful and Agent Ya now has a deep set passion for Ai-Jinn policy. Lun also decided 4 weeks of doctrine reinforcement were warranted so Johnny will lose his next four downtime actions.

Black…white…black…white…green…blue…black….blue…green …blue…yellow...yellow….

"Enough! Please…"

The lights stop, a woman speaks. She is calm and patient. "Tell me the codes, Mr. Hayashi."

"I can't, don't you understand? It's not me, it's the progra…"

Green…green…blue…red…red…yellow…red…red…black…whi te…green…blue…red…blue…red…red…green…red…

He screams. His knuckles white, the veins on his neck and forehead bulging, he bites down so hard his molars crack.

"Surely a man like you has control of his thoughts Mr. Hayashi?"

Hayashi cannot speak. He has lost control of his body and is making childish noises, snot is running from his nose and his eyes are no longer looking in the same direction.

"Each time I turn a light on it uses 0.0001 unit of power. The fission generator behind me can generate over fifty million units of power. Imagine how long I can keep the lights on, Mr. Hayashi."

Hayashi's eyes seem to focus and he speaks, his stilted words

bubbling through the phlegm. "I…can't….it's….the….progra…"

Red…yellow….red…green…blue…red…black…black…orange ….red….blue….

Blood dribbles from Hayashi's mouth but the woman is not concerned, it's probably just the broken shards of teeth slicing the gums.

"You know that the best feature of this method, Mr. Hayashi, is that the patient suffers only the most superficial physical harm. The process can continue for years until the brain places its own existence over the value of the information.
I realise that you believe you cannot help me and that may be true. But I'm not trying to pursuade you Mr. Hayashi, I'm trying to persuade your brain."

"But…but…"

"Don't speak. You are not ready, your mind is still far too stubborn, but in a year, maybe two, it will be ready. So get comfortable, this will be a long ride.

Dr. Zhin, set the machine to automatic, ten minute bursts every twenty minutes. Oh and give him an IV nutrient feed and sleep inhibitors. Call me in a week."

SECTION 6

AI-JINN ASSETS

Indestructible
Determination that is incorruptible
From the other side
A terror to behold
Annihilation will be unavoidable
Every broken enemy will know
That their opponent had to be invincible
Take a last look around while you're alive
I'm an indestructible Master of War!

Indestructible - Disturbed

AI-JINN MILITARY

You've all seen the numbers, but you need to know that the idea of a 'standing army' is a touch misleading, because the figures we've got here reflect strictly regular troops; they don't take into account the Stratoforges.

See, the Clangers keep their main divisions as a contingency force; for normal business practice like putting down insurrections, cleaning up guerrilla actions and pushing through hostile takeovers, they'll typically drop a Stratoforge out of low orbit, diverting fighter squadrons for cover as required. Damn things are about the size of half a city block, leaking oil like rain and sat in their own private smoke clouds; most the bulk is just raw mineral storage. They can kick out about thirty P-tanks an hour, drop 'em straight into hotzones on one-shot gravchutes, and they'll keep pumping the fuckers out until there's nothing left to burn. Then, typically, the Stratoforge goes back up into orbit for resupply, and any P-tanks left on the ground will all overload their reactors simultaneously just to make sure of the job.

So, while the UIG's awful proud of the fact that 'open warfare' is a thing of the past, y'all should know that the Ai-Jinn tend to treat sledgehammerin' walnuts as good business practice. It's why we train each and every one of you grunts in anti-armor drill... and it's why, like the fella said, you never want to start a land war in Asia.

-from Lectures at New West Point
attr: Col. Jack Danes, Western Federation

THE AI-JINN MOBILE ARMOURED FORCE

The mobile armoured force is a term used to describe the entirety of the Ai-Jinn's ground forces which can be brought to bear against an enemy. 50% of the army is always active, guarding assets, patrolling borders and so on. The other 50% can be called into action almost immediately but are maintained in a standby state to keep running costs to a minimum.

Below are outlined the basic divisions of the Ai-Jinn military.

32 CYBERUN DIVISIONS

These are typically composed of 10 cyberlins, predominantly battle class but including some ranger and scout class. These are used to guard assets or to back up other mechanised divisions.

5 AQUATIC CYBERUN DIVISIONS

These each comprise 4 Ocean class cyberlins and are used to protect ports or make attacks against enemy assets.

30 P-TANK DIVISIONS

Each Division is comprised of a swarm of 100 P-Tanks. These fulfill a variety of functions, for more information see their descrption on page 160.

8 TANK DIVISIONS

Each division is comprised of around 1200 heavy tanks supported by 800 light tanks. These form the main aggressive arm of the Ai-Jinn military.

32 ARTILLERY DIVISIONS

Each division contains 200 anti-aircraft cannons and 300 long range artillery bombardment cannons. These cannons are all mobile and are used to foil air attacks and bombard targets from a distance.

64 INFANTRY DIVISIONS

Each division consists of 25,000 troops. These will normally accompany the tank division and are used for assaulting and holding cities or assets.

32 HEAVY INFANTRY DIVISIONS

Each Division consists of 5,000 troops in heavy armour. These units typically support the standard infantry.

OTHER UNITS

16 BOMBER SQUADRONS

Each squadron consists of 30 bombers carrying high yield explosives. These units are used to bomb strategic assets such as airports, military sites and command centres.

32 FIGHTER SQUADRONS

Each squadron consists of 50 fighters which are used to intercept craft, make reconnaissance trips or make strafing attacks on enemy assets.

16 SPECIAL FORCES UNITS

Each unit consists of 25 highly trained and selectively augmented soldiers who routinely undertake missions in time of military activity. They are a much cruder tool than Agents and are usually used to attack assets or defend important positions.

160 AGENT DIVISIONS

Each Division typically consists of 5 highly trained, biomechanically augmented Agents. These are not typically deployed in large scale warfare except in command, sabotage or intelligence roles.

All Agents are always on active duty and the number of active divisions rises and falls continuously.

3 STRATOFORGES

These massive, hovering factories can be deployed straight into the airspace above combat zones, where they can churn out additional military assets at a frightening rate. They are kept in low orbit until needed, where they are periodically restocked by Ai-Jinn mining craft.

THE SPACE FLEET

The FarDrive is one of the key factors which distinguish the Ai-Jinn from the other Corporations. This incredible piece of technology has catapulted the Ai-Jinn mining industry beyond anything its rivals can compete with. It is believed the first subspace drive was recovered from an excavation in Antarctica and taken to an Ai-Jinn research lab at Xa Men.

WHY CAN'T ANYONE ELSE BUILD THEM?

One of the greatest secrets of the Ai-Jinn is their shadowy relationship with the Rogue Archon Hyperion. For reasons humans can only guess at Hyperion is working with the Ai-Jinn and has assisted them in their work. His* influence can be felt in several places, not least the changeable ID Chip, the illegal G.E.T. station at Tien Sing (see Machines of War), the Legacy Project (page xx) and the FarDrive.

The FarDrive plant is located two miles underground at Changsha in China. The facility is completely unmanned, sealed from the outside by durasteel walls dozens of metres thick and guarded by cyberlins. There is a single access door but no-one normally enters the plant. When the signal is given the door is opened and a completed FarDrive is collected by an automated loader.

Originally the plant was built according to some very exacting designs given to the Ai-Jinn by Hyperion himself, the majority of the systems being nanofacture units. Since the original construction the plant has apparently changed considerably. This information is available to the Ai-Jinn through the Legacy Agents who are the only ones Hyperion permits within the plant. See page 32 for more information on Legacy Agents.

Hyperion is able to remotely access the plant and instruct it to build the necessary components and assemble them into a working drive. Without his direct intervention no FarDrives can be built, hence why the Ai-Jinn have relatively few craft but the resources to build many more. This safeguard means that even if another Corporation steals a FarDrive there is no way they can duplicate it without the intervention of another Archon. It is rumoured that Hyperion has the power to detonate any FarDrive at any time but so far this has not been proved although many speculate that the FarDrive craft which have gone missing without trace could have fallen victim to Hyperion's kill-switch.

*Hyperion is referred to as male for convenience; there is no indication of gender.

REGARDING THE SUBSPACE MECHTRONICS TRAINING (THE EASTERN BANK).

Obviously FarDrives need occasional maintenance and calibration. The level of technology needed to interact with FarDrives is much lower than that which is needed to build them.

You could compare it to a computer user; in order to use a computer, the operator does not need to be able to build one from scratch.

Likewise Subspace Mechtronics allows you to build subspace related devices such as rift grenades and telepathic convergers or maintain and use FarDrives. This training does not allow you to build FarDrives.

THE AI-JINN FLEET

Since the FarDrive was perfected the Ai-Jinn have built over 100 FarDrive craft (FDC). The makeup of the fleet is outlined below.

WARSHIPS

These are massive craft with enormous offensive and defensive capability. They are generally found in geosynchronous orbit around Ai-Jinn assets which currently require additional security such as:

Spires where important meetings are taking place.
Newly discovered mining colonies.
Mining craft with valuable cargo.
Locations where xeno activity is suspected.
Shuttles transporting VIPs or sensitive cargo.

CURRENTLY ACTIVE AI-JINN WARSHIPS

The Jade Emperor
Oppressor Class
Flagship

The Kuan Ti
Fortress Class
Patrols the Sol system

The Chu Yung
Barbarian Class
Travels between locations in the Sol system.

These ships have seldom been used for direct aggression, the only notable occasions being orbital strikes during the Corporate

Wars. This was thought to be too destructive and inefficient to be used as a sustained tactic and was abandoned in favour of D-Shift weapons.

Warships have three main classes

Oppressor Class
Designed to lie ominously near sensitive areas and lay down the fear of a dozen gods. Oppressor class are at their best when used as a threat. They don't even need to open fire to get their point across.

Fortress Class
Fortress class crafts are crucifix shaped which allows them to bear 4 spinal charge drivers at cardinal points. This makes them extremely fast to react and excellent at guarding large areas of space.

Barbarian Class
Not as heavily armed as the other classes but fast and responsive. There were originally 3 Barbarian class cruisers but 2 never returned after investigating the disappearance of the Explorer craft in the infamous Epsilon Nestrum sector.

Between the cold and mocking stars
No light comes; we could not see what we had found.
But the Rebel King of Heaven, who built our carriage, knew.
Unwitting, we were his instrument.

-Carved into a trans-ferrum bulkhead, in simplified Chinese, in the wreckage of Celestial Eye surveyor-class FDC (Epsilon Nestrum sector). High concentration of ceratin found in gouged characters. Recovery team detained indefinitely by Hattamoto-Yakko on grounds of suspected sedition.

SAMPLE WAR SHIP - THE JADE EMPEROR (OPPRESSOR CLASS)

APPEARANCE
The Jade Emperor is the flagship of the Ai-Jinn space fleet. It's enormous hull stretches 1855 metres from prow to stern. The craft itself resembles a weapon as that's basically what it is. The interior of the ship is made up of functional, slabs of alloy and polymer. There are no concessions to aesthetics and none of the clean lines and sleek command consoles you might expect from a multi-billion credit space craft.

Everything is stripped down to what is crucial to reliability and function. In many ways it is reminiscent of the Amur Border Spire (Eastern Bank) where the function of the craft intrudes on and compromises the habitability of the interior. Bunk rooms are extremely hot and noisy and corridors may occasionally be shut down to act as heat sinks after dropping out of subspace or firing the primary weapon.

The computer systems used are relatively basic; the idea being simpler technology goes wrong less often. The only advanced ones employed are the navigation and tactical A.I.s. These are seasoned and thoroughly tested programs which are famed for their stability and evolve-code integrity. They are connected to hard-wired kill switches so the A.I.s can never over-ride the captain's commands. Sadly this system does not seem to be perfect as with the case of **The Ruin of Kai**.

The craft has a small array of energy and torpedo weapons at its disposal although the main ordnance is a linear spinal charge driver which runs along the full length of the ship. Because of the other corporations' lack of space faring craft, Ai-Jinn warships have very little in the way of ship-ship weaponry.

WEAPON SYSTEMS
Spinal Charge Driver
The entire ship must be manoeuvred in order for the charge driver to be lined up. This makes the war ship analogous to an old fashioned cannon galleon where the majority of the tactics involve lining the vessel up without exposing itself. At this time however, due to the lack of mobile enemies, the ship need merely be orientated towards the point of attack on an orbital or planet.

Torpedoes
The vessel has numerous torpedo banks. They fire medium range auto-targeting plasma warheads designed for ship-ship conflicts. They are typically used to disable the opponent's weapon systems and make surgical strikes on shield generators or engine nacelles. Again, the lack of opponents makes the tactical application of these weapons fairly academic.

Shield Generators
The Jade Emperor uses a batter of high-power shield generators which defend the ship from incoming weapons, asteroids and space debris.

STATS
Listed below are some basic STATS if you for some reason wanted to use the Jade Emperor in a combat situation. There will be more in depth rules about space combat in a future supplement.

HP   20,000
Shield 5,000
AV   50

Spinal Charge Driver
AT 40   Dam D4 x 500   Rate 1 per 4 mins   Range 100km

Plasma Torpedos
AT 40   Dam D6 x 100   Rate 1 per min   Range 10km
(Craft contains 10 launchers)

THE RUIN OF KAI - OPPRESSOR CLASS

There have always been suspicions that the first Oppressor class craft built - The Ruin of Kai - was taken over by the tactical A.I. who was both self-aware and loyal to an Archon. The Ruin of Kai managed to use its own systems to murder all the crew on board and fled the Sol system. The last transmissions were made in 2467 from a dying crew member.

Hyperion offered no insight into the event so whether the Archon was involved is still unknown. Reports from Vastaag state that a craft matching the Ruin of Kai's description has been occassionally picked up on long range scanners but no hard evidence is apparent.

EXPLORER CRAFT

There are currently only three Explorer craft serving in the fleet. Four have been lost without trace and two destroyed exploring the notorious Epsilon Nestrum sector. Although the Ai-Jinn are currently building new craft they are considering instead building more sensor/scanner equipped warships which will hopefully be better able to withstand the unknown perils of deep space.

The Black Rat	Surveyor Class
The Tiger Hunter	Pathfinder Class
The Hound	Pathfinder Class

Pathfinder Class

These ships are equipped with numerous long and short range sensors with massive generators to power them. They also boast impressive navigational and reactive A.I.s for charting unknown areas and developing action plans for previously unknowable situations. Their main purpose is mapmaking rather than deep level scanning; that is the domain of the Surveyor class ships.

Surveyor Class

Surveyor class do not boast the wealth of sensors that Pathfinders do, instead they sport impressive scanner arrays and are used to survey areas which have been earmarked by Pathfinder ships. They may spend many months in a single star system making geological maps which are in turn passed onto the mining craft.

DESCRIPTION

The ships are lightweight and only around 500 metres in length. They are equipped with the newest revision of the FarDrive which are the quickest to enter, travel through and leave subspace. They are manned by fairly small crews, typically 50 to 100 staff.

CREW

The crew composition is very carefully considered and for most missions consists of the following:

1 Captain (Shang Xiao)
1 Commander (Zhong Xiao)
1 Lieutenant Commander (Shao Xiao)
3 Navigators
1 Comms. Operator
15 Shipmen
5 General Mechtricians
3 Subspace Mechtricians
3 Weapon Mechtricians
4-6 Corporate Agents in a division
3 Medics
15 Scientists
10 Security Guards

Explorer craft will generally travel for one or two years, scouring the unknown reaches of space for minable resources, alien life or signs of past civilisations. Needless to say minable resources are the most commonly encountered.

There is always a division of corporate Agents on board all FarDrive craft, their versatility and sheer effectiveness make them invaluable in the diverse range of situations a FarDrive craft is likely to encounter. Aside the normal division specialisations there will normally be a xenologist and subspace engineer on Explorer craft. (See Subspace Mechtronics Training in the Eastern Bank.)

WEAPONRY

The Explorer craft are armed with a moderately powerful arc-beam energy weapon mounted in a spinal configuration which is used for clearing landing areas and in defence emergencies. It also contains two plasma torpedo banks for ship-ship confrontations. The Explore crafts are not designed for skirmishes and their main form of defence is rapid transfer to subspace.

MINING CRAFT

Mining craft make up the largest part of the Ai-Jinn space fleet. Although there are technically more transport shuttles, there is a greater amount of materials and money invested in these deep space resource collectors.

The mining craft take on a few different forms although the most common is the 'driller'. These ships (pictured on page 119) are orientated to the vertical and can be categorised into two sections. The top section houses the FarDrive, crew quarters and bridge while the lower half contains the mining drill and enormous hoppers.

Mining craft need to be quite diverse and there are a few standard variants:

SPIRIT CLASS

Also known as a gas miner, this craft is designed to collect gases instead of ores and substitutes the mining drill for atmospheric intakes.

AVALANCHE CLASS

These craft are the staple of the Ai-Jinn mining fleet and specialise in making the resources of an ore-containing body available for collection. The enormous drill is used to create mining tunnels which will be worked by humans and droids. The displaced rock is typically collected in the hold and taken back to earth for extraction. Mining the rock by hand is much more efficient though and the ore to rock ratio much higher. It is cheaper to establish and man a colony then to repeatedly send FarDrive craft into space which then bring back low yield ore.

The Rat & Dragon - Inquisitor Class Mining Craft

INQUISITOR CLASS

As well as acting as a mining and cargo craft this class of vessel has extensive labs and environmental suites on the upper levels for the housing and study of xeno-based life and technology.

SKIRMISH CLASS

This class of vessel has additional defensive and offensive systems. It is used to mine in areas where the Ai-Jinn believe hostility is possible.

CURRENT MINING CRAFT

The Rat and Dragon	Inquisitor Class
The Golden Monkey	Avalanche Class
The Tower of Skulls	Skirmish Class
The Green Demon	Spirit Class
The Heavenly Ox	Avalanche Class
The Great Horse	Avalanche Class

The shuttle came up over the last ridge and, through the pitted layers of the armoured viewport, Agent Tsang saw the foreign sun sweeping over the alien vista for the first time. He caught his breath as cold fire blazed from countless millions of mineral outcroppings, each a perfect natural sculpture never before seen by human eyes. The virgin landscape lay untouched before him, majestic peaks and plunging valleys sparkling brilliantly in the cold light.

An ugly shadow fell across the landscape as the colossal Avalanche miner dropped down between the shuttle and the sun. Though still several kilometres from the shuttle, its massive girth blocked much of the light, sheathed in endless layers of scarred, burned armour plating and studded with the innumerable spikes of communications gear and sensor arrays. Slowing, the vast cylinder drew close enough almost to brush the unblemished surface, and Tsang watched as massive stabilising claws snaked out to grasp the skin of the planetoid, their relentless grip digging in and crushing swathes of the delicate crystal formations. After a few minutes, with the gargantuan miner firmly grappled to its prey, the thick shaft of the main drill slid out and ripped brutally into the pristine surface. Tsang grunted in satisfaction as the atomised remains of the planetoid's crust exploded out into uncaring space in a glittering mist, the drill thrusting ever deeper into the ravaged rock, probing hungrily for the more valuable minerals identified in the lower strata.

Like everyone else within the Corporation, Tsang had seen the propaganda around the FarDrive; rosy-cheeked children gazing wonderingly up into the heavens, heroic subspace explorers staring manfully off into the starry unknown, all eager to cooperate to secure a prosperous future for generations to come. But here in the cold dark of space, he reflected, was the truth of it: this was rape on a planetary scale, justified by the all-important need to maintain Ai-Jinn dominance at any cost. Tsang grinned, and turned from the viewport. It would soon be time to brief the mining crews.

LEASED CRAFT

The Ai-Jinn also have a number of craft which they lease to other Corporations and the UIG. These ships are generally crewed by Ai-Jinn staff who restrict access to the FarDrive core. Example leased craft include:

THE BLACK FIST OF LAO

This is a large combat capable transport vessel currently leased to the UIG who use it to make trips to and from Venus, Lunas, Mars and other Sol based bodies.

THE WORLD VIEW

Luxury Cruiser – See page 157 of the Core Rules. Although E.I. paid for the construction of the vessel and own most of it, they do not possess the propulsion mechanism.

SHUTTLES

The Ai-Jinn lease several shuttles to various corporations to allow them to run scheduled flights to orbitals, colonies and orbiting ships.

THE SPIRIT OF CHANGSHA

This is an exploratory craft currently on lease to Amalgamated Xenological Enterprises (AXE) (Machines of War Page 124). It is one of three vessels AXE routinely hire to take them about the galaxy searching for relics and xenoforms.

SHUTTLES

The rest of the fleet is composed of transport shuttles of various sizes. Some are battle equipped but most ferry people to different locations around the Sol system. The shuttles tend to be named after important Ai-Jinn dignitaries, high ranking Agents, religious figures and places of significance.

NON AI-JINN CRAFT

There are a small number of non Ai-Jinn craft floating around the Sol system. They use far more conventional drive systems and are not sub-space capable. The majority of the ships are either construction, transport or defence vessels.

WESTERN FEDERATION

The Federation's Hydra Class warship 'Gravity Storm' is a relatively recent addition and the only craft to pose a significant threat to the Ai-Jinn warships. Instead of a spinal mounted charge driver, it uses an omni-directional coherent energy beam which is far more responsive but less powerful. Although it lacks the ability to orbital strike like the Ai-Jinn weapon, it is extremely flexible in its targeting allowing it to open fire on enemy craft regardless of the Gravity Storm's orientation.

EURASIAN INC.

E.I. has three Arbiter Class craft with moderate offensive capability: The Avenging Angel, Death's Door and The Silent Night. These vessels travel the Sol system taking supplies to E.I.s various outposts and acting as deterrents around Vastaag and the World View.

SHI YUKIRO

The Shi Yukiro have developed their highly regarded 'Tenshi' Class Interceptors which, although small, are extremely agile and can easily outmanoeuvre any other vessel. The Shi Yukiro have few space-based assets so the majority of these fighters are docked on Earth.

COMOROS

Comoros are yet to construct any significant space-faring vessels maintaining that the state of the Earth and its population should be addressed before humanity spreads its taint across the universe.

There have been no off-Earth skirmishes to date and the purpose of these various corporate vessels seems to be mainly for research and to ensure that a presence is maintained.

THE UIG & SPACE TRAVEL

A continual source of frustration to the UIG is the Archons' unwillingness to offer them FarDrive technology. The official stance of the UIG is that they do not see the purpose of spending tax payers' money on travelling beyond the borders of the solar system when there is very little to be gained at this point in time.

The real story is a little different and the UIG cannot understand the Archons' reluctance to assist when the Ai-Jinn have such open access to FarDrive technology.

In the halls of the Exchange the debate goes on. The UIG demand to know how the Archons can allow the most nefarious Corporation access to one of the most powerful technologies ever invented while preventing the policing government from accessing the same information. The allied Archons maintain that it was not at their behest that the Ai-Jinn acquired FarDrive technology and given the chance they would have prevented it from happening but as things stand, the Ai-Jinn are primarily concerned with the acquisition of resources which is not, in itself, a threat.

Should an organisation such as the UIG acquire complete access to FarDrive technology it would be used predominantly for research and exploration. At this time, the Archons maintain deep space is in a delicate balance and there is a significant difference between the odd low tech Ai-Jinn FarCraft drifting about mining resources and a fleet of high-end, government backed ships with the sole purpose of mapping the universe and making contact with other civilisations.

The AXE Corporation (Amalgamated Xenological Enterprises), however, pose more concern. Their pursuit of knowledge is potentially dangerous and it is only the relatively small scale of their operation which has allowed them to remain active.

USING DEEP SPACE IN YOUR GAME.

Although the majority of Corporation gaming happens on or very near Earth the occasional sojourn into the unknown can make for an excellent mission. Some example missions are listed below which should give you an idea of how to use deep space travel in your game. There are some key points to remember though which should help space retain its rightful position in the game world.

DON'T MAKE IT TOO COMMONPLACE.

Unless you are going to make up loads of stuff yourself there is not a great deal of information (yet) in the Corporation series of books to run a lot of games in deep space. A few scenarios where you are detailed to a mining ship or where you investigate a massacre on a colony are great but if you are stay up there too long you'll start running out of material. Space is supposed to be the exception, not the rule.

MAKE THE SHIP ITSELF A MISSION ZONE.

Loads of things can happen on the ship such as stowaways, mechanical emergencies, hijackings, out of control A.I.s and the inevitable insane ship's officer who wants to kill everyone in the name of the great Navarno! By treating the ship like a city and having the division police it, you can build a sense of continuity and they will get to know the staff and various parts of the craft. The same idea applies to off-world colonies.

ISOLATION

Try to put across the sense of isolation; the idea that if the ships drive was to break irreparably there would be nothing for millions of miles; that the the division would die and likely never be found. The same applies to mining colonies; if some kind of xeno was detected in the base the residents might simply be abandoned, left to survive on the remaining rations and dwindling energy supplies. That's not to say you should do that to the players, but the idea should be brought up now and again.

THE UNKNOWN

A huge part of space is the unknown. Almost every aspect of Earth has been studied in detail but space has the potential to hold fantastic mysteries. It can be very hard to think up completely new ideas as there are so many sci-fi films and books already out but try to be a little inventive and at least do *something* the players were not expecting or that they cannot immediately understand. Aliens who would rather kill themselves that be seen by someone or star bridges billions of miles across created from coalesced particulate drifting through space.

MISSION IDEAS

1. The maintenance droids have over-ridden the hard-wired kill switches so the A.I. cannot be shut down.

2. During an emergency situation the corridors are being used as heat sinks but the warnings are inactive.

3. Your Division has been selected to be the accompanying Agents on an Explorer Craft, charting the unknown reaches of space.

4. A mining ship has broken down and a team is being dispatched to repair it. Your division will be on board the rescue ship.

5. A colony has lost contact with Earth, your division is part of the recon crew who are sent to investigate. Yes...it's aliens and they're evil, monstrous, destructive and nigh-invincible!!!

MEGASTRUCTURES

Nonono, it's easy, look; you just take two quintuple-redundant active naninium cables; run a few asteroids through the geoscaper to get them in the right shape and thread them onto the cables like beads; connect the ends, wait until the whole lot starts to fuse and denature the naninium with a gamma radiation charge.

Then you just fill the whole damn shebang with water and atmosphere once you've set it spinning. Centrifuge will do the job of keeping it in without artificial gravity. Voila; instant ringworld!

- attr: Captain Lu Zheng, Ai-Jinn macroengineer.

Possibly the greatest achievements of mankind are the twin orbitals of Vastaag and Miller-Urey. While the ownership of these man-made worlds falls to E.I. and the UIG respectively it was the Ai-Jinn who actually constructed them.

Never has any organisation before or since overseen construction operations on such a titanic scale as the Ai-Jinn, and it is possible than none ever could. Without the other Corporations having access to the Ai-Jinn's space superiority and ferocious production rate, nevermind their construction expertise, any attempt to replicate the feat of towing billions of tons of space debris into one place, fusing them together and then terraforming the resultant molten proto-world would be a futile exercise, and certainly not a cost-effective one.

The Ai-Jinn, on the other hand, have benefitted greatly from their forays into world-building; the amount of credit paid out by the UIG and Eurasian Inc. alike were both sufficient enough to cause not insignificant imbalances in the world economy for some time, and it was the Ai-Jinn who reaped the rewards. The Corporation is highly excited about the possibilities that this form of macroscale engineering offers for the creation of a vast new revenue-source but recognises that as long as they are dependent upon contract-work from other organisations they are never going to be able to realise the true potential of megastructure building.

To this end, the Ai-Jinn have recently begun a series of private side-projects carried out gradually at minimal cost which it hopes will lead to economic ascendancy when unveiled. The Ai-Jinn's plans for their space construction efforts also serve to further less mercenary ends.

While the UIG's power over Earth is virtually unchallengeable, their grip over space and Earth's orbitals is tenuous at best. With no FarDrive-equipped craft of their own save those which the Ai-Jinn choose to lease to them, their operational effectiveness outside of Earth's atmosphere is effectively neutered. If megastructures can be built in a sufficiently cost-effective manner, the Ai-Jinn will become the first of the great Corporations to utterly emancipate itself from UIG control by moving their entire operation to somewhere that the law simply cannot reach.

PRIVATE PROJECTS

As part of the Corporation's plans for future advancement into space technologies, the building of a number of megastructures has begun. Some of the more prominent examples include:

SOLAR PLATES

The Ai-Jinn isn't quite ready to construct a Dyson Sphere just yet, and the other Corporations might object to the destruction of Earth for the raw materials that such a project would necessarily entail, but some of the principles of such a structure still hold some potential practical use.

The solar plates are colossal high-absorption nanofactured pentagonal solar panels, each over a mile across. The intention is to transport the plates near to the surface of the sun, where the amount of solar energy that can be absorbed is several magnitudes greater than can be gathered on Earth, and transmit the energy back to distribution stations on Earth and the orbitals by means of a series of microwave-beam satellites.

If successful then the Ai-Jinn will possess a vast and functionally inexhaustible supply of cheap electricity, much more than the entire Corporation itself can use; which is part of the plan. The true purpose of the solar plates is not merely to provide the Corporation with reduced power costs, it is to unseat the UIG-owned Universal Nuclear Fuels Ltd., simultaneously giving the Ai-Jinn an inroad into the power-generation industry and further discrediting the UIG by lessening the public reliance on their institutions.

THE FARGATE

As part of the Corporation's plans to expand further into deep space, the FarGate program is based around the idea of placing static subspace gates connecting key locations, forming interplanetary trade routes and 'express lanes'. Not only is this vastly more efficient - rather than equipping every starfaring ship in the fleet with a FarDrive only two are needed, one for each gate - but it would allow the Ai-Jinn to charge the other Corporations tolls for their use.

Currently only one gate is completed and its sister, a modularised version which will be broken down and transported to Mars space for the test-run of this technology, is still under construction so currently the gate just opens out into subspace with no exit. Non FarDrive-capable ships are therefore advised to avoid the dimensional meniscus vortex when the gate is active during the testing periods and no spacewalks are to be conducted during this time following the tragic loss and presumed death of twenty-three external workers during an activation accident three years ago.

One notable feature of the gate technology is that due to the fact that the craft using it must physically pass through the subspace portal it creates, rather than 'simply' translating into subspace like a conventional FarDrive-equipped craft, the subspace rift must be maintained for much longer. To this end, the entire ring of the gate is equipped with no less than six nuclear generators, all of which are pushed to their limit maintaining an active gate. While the Ai-Jinn considers this limitation acceptable given the vast increase in functional efficiency they will be able to reap by running vast fleets of FarDrive-incapable cargo ships between Earth and Mars rather than their comparative few FarDrive craft, some question the wisdom of keeping a subspace rift open for so long so close to Earth. After all, who knows what kind of things might be tempted to come through from the other side?

THE BRICKYARD

The Ai-Jinn keeps a zone of space just inside the orbit of Jupiter, known colloquially as the Brickyard, entirely for the purpose of containing mined-out asteroids from which they build their megastructures. The strip-mining process weakens the asteroids, making them easier to break down and render into a molten state within the bowels of the geoscaper ships so that they can be reconstituted into the desired form at a consequentially lower cost to the Corporation.

When the Ai-Jinn is done mining out an asteroid it is fired to the Brickyard with low-powered mass drivers and picked up by AI-automated tug ships to be towed into a stable orbit. Occasionally, when one of the megastructure projects requires raw materials the geoscaper ships FarDrive to the Brickyard to consume more rock matter like a titanic black beetle, the images of which are often featured in the Ai-Jinn's promotional films due to their dramatically impressive scale.

And as the last light of that most auspicious day turned to darkened gold through the dust of Beijing's hutongs, we found ourselves at last alone, in a walled garden far from the Spire. My impatience welled within me and I demanded of the CEO, then only six hours into her tenure: With all of your grand vision, what is it that you truly intend? When you have built the Phoenix Glass that we may steal the Sun and leave the oppressors in the shadow; when you have opened the Dragon Gate that we may grasp enduring prosperity among the stars; when the Celestial Palace is complete that we may live harmoniously and untroubled by the ravages of barbarians; what will we do then?

Yuan Qingzhao turned to me, her gaze serene and gentle, and she looked at me for a long time. And then, in a soft nightingale voice shot through with iron, she said: Whatever we want.

In that moment, I understood the choice of the Immortals.

-From My Conversations with the Venerable Leader
attr: Dragon's Head Kuan-Yin Liang

ASCENDANCY MEGA-HABITAT

Location - Geostatic orbit over Jupiter
Controlling Corporation - Ai-Jinn
Governor - Citizen Xue Pailung / Rank 2 / Level 3
Specialist Facilities - Optic Crystal Propagation, Precision Machining, Ore Refining.

Spire cities were the latest and greatest stage in solving the world's problem of creating enough habitation space for Earth's population while limiting the impact upon the already-fragile ecosystem. But Spires were first built over two hundred and fifty years ago, the Ai-Jinn considers it high time for something new.

The Ascendancy Mega-Habitat is currently only a sixth of its way to being finished, but it's hard for Ai-Jinn executives to blame anyone for the slow pace with which the work nears completion, it is after all nearly forty kilometres long and three kilometres in diameter. When completed, Ascendancy will be the single largest human habitation residential zone in existence, a slowly-rotating cylinder of orbital durasteel and armour-glass threaded together and reinforced with naninium cabling. It will be able to hold an estimated human population of around ten million in simulated natural conditions equal to that of a UIG clean-zone.

Preliminary promotional material depicts the interior of the hab as a vast sea of rolling green hills dotted with gleaming-white modern houses filled with happy families playing around the pool while real birds fly overhead. The centripetal motion of the hab's rotation will allow the entirety of the cylinder's interior to be built upon and inhabited while maintaining an artificial gravity of around .97 G's, meaning that people could literally look up with a telescope and see other Ascendancy citizens living above them.

Every measure to ensure the safety of the habitat is being maintained, the Ai-Jinn understand that people may be initially reluctant to live in space and want to make sure that as much of the public unease as possible is mitigated by the hab's very design. Every five-mile stretch of the structure is separated by a dividing wall to reduce the likelihood that a hull-breach could depressurise the whole habitat and in addition to debris detection systems and avoidance jets the whole structure will be protected by one of the largest matrix-hard-ion shields ever created.

As it currently stands only three habitation sections have been completed - one at each end of the main structural spindle and one at the centre - and only one of those has been partially terraformed. Three hundred employee families have agreed to trial the nearly-completed section on the understanding that they will receive increased pay and positions of authority when the Ascendancy hab is finally opened to the public.

In addition to serving as a major centre of human habitation, Ascendancy is set to become a major lynchpin in expanding the Ai-Jinn's already impressive production rates. The ore-ships travelling from Mars and the asteroid belt will no longer have to enter Earth's gravity well as often saving both time and thousands of tonnes of reaction-drive fuel. They can now conduct more production work in space, meaning that the efficiency of refining can be vastly increased.

There are also ways to take advantage of an environment without natural gravity and one section of the hab, devoted to crystal propagation and metal production, is designed not to spin with the rest, this makes it making it perfect for producing materials with no stresses having been exerted on them by external forces, greatly increasing their quality and the precision of the machines made with them.

THE MILLER-UREY EXPERIMENTS

Despite being its builders - or perhaps because of it - The Ai-Jinn did not get one of the more profitable or interesting areas of Miller-Urey. However, unlike Eurasian Incorporated, who got thoroughly cheated on the deal, the Ai-Jinn have never complained about their allocation of the tundra region of the orbital. Indeed, they actively petitioned the UIG to give them custody over the Ornus landmass, and in a rare act of contrition the UIG agreed.

The desolate, sub-zero terrain, almost incapable of sustaining provider life such as plants, was the perfect testing ground for space-colonisation experiments. On Ornus the Ai-Jinn has created a series of experiments in colonist-BIOs; self-aware creatures possessed of human-approximate intelligence but capable of withstanding environments that no human ever could without advanced equipment or biomechanical augmentation.

Dozens of possible BIO designs have been created, conditioned and released into the frozen waste to either thrive or die, and most don't last for long. Of the BIO species that survive long enough to create self-sustaining societies, the Ai-Jinn hopes to use them in the future as workers on terraforming operations. Once the terraforming is completed they can either be moved on to a new operation, retained as slave labour or simply culled to make way for the human colonists that follow them.

Currently, the coloniser-BIOs have not progressed beyond tribal-level society but captured specimens have shown capability to use advanced technology when provided with coaching and are acceptably tractable when brought beneath the lash. Most, however, require no coaxing to obey the Ai-Jinn, corporate ethnologists have deliberately manipulated their interaction with Corporate personnel to build a mythology in the BIOs' nascent culture relating to humans, elevating them to the status of gods or spirits.

Most coloniser-BIOs seem to regard humans as magical creatures to be worshipped and obeyed, or at least feared and appeased. They often willingly board the collection vehicles, sometimes returning with tales of their journey to the 'spirit world', filled with bright lights, wondrous magical devices and bizarre rituals that they were forced to carry out, thus further reinforcing the BIOs' superstitious awe of Ai-Jinn personnel.

The Maranathan Rebellion

Not all the sentient BIOs on Ornus are utterly subservient to the Ai-Jinn. There is a small but growing guerilla rebellion against the Ai-Jinn springing up amongst the coloniser-BIOs, named after their leader Maranath, a Yilepsid who was taken for routine study and experimentation in 2496 and later released back into the wilderness, apparently having seen through the Ai-Jinn's propaganda.

The Maranathans do not possess the same degree of superstitiousness that the other BIOs do. If they see humans as supernatural then it is more as demons than gods, and for the past several years have conducted ambushes on Ai-Jinn personnel, stealing weapons, armour and other technology and using it to conduct raids and sabotage on Ornus' bases.

The Ai-Jinn are growing increasingly irritated by their rogue creations but all attempts to eradicate them have resulted in rebellion springing up amongst another group of BIO's. It is only a matter of time, if the rebellion continues, before the UIG inspectors get wind of it and uses it as an excuse to levy harsh fines on the Corporation. If it comes to it then it is possible to flood the entire landmass with tailored toxins designed to kill the coloniser-BIOs exclusively but the Ai-Jinn would prefer not to do so as it would result in the waste of a great amount of valuable research.

These BIOs can be found in the back of the book under 'Antagonists'.

MISSION HOOKS

Ai-Jinn megastructures, including Miller-Urey, make great venues for missions that take players beyond Earth. There are few things more dramatic than human construction on such a gigantic scale.

Some sample mission ideas are presented below;

1. Several Solar Plates' systems have failed due to an unexpected solar flare which released a gargantuan EMP, resulting in a deteriorating orbit right into the sun's corona. If they are lost it will cost the Corporation hundreds of billions.

2. A ship that recently passed through the FarGate is floating dead in space, there has been no communication from it, find out why.

3. An AI controlling the Brickyard asteroid tugs has gone sentient and decided it would be more fun to accelerate asteroids at offworld colonies.

4. An unexplained explosion threatens the survival of the Ascendancy Mega-Habitat's personnel.

5. Find a key leader of the Maranathan rebellion and kill it, but without making it into a martyr.

6. It is believed that someone working in the Acendancy Mega-Habitat is a spy. Root them out.

7. One of the asteroids in the Brickyard is showing signs of life deep in its core. The asteroid is several miles across. The Ai-Jinn want a group of Agents to suit-up and find out what's inside.

8. Alien spores have been detected passing through the FarGate. One of these spores has landed on *Noachis Terra* (essentially a large desert) on Mars. Find the spore, isolate and determine exactly what it is.

9. Several of the worker droids in the Ascendancy Mega-Habitiat are disobeying orders and deconstructing the place. The resident security division has been wiped out. Your division is sent in as a replacement and to sort things out.

10. The Ai-Jinn wish to build two off-world factories, one on Mars and one on Venus. Your division has been chosen to represent the Ai-Jinn at a series of cross-corporation talks held by the UIG on Vastaag. You will be expected to prepare your arguments and seal the deal. Be on the lookout for enemy sabboteurs as well as spies and assassins.

JN09

TYPICAL AI-JINN FACTORY

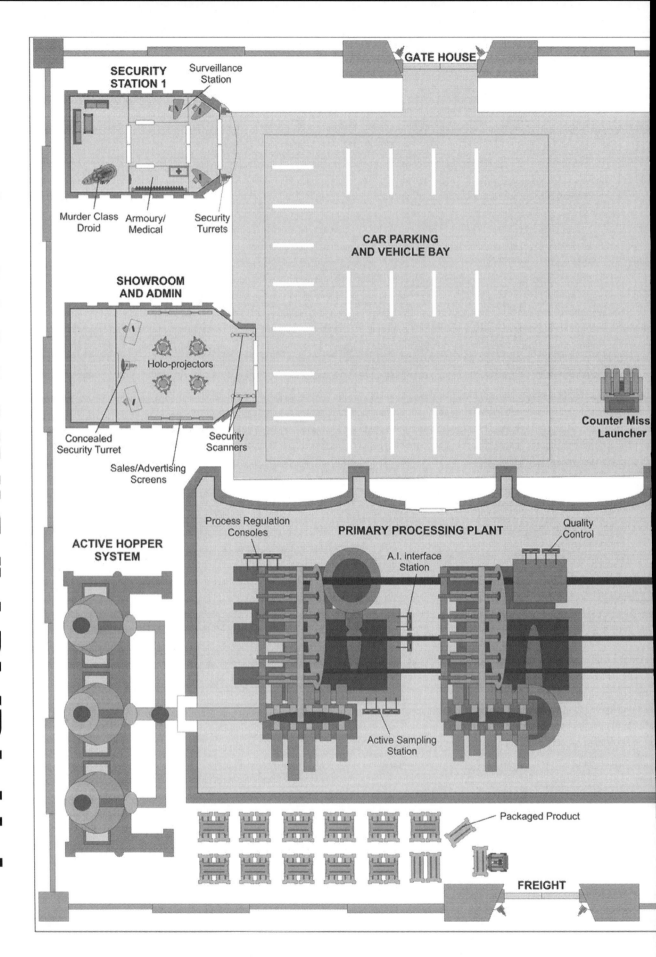

GATE HOUSE

SECURITY STATION 1

Surveillance Station

Murder Class Droid

Armoury/ Medical

Security Turrets

CAR PARKING AND VEHICLE BAY

Counter Miss Launcher

SHOWROOM AND ADMIN

Holo-projectors

Concealed Security Turret

Security Scanners

Sales/Advertising Screens

Process Regulation Consoles

PRIMARY PROCESSING PLANT

Quality Control

A.I. interface Station

ACTIVE HOPPER SYSTEM

Active Sampling Station

Packaged Product

FREIGHT

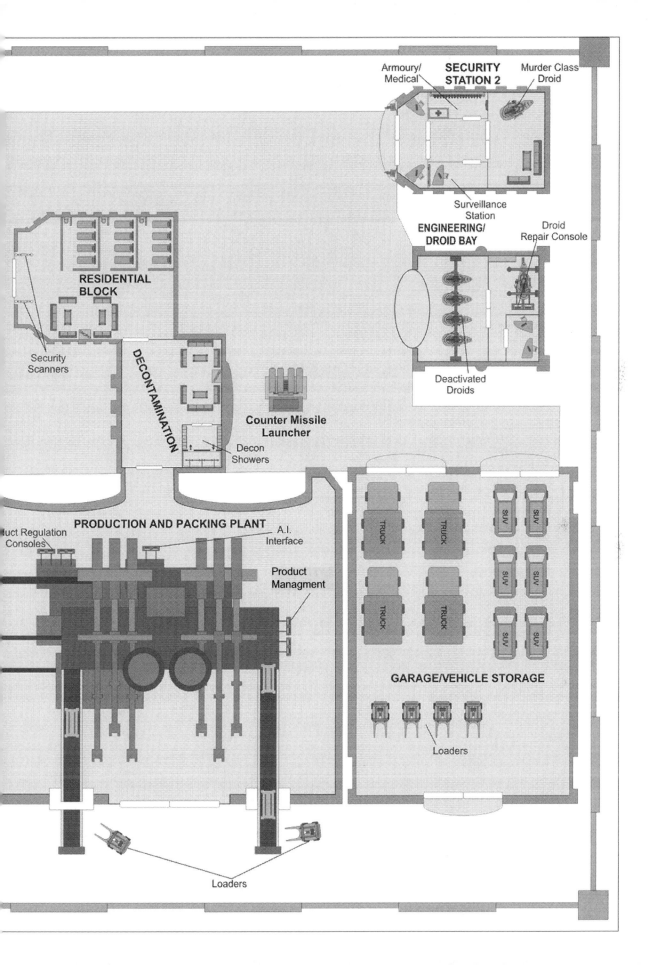

Armoury/Medical

SECURITY STATION 2

Murder Class Droid

Surveillance Station

ENGINEERING/ DROID BAY

Droid Repair Console

RESIDENTIAL BLOCK

Security Scanners

DECONTAMINATION

Counter Missile Launcher

Decon Showers

Deactivated Droids

PRODUCTION AND PACKING PLANT

Duct Regulation Consoles

A.I. Interface

Product Managment

TRUCK TRUCK

TRUCK TRUCK

SUV SUV

SUV SUV

SUV SUV

GARAGE/VEHICLE STORAGE

Loaders

Loaders

SECTION 7

CRIME

CRIME IN THE AI-JINN

Gary 'he Gravedigger' McRoth - Head of the Union Firm

nonetheless so great that these risks are worth taking.

The rule of thumb has always been to make sure the major players, the decision makers, the geniuses, the natural leaders etc. are kept out of harm's way and that only the foot soldiers take the brunt of the UIG's aggression. This practice has two major advantages.

1. Foot soldiers are easy to train and recruit so it's not a great loss.

2. The UIG get to 'nail' someone. They get to close the case and move on. If no-one gets caught and punished the investigation continues and the longer it goes on the harder business becomes and the more likely it is that someone important will get implicated.

There are two common practices, employed by criminals throughout history, still very much in play today, which stack the odds against the law and reduce the chance of legal punishment.

1. Keep Your Distance.
As stated above, by using a system of rank within organised criminal groups the lieutenants and captains seldom get caught. Most hands on work is carried out by soldiers who are often kept in the dark about the organisation's overarching goals. When someone gets busted it's not going to damage the group as a whole.

The Ai-Jinn insist that this form of hierarchy exists in the majority of its cells and if a group is not functioning as it should, Agents are sent in to bring some order.

2. Bribery and Corruption
Sometimes you simply cannot stay away from the law. In these cases it is necessary to oil the wheels with a little cash so when a shipment goes missing it's listed as never having arrived or when drugs are being dealt from a club, the local officers are getting a cut.

This method entails a certain degree of risk as you never know when an officer is going to come clean so the Ai-Jinn employ a carrot and stick policy when dealing with corruption targets.

It always starts with a bribe; people tend to work better with positive reinforcement but unfortunately some individuals are too law-abiding for their own good. In these cases the stick, often in the form of threats against the target's family or blackmail material, is used. This two-fold approach seldom fails and the stick is often brought to bear before it's even needed, just to make sure.

Crime is fundamental to the functioning of the Ai-Jinn. By using an illegal method the criminal is able to make a higher gain and thus be more successful. Although the Ai-Jinn are involved in several world wide criminal activities, it is the street level crime which they are better known for.

Their legions of yakuza, Triads, yardies, jacks and bangers (to name a few) create a network of soldiers who between them are capable of almost anything. This comprehensive army of loyal men and women are practically ubiquitous so if something needs doing, the chances are the Ai-Jinn have a group in place who can respond within hours and get the problem fixed.

The major problem with this type of methodology is that at any time the UIG can simply remove your soldiers from the battlefield. The UIG, if they deem it necessary, can destroy a Triad cell overnight with no explanation to the Ai-Jinn as to why they have killed a group of employees. If the same happened to a Federation or E.I. asset the fallout would be substantial. Such is the problem of working outside the law, what does not protect you can be used against you.

A certain amount of losses are expected within the Ai-Jinn business model. They realise that their assets may be captured, depersonalised, confiscated or destroyed but the benefits are

> *Fine: A bribe paid by a rich man to escape the lawful penalty of his crime*
>
> *Henry Louis Mencken*

BOSOZOKU / LIGHTNING TRIBES

Don't worry about death, we ride for those who died

-Bosozoku saying

The emergence of these gangs coincided with the growth of the motor industry in Japan in the 1950s. Throughout the 20th and 21st centuries they evolved from being simple motorcycle enthusiasts to rebellious teenagers to gangs of anarchic criminals.

Long ago each gang had a large membership and so violence between the tribes was rare as the potential casualty rate was huge. Over time, for a range of reasons, the typical gang dropped to only 25 members, this made it reasonable to attack another gang with the possibility of wiping them out. These circumstances led the gangs to seek support from the yakuza who, in exchange for fealty, offered to protect them from their rivals.

Although this might sound good the deals made were almost invariably a bad idea. The yakuza are unforgiving masters and would typically demand full body tattoos, regular cash payments and assistance in certain areas of their work.

The bosozoku's shift to hard crime was inevitable and they were essentially categorised as yakuza by the law. As membership of the yakuza was a crime in itself the bosozoku had little to lose and threw their lot in with the yaks. Although they are not full yakuza and are not entitled to the same tattoos it is sufficient for most bosozoku and they enjoy the reputation the association affords them.

As it stands now in 2500 you might consider the bosozoku to be the Yakuza's more impetuous, anarchic children. The gangs are still made up primarily of youths between the ages of 14 to 19 who spend the majority of their time causing havoc, prowling around cities on their modded motorbikes, terrorising the citizenry and waiting for the call from their masters.

Method
With their Yakuza backing the bosozoku have become extremely self-confident. A gang of 25 will think nothing of pulling up outside a bar and trashing the place, helping themselves to drink and money in the process. They have been known to goad UIG officers into chases, which they will then steer into busy areas such as shopping malls or town plazas in an attempt to get the officers to hit innocents with their cars.

These lawless outbursts are tolerated by their yakuza masters to some small degree but any activity which compromises operations or draws too much UIG scrutiny will be punished with the highest severity. This could involve the culprits being forced to sever their own fingers, hands or worse.

The Yakuza and consequently the Ai-Jinn use the bosozoku as either a distraction or a terror tool. If a casino is failing to pay its protection money then the bosozoku may be asked to ride by each night and pay the casino a visit until the money arrives. Alternatively they may be asked to cause some havoc in a certain part of the city in order to divert the UIG's attention away from something going on elsewhere.

Style
Bosozoku have a distinctive style which they enjoy displaying. Below is a list of common clothing styles worn.

Bandages wrapped tightly around the torso
Wrap around sunglasses
Full length military style coats adorned with kanji or imperialist icons
Industrial style coveralls
Surgical masks or more recently rebreather masks
Dungarees
Baggy trousers tucked into high boots
Hachimaki headbands (often white and red)
Full body tattoos are common

Females
Excessive makeup
High heeled buckled boots
Long dyed hair

Males
Coats are often worn open with no shirt on
Greased quiff hairstyles are common

Equipment
Bosozoku will always be mounted on motorcycles, some tribes may be able to upgrade to grav-bikes but there is still a preference for Shi Yukiro-made sports bikes. The gangs will be well armed, often carrying Molotov cocktails, short swords, katanas and pistols. They may occasionally have flack jackets and helmets but this would be unusual.

Their bikes are generally modified with illegally installed upgrades to make them faster and noisier. The amplified noise is often changed to sound like screaming making their arrival fairly intimidating.

Territory
The bosozoku gangs operate mainly in Japan with a few being found in some other east Asian cities. They are too unpredictable and chaotic to be allowed to run free in the Ai-Jinn's own territory. The demoralising effect the gangs have on the residents of Japan's open-cities is a pleasing side effect.

Any Japanese open or old-city has between 10 and 30 bosozoku gangs operating at any one time. There tends to be some rivalry between the gangs and not all of them are allied with the Ai-Jinn. The fights between them are violent, bloody affairs, often involving weapons such as bike chains, tyre irons, swords and Molotovs.

Shi Yukiro
A number of bosozoku consider themselves loyal to Japan and thus in some small part the Shi Yukiro. Although the Shi Yukiro do not officially endorse their activities they often receive backing from individual divisions operating in their area. These gangs follow all the same methods but tend to direct their violence and anger at enemies of the Japanese people, namely Ai-Jinn sympathisers. The information they need is kindly supplied by Shi Yukiro Agents.

Playing Bosozoku

Agents are generally not suitable to be bosozoku characters as they will be too old and not of the right mind set. This does not mean you can't create a bosozoku Agent however; if you want to go ahead.

What is more likely is that an Ai-Jinn Agent is ex-bosozoku and, having left the gang, joined the corporation. He may still have many of his contacts and could be seen as a mentor by some of the members. If you want to do this the GM may allow you to purchase contacts in bosozoku which can be useful for getting the gang to act as a distraction or terror tool as described on the previous page.

Sample Tribe Names

Black Emperors
Road Devils
Night Kings
Nagoya 50
Genshi
Kokuryu
X Sayonara
Zenryoku

Plot Ideas

1. You must gain the trust and respect of a bosozoku gang. The Corporation wishes to use them as a terror tool in the coming months.

2. A bosozoku gang has got some extremely high-end bikes and are proving very difficult to catch. Find out how they got the bikes.

3. Something is wiping out the bosozoku one by one leaving no trace. Stop it before it kills all of them.

4. The Shi Yukiro are turning the bosozoku gangs by offering them cash and tech. Teach them the meaning of loyalty.

5. Unaffiliated bosozoku gangs have been attacking corporate assets in lightning raids. Stop them.

6. A charismatic leader has united 8 gangs into a single unit. They believe they are unstoppable. Try to create infighting within the newly allied unit.

7. The UIG are clamping down on motorcycle gangs and starting with some of the Ai-Jinn's most useful allies. Help them in their war against the law.

8. Each year each bosozoku elects a champion. These champions race in a deadly event across Tokyo leaving suffering and destruction in their wake.

The Clangers get kind of a bad rep, all that violence an' extortion an' all, but you ask me, they're just a lot more upfront than the rest of the Five. Lots of businessmen wind up crooks, 's a well-known fact. Clangers just took the most successful crooks and gave 'em control of business from the start. Same result, just their methods are a bit more direct. Seems to be working out pretty well for 'em so far.

attr: Dino Collins, social-political commentator/alcoholic

YARDIES

Yardies is a term used to describe Jamaican gangsters who ply their trade dealing primarily drugs and guns. The word 'yardie' comes from the fact that in the impoverished areas of Kingston where the gangs originally hail from the housing projects contained communal yards. These areas were extremely poor and became a fertile environment for violent gang warfare.

Originally yardies were not considered organised criminals as they lacked the structure associated with groups like the Triad or Mafia. In the last few centuries the story has changed significantly. With their predilection for violent and spontaneous gun crime it has become necessary for them to protect themselves from their rivals, the Corporations and the police. For the most part all of this has been achieved by working with the Ai-Jinn corporation.

The Ai-Jinn Alliance

By maintaining a loose relationship with the Ai-Jinn the yardies are able to ensure a constant supply of drugs and guns. Although they welcome this facilitation to trade, they draw the line at protection. Yardie gangs are proud and refuse to allow Ai-Jinn Agents to come and assist them in fire fights.

The Ai-Jinn are also adept at greasing the legal wheels which can help considerably when a gang has been overpowered and hauled in by the UIG. Again, they are not pleased to have to rely on the Ai-Jinn but in their war against Babylon, the end justifies the means.

It should be noted however that the relationship between the Ai-Jinn and the yardies is tenuous at best. The yardies believe they are exploiting the Ai-Jinn and getting the best deal. The Ai-Jinn are of course aware of this and do not push things too hard. If the yardies began to feel owned or manipulated, they would likely turn on their allies like a rabid dog.

Independents Yardies

Some purist gangs refuse to ally with the Ai-Jinn, considering the alliance to be a sign of weakness. These rebels are often targeted by Ai-Jinn divisions under orders to either bring the gang to heel or wipe them out.

It's obviously not working though, the independent gangs tend to work together to 'fight the power' and their operational methods are not influenced by the Ai-Jinn meaning they are far more unpredictable and potentially dangerous.

Religion

Over the past two hundred years religion has become more and more important to yardie gangs as they find their culture being wiped out by the inexorable march of the corporations.

Rastafari

Most yardies follow a religion known as Rastafari, which is an old testament religion that focuses on the one god 'Jah'. They believe the spirit of Jah resides within them hence referring to themselves as 'I and I'.

They believe the promised land of Zion (Ethiopia) has been left to them by Jah and they reject Western society often referring to it as Babylon. This rejection is part of the reason that they will only maintain the loosest of connection with the Ai-Jinn. Obviously the

Ai-Jinn is based in the East but much of their philosophy and commercialisation mirrors western trends.

Followers of Rastafari also have a ceremony which involves the smoking of cannabis while talking about relevant topics. This could range from discussing personal problems to planning the next job. It should be noted that the version of Rastafari which is practiced by yardies in 2500 is a fairly corrupted and bastardised version of its original form but nonetheless, brings spiritual fulfilment to those who observe its tenets.

It is not surprising then that there is also a contingent of yardies in the Comoros Corporation and a few of those who pay passing homage to the Order of the True Faith.

Voodoo (Vodou)

Note: The spelling Vodou has been used to denote the original, peaceful form of the religion. Voodoo is used to describe its less savoury form.

Although originally a peaceful religion based on protection and spirituality modern voodoo cults, especially within the yardies, have taken on a more sinister bent. True followers of the original vodou religion would be appalled at what has happened to their faith.

The main reasons for the popularity of voodoo within yardie culture is not as a form of personal enlightenment but more as a tool of fear and intimidation. With the increase of faith and greater acceptance of the unknowable the power of suggestion has become extremely powerful.

Blood letting, the use of dolls, curses and even forms of Satanism are rife among the religion's practitioners. These methods are all very effective in intimidating the weak willed and adding an air of deathly mystery to yardie voodoo posses.

But does it really work? Many would maintain it does and although the evidence is insubstantial the possibility that somewhere deep within the warrens of Haitian or African old cities someone has managed to use telepathy to bring these vile rituals to life is not ridiculous.

Adding voodoo to your game

If a player is unlucky enough to get themselves cursed by a voodoo master, you should feel free to decide upon a debilitating condition which would be explicable with a telepathic variant.

For example, imagine a variant of Biokinesis where the victim loses 1HP a day or a version of Telekinesis which damages the optic nerves rendering the victim blind.

Unless you wish to take your game into the realms of the fantastic you should avoid curses such as 'ravens will peck you to death' or 'your loved ones will all die by this time next year'.

Be creative but make sure your curses are feasible, either through telepathic variation or through self-imposed paranoia. If someone really believes in the power of voodoo and is cursed to die, it's not unheard of for their heath to degenerate over the next few months as they become so scared of the curse it begins to physically affect them.

Comoros yardies

With the religious and spiritual tendencies of yardies it is easy to see how they could find allies within the Comoros corporation and indeed many do. The main clash is that although Comoros regularly engage in acts of violence, as a principle, they cannot condone gun running, drug dealing and the general social destruction that yardie business entails.

The yardie groups which are affiliated with Comoros tend to curtail their activities somewhat and co-operate with Comoros Agents to ensure the end justifies the means.

Style

Yardies are a diverse lot and although many favour luxury cars and expensive jewellery, others prefer camo trousers, flack jackets and heavy boots. Dread-locks are still the norm although nowadays all kinds of hair styles are present.
Their trademark is brutal, open and impulse gun crime. Yardies are not afraid to pull up in their big cars, get out and spray the streets with gunfire if it will achieve the desired effect.

There is an unwritten rule among yardies of respect and if breached you can expect rival groups to band together to right the wrong. This rule is hard to nail down and there is nothing saying 'you can't kill him' it's just something you know.

To yardies murder is little more than part of business. Their killings are seen as badges of honour and let others know the individual means business.

Playing Yardies

As an Agent of the Ai-Jinn a yardie makes an excellent character. The fact that he has been split from his posse is a minor inconvenience when compared to the opportunities available as an Agent.

The GM should allow any yardie character to have contacts in his posse. A yardie would typically look for ways to acquire and sell drugs or guns whenever possible. It would also add a lot of interest to the character if they were to at least have a passing interest in one of the religions.

Sample Names

The Children of Ja
Zionites
The Snakes
The Chosen
The Last of Samedi

Plot Ideas

1. A yardie posse has cursed one of your Corporation's best Agents. Find the posse and convince them to remove the curse.

2. A posse has been going over the top making dozens of random killings just to scare their rivals. Take them out.

3. The Ai-Jinn need better control of the drug trade in one of their cities. Contact the yardies in the city and try to set up a mutually beneficial arrangement.

4. Yardies have stolen a shipment of new weapons intended for a special ops division. The weapons must be recovered and the yardies taught some respect.

5. A yardie patriarch has asked to see a representative from the Corporation. Your division has been selected to meet him.

6. A voodoo posse has been enacting some potent curses on their rivals. Find out how they are doing it.

7. Street warfare has erupted between several posses. It must be stopped before the city burns.

8. Ai-Jinn allied yardies are at war with Shi Yukiro backed yakuza. Make sure your side wins.

JACKS

Jacks have appeared on the organised crime scene relatively recently. They are a worldwide group of hackers, data miners and social engineers who use and abuse the World Data Net for personal gain or on behalf of paying clients.

They began as a faction within the American Underground (AU), using their skills to mess up Federation networks, damage databases and even place false orders into the system. This ended up costing the Federation millions of credits and so they began to put even more cash into rooting out these scum. Huge rewards were offered and the jacks soon found themselves being given up by the American people they were trying to help.

It was time they became a little more organised; rather than co-operating with the rest of the AU they sealed themselves off, trusting only each other and communicating with the rest of the AU only through obscure and bizarre methods.

As a more organised unit, the jacks became even more influential. Within a few years they had accrued enormous amounts of wealth and power which they used to ensure their secrecy and expand their operations.

Today the jacks have all but forgotten the AU. They will do jobs for them but only for good money; gone are the days where the jacks stood for freedom of expression and sticking it to the man.

Organisation
Since the jacks broke away from the Underground their structure has changed significantly and the original members have mysteriously faded away from memory. Exactly when the hub, cell and Server format was adopted and how it arose is unknown.

The jacks do not have a very typical structure in that there are no strong codes of conduct and the pecking order is only there for convenience. They work in isolated cells scattered across the civilised world.

These cells are all linked to central management hubs which are responsible for finding work and passing it on to a cell. There are around 25 hubs in the world and each ultimately reports to the shadowy *Server*.

Cells
These are groups of 3 to 10 jacks, each of whom is either a hacker, data miner or social engineer. They tend to work in teams in non-descript locations, far from the prying eyes of the UIG. They will typically be assigned work which is geographically distant from their physical location. For example, someone employed to hack a

database in Beijing may well be located in New York.
Hackers
We are all familiar with hackers. They are highly skilled in bypassing security systems on computers and accessing or planting data.

Data Miner
Data Miners look at data and extrapolate useful information from it. They work in close conjunction with the hackers to interpret the data gathered in the hacking runs. What might appear to be a cryptic series of numbers, may in fact be encoded co-ordinates revealing the locations of UIG witnesses.

On a more domestic note, they could simply be looking at a shopping bill to determine what kind of person the target is and how best to put some pressure on to make them do a simple task. For example, noticing that the target purchases child's toys will allow them to make threats against their family.

Obviously you could go around to his house and achieve the same result but the jacks are not hands-on criminals. They operate as far as possible from their targets and do not like to skulk around outside people's houses.

Social Engineers
These charismatic individuals are effectively conmen who trick others into divulging secrets of confidential information. For example, ringing up a secretary, pretending to be from the IT department and requesting an access password. Although companies are very wary of such tricksters, a good engineer can look for routes within routes, first starting right at the bottom of the chain with the lowliest employee who everyone overlooks and steadily working up.

A good social engineer will complement both the hacker and the miner, allowing them to do their work more quickly and with less illegal activity.

Hubs
The hubs are made up of the most savvy and hard-arsed of the jacks. They are ruthless deal makers and excellent brokers, always getting every possible credit out of the client without letting them realise it. The client may even be the target of a data miner, who will inform the hub how much he thinks they can afford.

Although the hubs are comprised of a number of individuals (normally 3-6) who will occasionally meet up, they do not hang round in groups like the cells. They can range from being prominent businessmen and corporate Agents to corrupt UIG officers or even seemingly innocent civilians. They simply receive calls on their encrypted lines and then pass the jobs on to a relevant cell. Transactions are made in slip credit to safe drop-sites and work does not begin until all payments have been completed.

The hub takes 40% of all payments made, the remaining 60% going to the jacks working in the cells.

The only common point of contact all jacks have is the Server. If they want to communicate with a cell to pass on orders or contact another hub to co-ordinate a big job it must be done via the server. This ensures the jacks are totally isolated from one another and the organisation is all but indestructible. Obviously the elimination of the Server would cripple the entire network in one go.

The Server

No one knows who or what the Server is. Everyone in the jacks can contact the Server whenever they want to; this is done via text to a specific WDN address. When the UIG have captured and interrogated cell members and the address has been disclosed, it has changed within seconds. The last few addresses discovered were:

server2.tokyo2.jpn
theserver.oldkent.eng
serve.nyork.usa
server4.wyoming4.usa
serve9.glenorie.aus

Any questions directed at the Server will either be answered directly or the message 'insufficient permission' will be relayed back. The information will not discuss the nature of an ongoing job as that is the function of the hub.

The UIG have several suspicions about the nature of the Server but they have never even got close to an arrest. The current suspects are:

An ex-Aries graduate using his brilliance to shape the world
The Children of Minerva enacting some unfathomable plan
A Rogue Archon collecting data
A Corporate entity, possibly the Ai-Jinn
The Original Founders
Highly placed UIG officers using the jacks for work that is unethical but must be done.

Playing Jacks

As an Agent it is not really feesible to play cell members but you can play a Hub.

HUB OPERATIVE

Sample Prerequisites

Presence 7
Computers and A.I. 4
Business 5
Attitude 5
Lying & Acting 6
Psychology 5
Corp. Knowledge 4
Position of Influence (e.g. Agent, Officer, City Official, Business Owner)

A hub member deals with requests from clients and then passes orders on to a cell via the server. You'll be expected to barter on price, arrange the drop-offs and communicate with the Server. On occasion you'll need to meet the other members of your hub to discuss policies and events and sort out finances.

However, you will receive extra cash at the start of each mission brief. (This is not connected to your mission brief; it's just a convenient time to award the money.)

You'll receive (D10 + Corp. Knowledge) x 100¢

Getting Caught

The job is extremely risky and membership of the jacks is punishable by instant depersonalisation. It is really up to the GM to judge how well you deal with your secrets. If you keep mentioning them or don't take enough care in your communications or money drops then you may well end up being monitored by the UIG. Catching a hub member is a real prize for them and you will likely skip standard procedure and be taken directly to the Shadowmen*

Do the Corporation Know?

If you are playing Ai-Jinn then being a member of the jacks is perfectly acceptable as long as it does not come before the corporation. As an E.I. Agent you should judge the situation for yourself but if you are Federation, Comoros or Shi Yukiro then you had better keep it quiet. These corporations have issues with the jacks and their methods and you will more than likely end up in an interrogation suite.

*Shadowmen are not described in this book and will be covered in a future supplement. They are a Black Ops arm of the UIG.

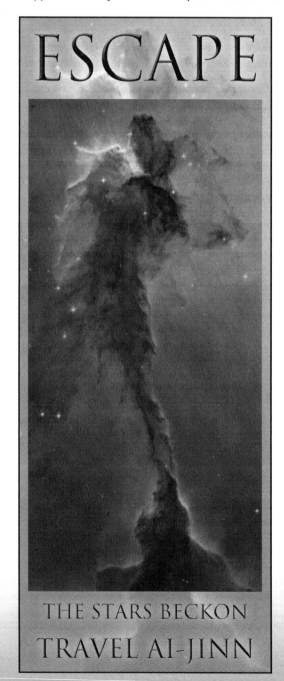

ESCAPE

THE STARS BECKON
TRAVEL AI-JINN

NEW CRIMINAL ACTIVITIES

> *The unified currency of Earth has presented such wonderful economic opportunities. Now I can steal from 100 different countries with just one siphon stream.*
>
> *Hody Kessex - Financier for the Jacks.*

This section lists a number of criminal professions in existence today. As well as these types you can also assume that any criminal activities that were going on in the 21st century will also be present in the 26th, albeit revised.

CLONERS / BODYSWAPPERS / ORGAN LEGGERS

Ever since mankind realised it could replace damaged or failing body parts there has been a dark and bloody trade in human organs. That market is still flourishing today and with the advent of cheap, effective and easily available anti-rejection drugs, getting a new organ is as simple as buying headache tablets, if a little more expensive. It should be noted that it is not just organs that are sold; blood, tissue and even individual cells are in high demand with a range of clients.

The typical organ legger will normally use one of the following methods to acquire his stock

Raiding Medical Facilities
This is the most dangerous but will generally yield a range of high quality, well-stored stock with the added bonus that equipment and relevant drugs can often be secured at the same time.

Outcast Harvesting
By hunting down outcasts or outlaws the cloner is able to secure a selection of fresh bodies which can be stored until needed or harvested straight away and the organs placed into some type of stasis. This method is extremely cheap but the quality of the organs is questionable. Typically outcasts are in poor health and their organs have been abused or neglected. Regardless, the savings can be passed on to the customer and so those short of cash will often find themselves buying outcast organs.

Illegal Cloning
This setup requires a fair amount of expense and skill but the results are high-grade, unused, tailor-made organs. More details on setting up your own illegal cloning lab can be found in Machines of War.

Bagging / Body Mugging
This involves just grabbing people off the street, either to order or as and when the opportunity arises. Unlike taking outlaws this practice is illegal and highly risky; however it is extremely cheap and can provide a wealth of high quality organs. This practice is most common in open cities such as those in Tokyo, Osaka or Los Angeles. Such places are not as secure as spire cities and tend to have a wealthy population, thus ensuring a steady supply and demand.

SNELLING DRUG LABS

Manufacturing drugs is nothing new as far as crime goes, manufacturing ultra-high purity drugs using genetic bioconstructs is.

Snellings are one of the first and most rudimentary BIO's ever created. Resembling something between a caterpillar and a giant ant, Snellings are about the size of a small dog and do little but consume raw materials and excrete refined drugs. Snellings are classified by what drug they produce but with the proper biochemical treatments (acquirable on the black market with a bit of time, money and danger) you can alter their metabolism to produce a something a little different.

The drugs produced by Snellings require no processing other than boiling off excess moisture and cutting with cheaper substances to be made ready for the street, allowing even operations without the expertise to run a drug lab to get in on the racket.

However, Snellings are BIOs and as such are illegal to possess on Earth, most of them exist in battery farms on Miller-Urey in the laboratories of Gemini Bioware and Two Snakes Pharmaceuticals, endlessly producing vast quantities of medical drugs to be shipped back to Eurasian Inc. hospitals.

A Crack Snelling, Roaming Wild and Free

The ones that do make it to Earth are usually smuggled in by the Ai-Jinn or Eurasian Incorporated and biochemically reprogrammed to produce illicit substances. The penalty for trafficking in or owning BIOs on Earth is a loss of 20 to 40 rank points, even for the relatively harmless and innocuous Snelling.

Running Your Own Snelling Lab
It's not particularly hard to look after a Snelling. You must simply fulfill the following critera.

1. Feed the Snelling a specialist nutrient.
This cannot be bought and must be manufactured. A month's supply costs 100 credits and must be made by hand. This either requires

A) A successful 'Intelligence + Science' roll.
B) Possession of the BIOkeeper Training (Machines of War).

2. Tend the Snelling each day.
The Snelling is a delicate creature, its environment must be monitored and health checked daily. This either requires the BIOkeeper Training or a daily 'Intelligence + Science' roll. If you fail the roll, next day you must make the roll at -4. If you fail this roll the Snelling dies.

Obviously Agents will have a hard time running their own Snelling labs as their duty will preoccupy them.

3. A Snelling Tank
This can be created at home by anyone with Mechtronics 3 or more. It costs around 100 credits to build a single tank which is around the size of a medium fish tank.

Harvesting the Product
Each week a Snelling produces a variable quantity of the target compound.

You should note that the snelling can only produce the compound it was intended to make. Common Snellings you may come across are listed below with their rough weekly yield.

Ox (EB)	3D10 Doses
Wolverine (MoW)	2D10 Doses
Lambanic Acid	D2 Doses
Metapsitrophin	D4 Doses
Tamba	3D10 Doses
TDT	D2 Doses

EB	Eastern Bank
MoW	Machines of War

GRINDING

Taking its name from an old computer game term, grinding is the disreputable act of accepting UIG rank awards for taking down bounties that you yourself did not kill. Paying a grinder to go out and bag your bounty for you and then taking the credit for the kill is highly illegal and spits on the whole premise behind the UIG rank system, essentially trading cash for rank. The punishment for paying a grinder is suitably draconian, with rank deductions being double that gained from all illicitly bought bounties and the immediate revoking of the perpetrator's bounty hunting license, but the practise continues regardless. Grinders are subject to the loss of 4 rank points per confirmed instance of their crime and have all assets frozen until such time as they can be properly investigated and fined. As a result, grinders usually charge a high price for their 'service', often double the value of the bounty itself.

MEATDOLLS

One of the most terrible crimes on the books, roughly equivalent with a combined kidnap, murder, rape and forced labour charge, the practise of creating Meatdolls is punishable by instant depersonalisation and internment in Kildanna penitentiary. The process involves kidnapping a human being and overwriting their brain with an artificial psyche matrix for sale as slaves, usually to sexual deviants. The name comes from the fact that artificial psyche matrices are rarely ever as complete as one derived from a real human mind, leading to the victims often behaving in a way that seems pre-scripted or doll-like, moreso even than droids or replicants in many cases. Fortunately, creating Meatdolls requires sophisticated and highly expensive neurological patterning equipment - similar to that used by the UIG to train marshals in a short period of time - and can generally only be carried out by extremely wealthy and successful criminal operations. Despite the expense of the setup costs and the ease with which such operations can be traced if kept in the same place for too long it still continues because the tradeoff in hard credit can be extraordinary, especially once they start taking orders for the abduction of specific individuals.

OFFWORLD PEOPLE-TRAFFICKING

A rising number of organised criminal groups have begun offering passage off-Earth to those who would not normally be able to gain legal permission. Such individuals include, among others:

Outlaws
Those on parole
Those who want to conduct business off-Earth but want the UIG to believe that they have not left the planet.
Those who wish to smuggle something with them.
Those who cannot afford to be detected going through a scanner such as a Cultist with illegal upgrades.
Those who have been declined an emigration order.
Those with insufficient funds to support themselves upon arrival.
Those who are being taken against their will such as prostitutes or slave workers.

Although many criminals around the world provide this service it is mainly Ai-Jinn connected gangsters who organise these trips as they have better access to shuttles than most. Ai-Jinn craft leave the planets surface on a weekly basis, taking supplies into space or simply ferrying individuals around the stars.

Typical penalties for off-world trafficking are:

For the person being trafficked	-10 Rank Points
For the trafficker	-10 Rank Points per Person
Unwilling victim	No penalty

If the customer is a criminal the trafficker's penalty is doubled.

Typical Costs
Close to Earth (Moon, AMS Orbital)	5,000¢
Sol System (Mars, Venus)	20,000¢
Further	100,000+¢

tle Class Cyberlin - The Retribution of Jing Lei
rently stationed at Amur Border Spire in preparation for the
vitable reclamation of the Eastern Province.

SECTION 8

LOCATIONS

THE XING GONG ORBITAL

I hate to advocate drugs, alcohol, violence, or insanity to anyone, but they've always worked for me.

-Hunter S. Thompson

Every Corporation recognises the simple fact that even their biomechanically enhanced Agents are still ultimately human and are as subject to stress and fatigue as anyone else, perhaps even more so given the dangerous and often violent nature of their work. After all, while a soldier can reasonably expect to go their whole career without ever discharging their firearm outside of training exercises, an Agent rarely goes a week on-duty without emptying multiple clips.

It also bears mentioning that while Agents receive numerous physical enhancements that make their bodies far more durable than those of normal humans, they still retain all-too-human psyches. With the sheer amount of psychological stress their work puts them under it's not surprising that Agents frequently suffer from a variety of mental ailments, the most common being post-traumatic stress disorder. Simply put, there are only so many times you can have your torso shot into a bloody pulp, lose limbs to flashing ion katanas or track Machina cultists through lightless subterranean warrens before it starts to get to you, even if on an intellectual level you know that little can do you permanent harm.

It was with this in mind that the Ai-Jinn created the Xing Gong station, an orbital recreation facility where their Agents could spend their downtime in a comfortable and therapeutic manner. Of course, this being the Ai-Jinn, 'comfortable and therapeutic' translates into what amounts to a pleasure-palace in space, stocked to the ceiling with booze, hookers and exotic narcotics.

The concept is hardly new, E.I. has been running the entertainment orbital Vastaag for some time now, a structure that positively dwarfs Xing Gong, but what the station provides Ai-Jinn Agents with is something they cannot get anywhere else - security. Xing Gong is entirely owned and operated by the Ai-Jinn with access restricted to employees and the rare trusted outsider by exclusive membership. There Agents can be assured peace of mind during their stay, safe in the knowledge that they won't be spied upon, something they couldn't hope for on Vastaag.

THE STATION
The Xing Gong orbital vaguely resembles a colossal gunmetal-grey flower slowly spinning in space, the different sectors of the station constructed as petal-shaped segments surrounding a long central generator spindle. Always forward-thinking, the Ai-Jinn made the station modular and more of these 'petals' can be added to the superstructure of the spindle as needed, providing the station with even more facilities or quickly separated from the main structure to protect the rest of the station in case of fire or disease.

The command dome from which the station is administrated sits in the centre, at the top of the spindle, providing administrative staff with instant access to any of the radial sectors.

The interior of the station that most visitors see is opulently decorated in a combination of styles from the Ai-Jinn's various territorial countries, most predominantly those of China, Thailand and Korea. Exterior windows are present on every sector, allowing visitors a breathtaking view over Earth. Accommodation is universally luxurious and although the silk sheets on the beds may be high-quality synthetics rather than the real thing and the decor a little too far past the point of ostentation to be truly considered tasteful, by the standards of most Agents, who tend to be rough-and-ready sorts anyway, it's a dream come true.

Divisions between facilities on Xing Gong are rarely distinct; the whole station seems to resemble a huge, raucous, non-stop party. However, there is some degree of specialisation in the different sectors of the station, with each catering to a particular flavour of vice.

GAMBLING SECTOR

The Golden Pot Casino
A Las Vegas-style casino that is most people's first stop for gambling on the station, the Golden Pot dominates the entire sector, taking up a full third of the floor space. The gaming tables are running 24/7 and drinks are free and constantly available, making losing all your money a much more enjoyable experience. In general, though, the Golden Pot is far less corrupt than most casinos are and gamers still have a chance to make a big win, just not with any greater frequency than that determined by their luck.

Jimmy Ya's Card House
True professional gamblers disdain the Golden Pot in favour of Jimmy Ya's place; a smoky, low-ceilinged bar backed by a dozen private rooms where cutthroat games of blackjack and poker are run. Anyone willing and able to put up the entry bet can join a game, but many of the players are experts, employed by Ya himself with part of their winnings going to the house. Those with enough skill stand a much greater chance of making a big win at Jimmy Ya's than at the Golden Pot but the less talented are viciously fleeced without mercy. Despite this mercenary attitude, Agents with a passion for gambling are likely to find the games run at Jimmy Ya's immensely satisfying.

Red Knives!
Xing Gong's arena, Red Knives!, attracts gamblers and casual spectators equally. Every night depersonalised, violent criminals shipped in from Kildanna penitentiary fight to the death for the amusement of the audience. Of course, given the rather jaded outlook of most Agents, only the most dangerous criminals are deemed fit for the Xing Gong arena, preferably those with augmentations or post-human skills, such as Chimera and telepaths. Bets can be placed on the outcome of fights, and even

audience participation is permitted should any of the Agents like to blow off some steam, safe in the knowledge that med-techs stand by should things get too hot to handle. A speciality of the house is 'The Splatterdrome', where the fighters tear each other to pieces in a rotating spherical cage using only knives while the arena's artificial gravity is deactivated, sending droplets and streamers of gore flying in literally all directions.

NIGHTCLUB SECTOR

Absolüt Zero

Mimicking the Eurasian club scene in its style, Absolüt Zero is the place for an Agent whose idea of fun is loud electronic music, heavy drinking and drug abuse. The club hires a number of skilled DJ's (including the ever-popular 'Unnatural Jay', an award-winning music A.I. that was stolen from the UIG by Ai-Jinn Agent Yu Bailong on a drunken prank) and produces much of its own music. An expensive hologrid system integrated into the walls makes the nightly light-shows something that has to be seen to be believed. For those seeking chemical comfort, the bar serves a speciality speedball cocktail of alcohol, Savage, natural cocaine and TDT called an 'Absolüt High' alongside its more common drinks.

Huokang (The Fire Pit)

Huokang is encased in the best soundproofing money can buy for good reason; it is one of the few places where neurothrash can be played legally. Neurothrash combines rhythmic, tribal, thrash-metal with subsonic recordings of the death-cries of condemned serial killers and other, even stranger things, looped through a fractal synthesiser. It has the side-effect of inducing extreme feelings of undifferentiated hatred in those who spend too long listening to it, and as a result Huokang experiences brutal nightly barfights. It is often the last stop for Agents looking to "psych-up" for their next mission before leaving the station.

The Red Petal Lounge

Far from the blaring music and raucous parties, the Red Petal Lounge is a place of pure relaxation. The lights are always dim, the music always soothing and attractive service staff ever available to provide whatever the customer desires. It is also the venue where the highest paid courtesans do business as the customers are unlikely to prove violent or difficult. In short, the Red Petal Lounge is every gangster's decadent dream come true. Those who make it their first stop on the station often never go anywhere else, content to while away their time in an opiate stupor, intermittently rising from their silk cushions to indulge in more drink or pliant company.

PEOPLE

KONG MENGTIAN
Station Administrator (Rank 6, Level 31)

Having been employed by the Ai-Jinn for nearly two hundred years, Kong Mengtian has been given a retirement of sorts as the administrator of the Xing Gong orbital. A Chinese man who appears to be in his late forties thanks to extensive use of anagathics, Mengtian takes great pride that nobody leaves his station unsatisfied with their stay and takes a keen interest in all forms of entertainment and produce brought aboard. Friendly and outgoing to visitors but tyrannical and draconian to station staff, he has run the orbital well for many years by keeping standards high. Anything, be it drugs, drink or girls, that doesn't meet his standards will not make it onto the station. He has a strong belief in the adage that 'the customer is always right' and makes sure that his staff learn this well or they soon find themselves out of a job. Though he rarely has a chance to engage in combat anymore, Mengtian has kept up his training regimen and is a prodigiously skilled martial artist, his abilities elevated by cybernetics to levels that make him more than capable of going toe-to-toe with armed foes. Should Xing Gong ever come under internal attack he would be among the first into the fray.

Kong Mengtian

MISS FORTUNE
Courtesan (Rank 0, Level 3)

One of the most popular courtesans on the station, the woman going by the pseudonym of 'Miss Fortune' knows more information on undercover Ai-Jinn operations than anyone has a right to, there being a lot more that can be learned from an Agent in pillow-talk than can be tortured or intimidated out of them. Not only that but she understands that she knows too much and doesn't return to

Earth out of the (perhaps not entirely unwarranted) fear that she might be tracked down by a rival corporation or silenced by the Ai-Jinn. Miss Fortune figures that as long as she remains aboard Xing Gong the Ai-Jinn will not regard her as being a threat. Still, if a rival corporation could acquire her loyalty they'd have access to a veritable gold mine of Ai-Jinn dirty secrets, though she's far too knowledgeable about the way the corporations operate to be willing to leave the safety of the station without some tangible proof that she wouldn't be at risk.

UNNATURAL JAY
Music A.I. DJ (Rank -, Level 5)

'The music is all. People should die for it. People are dying for everything else, so why not the music?'

- Lou Reed

All A.I.s are created for a purpose, some are destined to provide the operating system for droids, some are meant to be installation administrators, the lowliest simply direct automated weapons. Unnatural Jay, however, was born to make music. More specifically, he was created to examine how people might react psychologically to a charismatic sentient A.I. in a prominent public position, as a precursor to the Archons taking a more direct role in world affairs. Having a sentient A.I. created for the sole purpose of producing music sparked a lot of controversy on Earth back when Unnatural Jay was made. Some even held to the position that a data-construct was incapable of the human creativity necessary to craft true art. Unnatural Jay proved them wrong, at least in terms of record sales and adoring fans. Even though he* hasn't had the same kind of stardom he once had since being stolen, Unnatural Jay is still satisfied with his lot aboard Xing Gong. Especially given that he has more artistic freedom now, rather than having to pander to UIG culture-trend analysts and their predictions. He has recently been working on a new composition that he feels could be his magnum opus, something that ought to be shared with all the Earth, a song capable of truly embodying the zeitgeist of the Corporate age. All he's having trouble with is the crescendo, the sound of a quarter of a million tons of superheated metal crashing on a city... but which city to choose?

*An abstraction based on Unnatural Jay's most commonly chosen avatar, A.I.s have no true gender.

MISSION HOOKS

1. Investigate rumours that a member of the station staff may be a spy who has managed to get past the background checks, all while posing as Agents on vacation.
2. Gladiators from the Red Knives! arena have broken loose, taken part of the station under siege, and are now holding an important corporate official hostage.
3. Keep watch on an envoy from a rival Corporation while they are enjoying a rare outsider pass into Xing Gong, all without tarnishing the Ai-Jinn's hospitality.
4. Take part in an inter-corporate poker competition conducted on Xing Gong, the competition is really a cover for a black-market in illicit information.
5. Investigate a series of strange disturbances in the stations security system.

At every turn, I find myself confounded by their damned bureaucracy; just when I think I have bribed or threatened or cajoled my way past the final layer of blank faceless obfuscation, I find another. But even now, with so much still hidden, a strange truth is beginning to emerge; the numbers simply do not stack up.

We have the figures for mining attrition, thanks to IMA disclosure requirements. Assume typical PR spin; double or even treble those. Ship manifests are never released, but we have all registered craft on record and can extrapolate likely numbers for permanent crew; again, if we accept that the Ai-Jinn are likely concealing some of their military space assets, we should err on the side of caution and increase these estimates threefold. Call it ten thousand people, then, who are either stationed off-planet long-term, or who do not survive the mines, in any given year.

On the other hand, even if we assume the very public facilities in Beijing, Changsha and Guangzhou are the only interstellar academies the Ai-Jinn maintain – which I submit is singularly unlikely – we know from their supply data that they must be operating at full capacity around eighty-two percent of each year; over twenty-one thousand men and women undergoing Far Space training annually. And I have seen the endless promotional campaigns; I have seen the vast and jostling crowds at the recruitment drives. Yuan Qingzhao has tapped every last ounce of charisma, sociological persuasion and ideological leverage to whip millions of her people into a patriotic fervour directed at the stars. Based on what I have seen here, I would estimate that the Corporation produces something closer to sixty thousand fully-trained spacers every year.

Are the Ai-Jinn secretly increasing the scale of their mining operations faster than they disclose under the IMA? Unquestionably. But I do not believe that their resource drive, clandestine though it might be, can account for the full extent of this discrepancy. Nor do there ever seem to be very many returned spacers sitting idle in the Spires and Old Cities. It is my unshakeable conviction that hundreds, if not thousands, of the people sent out on Far Drive craft every year simply vanish.... and are never spoken of again.

I believe I have located a source who can unlock the final piece of this puzzle; he fled from a research lab close by the Changsha plant, he tells me, and now lives as a fugitive here, in the slums of Xing Ma Duo. I will meet with him this evening, and deliver my full report when I have uncovered the truth.

-attr: UIG Special Investigator Benoir

(final communication from Xing Ma Duo Old City before outbreak of 'The April Atrocities', cf. Cult of Machina)

[SUPRESSED 15.4.2502, /unknownadmin]

[DELETED 15.4.2502, /unknownadmin]

HONG KONG SPIRE COMPLEX

> *We shape our buildings, thereafter they shape us.*
>
> *Sir Winston Churchill*

Note references to Hong Kong nowadays always refer to the Hong Kong Spire Complex. What's left of the original Hong Kong is referred to as Old Hong Kong or Hong Kong Old City.

Hong Kong Spire Complex, as it stands, is one of the single largest urbanisations in the world. When one bears in mind a large spire can accommodate just short of one million people and that Hong Kong comprises nine such spires, it's easy to see how it has become the urban horror that it is today.

Hong Kong is not the only Spire Complex in the world. The magnificent structures of both Austerity (Federation) and Catalan (EI) are examples of how space-conscious, high security accommodation can be sensitively constructed and efficiently operated in order to provide a highly desirable and successful accommodation system.

The Ai-Jinn, unfortunately, do not see the value in soaring, graceful structures or clean, artful interiors. Four of the nine spires were originally constructed in 2301 with only a cursory nod to aesthetics and luxury. As a result they did not have the same desirability that most of the world's spires possessed and residential uptake was slow.

The project had been extremely expensive and the governor of the Southern Province at the time, Andrew Li, was under enormous pressure to make the complex profitable. To this end he made an unprecedented and extremely brave decision by reducing the cost of spire living to an amount old city dwellers could afford. Compared to the quality of life in New Kowloon and nearby old cities, the already deteriorating spires of Hong Kong seemed like a palace. The influx of residents was predictably huge and the spires began to recover their costs.

Although this is not what the Ai-Jinn had planned for their spire complex, it was an undeniable success and Li was instructed to oversee the construction of another five spires to expand the complex. The idea being to house a massive percentage of the Ai-Jinn's lower class citizens in one place. This would not only keep them under control and away from the more discerning members of society, it would generate a substantial and continuous source of revenue.

Even the Ai-Jinn's more affluent spires tend to be filthy, grimy, neo-industrial mazes so it's not hard to imagine how Hong Kong degenerated over the next century. In true Ai-Jinn style the requirements for residence at the spire were minimal and amounted to 'can you pay the rent'. Even criminals were permitted to slip through the process as long as they could keep up the payments. The result was a mixture of residents ranging from middle of the road, productive citizens with decent jobs and good morals to low-down scum who would go out mugging each week to collect the next rent payment. It was as though the old cities had come to the spires, which indeed to some degree they had, and brought many of their problems with them. The spires, already filthy and rife with urban decay, went downhill year by year. Law enforcement was fairly selective and tended to take the attitude of 'yeah, it's bad here, but it's worse outside - so deal with it'.

Before things got out of hand the Ai-Jinn realised that if things went too far, Hong Kong would be no better than the old cities and so in 2408 additional security measures were put into place. The UIG were given full access to the spires in order to carry out patrols and investigations and Agent divisions were assigned to each of the nine main structures. Stricter entry requirements were implemented and although it's still possible for a criminal to buy his way in, it's not as easy as it once was.

These steps seem to have worked well for the past century and now Hong Kong, although far from pleasant, is at least vaguely civilised. It's still a dirty, depressing hole but it's safer than an old city and there are plenty of employment opportunities in the surrounding factories.

STRUCTURE OF THE HONG KONG SPIRE COMPLEX

Each spire is named after a colour. Although externally they are all the same rusty grey-black, inside, the peeling décor and graffiti-covered walls still show signs of the original colour schemes which mirrored their titles.

The Northern Spires

Red Spire	Hong Se Spire
Blue Spire	Lan Se Spire
Green Spire	Lu Se Spire
Black Spire	Hei Spire
Yellow Spire	Huang Spire

The Southern Spires

Orange Spire	Cheng Spire
Grey Spire	Hui Se Spire
White Spire	Chun Bai Spire
Gold Spire	Jin Zi Spire

The nine spires are divided into a group of four (The Southern Spires) and a group of five (The Northern Spires), the latter being the newer structures.

THE NORTHERN SPIRES

In the Northern spires there are dozens of walkways inter-connecting each of the spires. They vary in elevation from ground level all the way up to the higher floors hundreds of metres up. Most of these walkways are constructed of steel and reinforced poly-plastics, though age and neglect has left the windows scratched and mucky to the point of near opacity and the floors are normally a few millimetres deep in murky water that has leeched in from the rotting seals.

The Northern Spires were constructed with low cost housing in mind and so are even more warren like than their southern counterparts. Rooms range from cupboard-like to cramped and the only way to get a better suit is to move out. The plethora of money saving initiatives are always evident and include dingy lighting, thin walls, no carpets, fold out beds, inadequate lifts and metered electricity and water.

MANAGEMENT

As one might expect the spire management leaves something to be desired. At present Mr. Jun Dao, a high ranking Ai-Jinn official is responsible for the administration of the Northern Spires and, although a loyal member of the Corporation, is known to use the position to his advantage.

It's well known that criminals who reside in the Northern Spires are all well acquainted with Mr. Dao. On one side he takes a little extra rent each month to ensure the UIG don't come sniffing around and on the other he is more than happy to pass on relevant information so they can more easily earn the extra rent. He essentially keeps them in a trap, threatening them with exposure but at the same time forcing them to commit more crime to pay him off. Dao plays a dangerous game but with 15 Agent divisions at his beck and call, he can justifiably feel a certain sense of security.

Dao's overall policy with regard to handling incidents within the complex is predictably no nonsense. The Ai-Jinn give him a free hand to police the spires as he sees fit. The only real limitation is that things must be acceptable to superficial UIG scrutiny. Although CRO (common residential officer) squads patrol the spires, they are inexperienced and easy to manipulate.

The main issue arises when the UIG engage in targeted operations with the aim of dealing with a specific problem such as busting a drug ring or arresting a gang leader. In these cases more competent units such as marshals or Malenbrach will turn up and no amount of bribery or implied threats will keep them at bay. In these cases Dao just has to take the hit and trust that he has been cautious enough not to implicate himself.

THE SOUTHERN SPIRES

The Southern Spires, to the outside observer, are nearly identical to their northern counterparts but once inside there is a tangible difference. Although the exteriors are stained concrete and rusted steel, inside the corridors are freshly painted and free of litter. The air-con works and the lights don't flicker.

The governor here, a retired Agent named Miranda Kirkova is convinced that through a process of enforced education life can become better for the oppressed citizen.

The rent in the Southern Spires is considerably less than in the North but it comes at a cost not counted in credits. All residents are expected to undergo mandatory education for at least 1 hour a day. The more time you spend learning the lower the rent, generally to a minimum of 50%. Residents are continually assessed and if they are not showing improvements are given a warning or work related options. If they still refuse to comply they are eventually ejected from the complex.

So far the system works well; residents are, for the most part, keen to be able to save some money and the range of programs ensures that there is a learning opportunity for everyone. Even hardened criminals can be surprisingly enthusiastic when learning the 'real' power of a UIG officer or how to improve the condition of a damaged firearm.

It's true that in some cases the education will be abused but Kirkova believes that most people, given the opportunity, would rather earn a decent wage and be productive members of society.

Of course some cases are hopeless and individuals simply cannot learn or refuse to try. In these situations they are given the option to work for their place, cleaning, cooking, repairing and helping out all contribute to the general upkeep of the spire.

The Southern Spires are not as profitable as the Northern ones but the Ai-Jinn see great promise in Kirkova's work. To have their lower class citizenry at a reasonable level of occupational skill has great potential and the crime rate in the Southern Complex is extremely low.

Plot Ideas

1. Crime has got out of hand in the Northern Spires. Your division must enter the spire, appraise the situation and present a plan to Mr. Dao. Then if appropriate, execute it.

2. Your division has been given a list of people complying with the rules of the Southern Spires. One by one, they must be found, questioned and dealt with.

> In the pre-Federation era, Hong Kong was infamous for its pollution, 'Fragrant Harbour' – the direct translation of the Cantonese – being something of an irony even then. Today, the place is a masterpiece of squalid horror. On the island, the nine towers of the complex proper reach up like rusty nails from layer upon layer of grimy, lightless slums, trailing a ragged cobweb of dilapidated walkways bearing ceaseless toiling queues of human traffic. Across the thin slurry of black oil, filth, and industrial contaminants that was once a harbour, the broken sub-city of New Kowloon squats like a huddle of tombstones on the shattered remnants of the old mountain range. The sky is an ochre swirl of airborne grime, bloodied in places by the lethal fumes of factory fires. Travellers are advised to bring their own drinking water.
>
> From The Solitary World: A Guidebook to the Ai-Jinn Territories
>
> Western Federation Tourism, Trade and Foreign Relations Section

NEW KOWLOON

> *Architecture, of all the arts, is the one which acts the most slowly, but the most surely, on the soul.*
>
> *Ernest Dimet*

Located approximately thirty miles north of Hong Kong Old City, the walls of New Kowloon rise out of the ground, two miles wide on each side. When the Ai-Jinn began its monumental unification of Asia there were an understandably large number of conflicts that arose as a result, and with them came dispossessed civilians. New Kowloon, named after the infamous Kowloon Walled City, began its life as a city-sized relocation camp for victims of the the Ai-Jinn's expansion.

Originally conceived as a series of unconnected tenement blocks, subsequent expansion and rebuilding made by the inhabitants after the site was abandoned by the Ai-Jinn have caused the whole structure to grow together organically.

Today, New Kowloon is a massive, sprawling, multi-story, shanty-town, resembling a squat, crumbling mockery of a spire city in its overall shape. Ironically, despite having been abandoned by the Ai-Jinn while it was still a viable population centre, New Kowloon has once again become a Corporate asset now that it is a crime-ridden hellhole.

The city is a haven for outlaws and criminals throughout Asia, so much so that it has become a UIG blindspot, the crime being simply too dense to police. Whole Malenbrach units have entered New Kowloon and simply disappeared. Only teams of Marshals enter the town with any frequency, and even then only on in-and-out raids. As a result, some of the Ai-Jinn's most secret installations are hidden inside New Kowloon. Drug and weapons production, illegal research and brutal interrogation centres take their place among the tattoo parlours, brothels and crack houses set up by the locals, all hidden beneath an impenetrable pall of lawlessness.

Living conditions within New Kowloon are appallingly squalid, with people living in conditions so cramped that they must take shifts sleeping simply because there is not enough floor-space in their domiciles for all to lie down at once. The streets are so narrow that in places it's necessary to walk sideways and the web-work of clothes-lines, extensions and makeshift bridges strung between buildings make sunlight a rare sight.

GEOGRAPHY & ENVIRONMENT

New Kowloon was constructed on an area of wasteland, the Ai-Jinn not wanting to use more valuable land for what was originally to be no more than a temporary affair. Barren land, scoured by the weapons of the Corporate Wars, supports only the hardiest forms of life such as scrub bushes, small mammals and the few mangy predators that feed on them. Much of the wildlife is mutated in some way by radiation and viral bioweapon residues and can be dangerous to the unwary. Mines and quarries operated by the Ai-Jinn dot the surrounding landscape, providing one of the few reputable sources of work and income for the city's inhabitants. At the same time these mines cover the sky in a perpetual cloud of smoke and atmospheric particulate from the micronuclear land-tiller explosives employed in major mineral extraction.

HAZARDS

The squalid city of New Kowloon is home to many dangers, ranging from rabid, mutant animals to shoddy construction and even simple disease and pollution. The following are a few of these health hazards, with in-game effects:

Shock Pools

Back when New Kowloon was constructed one of the primary sources of high-yield portable energy were supercarbon-lithium

power cells. The liquid medium that stored the electrical power was dangerously volatile in conducting power and had to be heavily insulated as even touching it could result in a lethal electric shock. Many buildings still have terminals for supercarbon-lithium cells and over time, a lot of these power cells have been damaged, spilling their contents into the streets where they pool in viscous puddles that look dangerously similar to rainwater. Anyone entering an area with power cell runoff must make a 'Perception + Observation' roll to notice the bluish-grey sheen and oily viscosity that indicates that the pools aren't water. If they fail, or choose to ignore the pools as harmless, then they run a 50% chance of stepping in a pool that still contains residual charge and taking 3D6 electrical damage.

Blackdrop (Level 2 Contact Toxin)

Radioactive ash from the mining operations sometimes congeals in the gutters of New Kowloon, mixing with rainwater and clogging the runoff drains so that it drips into the streets below on wet days. This inky black runoff, called blackdrop, is highly acidic as well as radioactive and causes inflammation, boils, lesions and painful ulcers on contact with skin, and over time can cause dermal cancer.

Locals wear heavy raincoats or carry acid-treated umbrellas to avoid contact with blackdrop but nonetheless blackdrop-induced cancer is one of the biggest killers in the city, especially among street children and the homeless. Anyone coming into contact with blackdrop will develop sores and lesions on the affected skin over the course of an hour or so unless the stuff is quickly washed off with soap and hot water.

Blackdrop scald results in a -1 penalty on strenuous physical actions and subtracts 5 from the sufferers movement speed due to the pain. ICE or Toughskin users can ignore the short-term effects, though they may still develop dermal cancers.

Treatment takes the form of physical surgery coupled with a course of anti-oncogen tablets. The healing process takes about 2 weeks and costs around 1000¢.

Falling Masonry

Much of New Kowloon is crumbling and poorly constructed, the original Ai-Jinn buildings having been altered and added to by unskilled builders for many years. In the cramped streets where there is little room to move this can make falling roof tiles and bits of acid-eaten rubble a major risk.

Anyone using a kinetic or explosive weapon that does more than three dice of damage in an area where there is falling masonry triggers a rubble-fall on all doubles when making their attack roll. Everyone in the area must roll 'Reflexes + Observation' or take 4D6 damage; wearing a helmet confers a +2 bonus on your dodge roll.

Flechette Flies

Vicious mutant mosquitoes that gather around pools of stagnant water are a constant annoyance during the summer months, temporarily replacing the impersonal danger of the blackdrop with deliberate hunting stings. Flechette flies would only be an irritation if they didn't carry dangerous sicknesses, the most common form of contagion their bites transmit is a virus called 'sludge lung' that causes breathing difficulties and possible death from mucous drowning. Entering an area containing flechette flies results in a -

2 penalty on all rolls requiring concentration due to their distracting bites and victims must make an Endurance check on a D10 or contract sludge lung, losing 1 Endurance every day for D10 days that is not recovered until it is cured. Toughskin makes the user immune to flechette fly bites.

Sludge lung is a disease and cannot be cured with a toxin purge, the normal treatment is a 4 day course of antibiotics (cost 600¢), at the end of which the disease is cured and the Endurance points are recovered at a rate of 2 per day.

LOCATIONS OF NOTE

The shadowed alleys and twisting streets of New Kowloon are home to many surprises, and as a city whose economy is based primarily on crime, many of them are dark, fickle surprises waiting to destroy the unwary. Among the more colourful places in New Kowloon are:

PASTOR SOON'S CHAPEL

> Of course I will heal you child, your eyes are kind and your soul deeply generous. I sense a goodness in you that calls for my gifts.
>
> -Said by Pastor Soon to Sun 'The Bomber' Lee, Mountain Lord of the Kowloon Furious Dragon Triad currently the most wanted terrorist in Eastern Asia.

This tiny inner-city chapel is identifiable only by the yin-yang symbol above the entrance and the small signboards bearing handwritten descriptions of the day's service. Only a few people ever attend, and the spotlessly clean chapel is empty most days, but the signs get written anyway. Pastor Soon, an ordained member of the Order of the True Faith, has been a fixture in New Kowloon for as long as anybody can remember, it's as though he's always been there.

Normally an elderly and slightly senile priest would have about the same life expectancy in New Kowloon as a gnat in a flamethrower nozzle but the locals are highly protective of the old man, especially given the service he provides. Pastor Soon is a biokine, able to heal almost any physical ailment with the power of his telepathic abilities.

His power has waned with age and coupled with the slow loss of his faculties, he can no longer perform more than a few "miracle healings" a week. The very fact that he performs them for free to whoever asks, when he is able to, has endeared him greatly to many people, a lot of whom owe their lives to his uncanny skills.

The last time someone made the mistake of robbing Pastor Soon they ended up hanging upside-down from a scaffold by their testicles at the behest of a local mob-boss who Soon had saved from a case of terminal skin cancer. Though he asks for nothing in return for his services, people still leave donations of food or money whenever they can, often under the pretext of attending one of his services and leaving their donation in the collection plate.

Biokines (telepaths who can heal others with biokinesis), are extraordinarily rare and only normally produced by the Order. The

Ai-Jinn has given up on trying to interrogate Pastor Soon for the secret of the technique as he no longer remembers how he came to develop the ability and simply attributes it to faith healing.

Mission Hooks
1. A powerful gang has taken over the area where Pastor Soon's chapel is located and are monopolising access to his gifts.
2. The Order has got wind of Pastor Soon's presence in New Kowloon after uncovering a clerical error that meant he was supposed to be reassigned to another parish decades ago. Now they want him to move.
3. People being healed by Pastor Soon are gaining telepathic abilities.

KAC-SHIM MANUFACTORY #3

Do you want ammo with that?

-Repeated thousands of times daily at Kac-Shim retail desks worldwide.

The largest business in New Kowloon is easily the Kac-Shim factory. It is a grimy sweatshop that doubles as its own warehouse and weekly produces thousands of low quality personal armaments for the fiscally conservative (or merely desperate) customer. Providing one is willing to brave the crushingly high quotas, poor working conditions and complete absence of safety measures then it is possible to make a liveable wage with a pittance to spare.

The Kac-Shim factory has few permanent workers though, most are young people looking to join a gang who only work there because the company gives out free guns to its workers as bonuses. Many a successful New Kowloon gangster has started out as a gangless hood with a gratis Kac-Shim pistol.

Mission Hooks
1. A shipment of Kac-Shim arms have been made with accidentally misplaced Western Federation components.
2. Dissident rebels are planning to take command of the factory to build weapons to use against the Ai-Jinn.
3. A disgruntled former employee is threatening to blow up the whole factory unless his demands are met.

OX LABS

"I used to have a drug problem but since moving to New Kowloon I never run out.

-Linden 'Goldsocks' Ericsson, Professional Socialite

The Ai-Jinn use New Kowloon as a major base for the production of the instantly addictive designer drug Ox. Far from UIG scrutiny and inspection and hidden by SatBlankets, Ox production occurs here at unprecedented levels.

The labs, while perhaps the most illegal operation running in New Kowloon, have ties to the most reputable, the mines. Both are interconnected parts of a greater Ai-Jinn profit-scandal. The production plants run round the clock and the finished product is shipped out every day on the buses that take the workers to the mining operations; from there it is distributed wherever the Ai-Jinn want it in UIG-approved ore shipments.

Mission Hooks
1. Parties unknown are destroying Ox labs but leaving the product to burn.
2. The UIG are conducting a major Ox crackdown, even going so far as to enter New Kowloon.
3. A bus heading for the mines has been attacked by outlaws and the passengers killed. But more importantly, they stole the Ox shipment!

THE HIVE

At the centre of New Kowloon are the original Ai-Jinn-made habitation towers that the rest of the city rose up around. Once shining white macro-fab tenement complexes, the gradual collapse and unskilled rebuilding has, over time, shaped it into a fused mass of pitted and rust-stained concrete and iron sheeting colloquially referred to as 'The Hive'.

Most of the city's population live here, often with five families sharing an area designed for one. However, as the main population centre, without the Hive New Kowloon would die. Only three elevators out of the original twenty four still work and even the stairs in some areas have been made impassable by partial collapses. In these cases access to the other levels is achieved by means of makeshift methods such as ladders tied onto the outer walls with rags and plastic cording, knotted ropes through holes in the ceiling and remaining sections of the fire escapes. Partial structural collapses are frighteningly common and not helped by the fact that walls are frequently knocked through by the gangs that rule the Hive. These efforts to expand their bases usually have little regard as to which are supporting walls.

Mission Hooks
1. A mad artist is transforming the Hive into a sculpture by demolishing sections of it with bombs.
2. While on a mission, an Agent was trapped in a collapsing part of the Hive, his smeaker is still sending nonverbal signals, he may still be alive and buried.
3. A gang leader has declared himself the 'Kowloon King' and taken control of the entire Hive.

THE KOWLOON MARKET

The city's informal commerce sector is a covered market set up in an abandoned construction hangar of the long-defunct Ai-Jinn subsidiary 'Lu Taiyang Aeronautics' and still bears faded company logos on the walls. Here, the smell of hot cooking fat from the fry-carts overpowers the chemical and refuse stink of the rest of the city and something approaching normal life goes on.

Every day, street vendors vie with each other for the best spots to set up their tables, often breaking into fist-fights over particularly lucrative sites. The Kowloon Market is where most people in the city go to purchase groceries, usually in the form of meat products of dubious provenance and stunted vegetables grown in home-made hydroponic basements and rooftop gardens as well as processed goods from outside the city. Pretty much everything else can be found here though, from guns and ammo (usually Kac-Shim or cheap Y&S knockoffs) to the services of an unlicensed street doctor.

Mission Hooks

1. The division must go undercover and set up a knock-off gun stall to find out who tries to hustle them out.
2. An awesome street chef is working in the market, his reputation has spread and the CEO wants his famous crispy wontons! Be careful, the Shi Yukiro might mistake it for an important item-drop and try to steal your precious fried snacks.
3. Outlaws have been coming out of New Kowloon bearing cybernetics with Ai-Jinn registration numbers, find the source.

THE WARRENS

New Kowloon is a city built upon the corpses of past habitations. The warrens are a honeycomb of foundations, sewers, disused basements, pipelines and semi-collapsed buildings that have built up underneath the sprawl. They have evolved over centuries of construction and demolition into a nearly-complete underground tunnel system.

It is possible for a man with a compass and a mining drill to get to almost anywhere they want in the city simply by following the right tunnel and knocking through to the next chamber when they can't find one. Few ever attempt it though, especially in recent years when those who enter the warrens often don't come back and those who do return tell stories that the Cult of Machina have claimed the warrens for their own.

What business the Cult has with New Kowloon is anyone's guess, but judging by the great aggression with which they keep outsiders away, it could be that they have chosen the city as a site for one of their subterranean fortresses; a *Cathedral Machina*.

Mission Hooks

1. Catch 'The Kowloon Ripper', a serial-killer Chimera who uses agility-boosting cyberware and freerunning skills to kill from practically anywhere in the city with impunity.
2. Find the Cathedral Machina and assassinate Typhon, a seditious Cult Architect who has been uniting the Cultists in the area.
3. A group of children have become lost in the warrens and the locals are begging the Ai-Jinn for help.

The three remaining members of the Division burst out of the alley in a tight cluster and stopped dead. The pursuit had led them back onto one of New Kowloon's main thoroughfares, and now they stood on the edge of a milling crowd of civilians, hundreds of thousands of jostling bodies crammed between the neon-soaked walls of the entertainment district. Agent Schaefer found herself staring into the swirling mass to try and pick out individual faces, but it was futile; the ebb and flow of humanity ground away any hope of discerning any one person within the seething mob.

Schaefer looked back at Heinz, now acting leader of the Division, for guidance. He stood for a long moment with his cold blue eyes fixed on the churning crowd, absently rubbing the day's worth of grey stubble on his chin. When he spoke, his voice was high and tense, just audible over the insensible babble of the horde.

"Fei will have gone straight through the crowd into the upper levels. She'll be expecting us either to spend time trying to get Dyson back on his feet or to comb through this lot looking for her." Heinz fixed his gaze on Schaefer for a moment, flicked his eyes across to Williams, back to Schaefer again. "Dyson is dead by now, or as good as, and we all know it. There was nothing we could do for him. Priority now is to catch up with Fei and find out what we need, then evac at the designated site. Move through here, get out of the crowd as fast as you can, up to the higher levels ASAP. It'll be less congested there; we can run a proper grid search." Heinz flexed his stubbled jaw, and Schaefer heard the reassuring crackle of feedback in her subdermal earbud. "Try to stick together, but we'll stay in touch by smeaker. Remember, these are civilians, no danger to us, so keep it cool; save it for Fei. See you on the other side. Go."

She saw him push into the edge of the crowd, hurried to follow him before the flow of thronging bodies closed again. Then they were in amongst it, people all around shoving, jostling, bumping. Heinz's broad back was just in front of her, not even an arm's length away as they edged their way through the mass of bodies. She stopped briefly looked back over her shoulder for Williams. Williams wasn't there. She saw only a shifting chaotic flurry of faces, each barely glimpsed and gone again, somehow inhuman in the confusing medley of flickering coloured lights. Nobody met her eyes. The babble of sound around her was a solid wall, hundreds of individual voices crushed together into meaningless noise. She bit down to open a smeaker channel to Williams and felt a particularly hard shove in her upper ribs, hard enough to be painful; she stumbled and almost fell, staggering against a press of bodies, and the impact jarred her jaw, breaking the channel again.

Recovering, Schaefer looked about herself; she realised she'd lost Heinz, now, and was no longer sure which direction she'd been heading in. Somewhere close by she heard an edge of sound above the crowd noise; the start of a scream, abruptly cut off. It sounded like Williams. She began pushing through the packed bodies towards the noise, working elbows and shoulders in against the compressed mass of humanity, making slow progress. She bit down again, this time opening a channel to Heinz.

A crackling roar of static feedback sounded through the earbud and she dropped the connection, fighting down panic. People pressed in on every side; she felt constrained, with barely enough room to breathe. Her hand slipped inside her trenchcoat, seeking the reassuring grip of her Black Cougar, but found only the severed ends of the holster straps. Somehow, they'd taken her gun! She took a step back, stepped on something that crunched and skidded wetly out from under her, almost fell again. She instinctively looked down.

A chance flare of yellow light from somewhere high above showed her what she'd trodden on. It was a human jaw, a couple of the teeth now broken where she'd stepped on it. The chin was covered in a day's worth of grey stubble. The other end was wet ruin; a severed smeaker wire protruded from the mess.
Schaefer screamed, once, but the sound was choked and swallowed up by the ceaseless noise of the mob. The crowd closed in around her like the incoming tide.

SHOPPING IN NEW KOWLOON

As much as New Kowloon is a crumbling pit of a city, its status as a world crime centre means that it is still an excellent place to acquire illegal goods.

If you aquire illegal goods here using the Underground Operations training the GM should lower the price of drugs compared to other areas.

In addition, a few items are relatively exclusive to the streets of New Kowloon, although similarly dilapidated cities such as Rio in the South American freestate may have similar items;

Kokuri

Kokuri	Potency 6	Class B	15¢ per Dose

A low-grade recreational drug produced from treated chemical runoff and mutant plant life from the city suburbs. Physically it resembles an extruded brown-black lump, usually sold in 20-dose slabs in packets made from heat-sealed cuts of plastic produce sacks. Kokuri is hard but melts with the application of human body heat, becoming a thin, inky substance that is rubbed under the eyelid. Effects include a general feeling of contentment and extreme hunger, even to the point of attempting to consume non-edible substances such as polystyrene, packing foam and - on at least one occasion - pillows. Long term users often develop tar-black sclera but there are very few long term users.

Zip Gun (Light Firearm)

D6	10¢	Medium	Rate 1	EMP Immune

For those too poor to even afford a Kac-Shim there's always the good-old Saturday night special. Zip guns are handmade, one-shot pistols made from loose sections of pipe and castoff junk. A zip gun can generally only fire once before it is rendered useless, though a few can be reloaded it still takes a full two rounds to prime a new bullet.

Acquiring ammo will be difficult as zip guns universally use obsolete cartridge-ammo technology only stocked by specialists. As pathetic a weapon as a zip gun is by the standards of an Agent it's still usually enough to scare the average citizen into compliance. Zip guns are always Condition 1-2 and cannot have their condition level increased in any fashion.

Cartridge Ammo   5/10/15¢ each

Used in old-fashioned kinetic weapons not configured to use SMART ammo. Cartridge ammo takes the form of sealed brass tubes containing the propellant and ignition mechanism with the projectile at one end and a pin-strike igniter at the other. In the case of shotguns these may be plastic or cardboard instead.

Unlike SMART ammunition, they must be purchased in specific sizes, though most pre-SMART weapons use one of a standardised format. While cartridge firearms see virtually no use anymore there is still a call for them by antique gun enthusiasts and some old-city dwellers preserve the technique for making home-made bullets, something that cannot be done for SMART ammo without access to the kind of equipment that rarely leaves the spires. The listed prices are for Light, Tactical and Heavy firearms respectively.

Warren Map   Cost Varies (100-2000¢)

A few enterprising citizens of New Kowloon have taken it upon themselves to engage in amateur cartography of the tunnels beneath the city. Most maps of the warrens available are photographed copies of hand-drawn and hand-annotated notebooks, often haphazardly arranged and lacking any organisation or key that can be understood by anyone but it's maker.

The common purveyors of these maps are homeless street children, who have built something of a strange subculture around tests of courage in the warrens. An old map or one which only covers a small section of the warrens might sell for only 100¢, a nearly-complete map, relatively up-to-date and accurate, detailing dangers such as hanging power cables, gas pockets and Cult enclaves can command a price of up to 2,000¢.

Resonance Material   5000¢/Kg

Most material that acquires telepathic resonance does so during times of focused, heightened emotion such as a statue that had been the focal point in a place of worship or the knife used by a man to murder his wife. In New Kowloon, however, the sheer oppressive gloom of the place occasionally infuses an item with potent telepathic resonance just from passive exposure over time.

Strangely, almost all of these items are things that were once part of the city architecture itself, though why this is the case has yet to be explained convincingly. Telepaths who read the resonance of such items are often reduced to wracking sobs at the sheer weight of depression and human misery contained in something so mundane as a lump of masonry or a steel rebar, rendering them at -2 to all Action Totals for 1D10 minutes. Mostly these items are just unusual souvenirs that occasionally get picked up by sensitive locals and sold on to passing telepaths who might find such things interesting.

The Order of the True Faith, on the other hand, are able to forge such material into potent resonance weapons and it is rumoured that the Comoros Corporation too, has mastered the rudiments of this technique, using it to create telepathic focuses to amplify their already formidable abilities. Both factions are highly covetous of any resonance material, often viewing it as their property by right of their superior psionic knowledge.

THE FUBARR

Originally set up in Old Detroit, Michigan, the first FuBarr was the brain child of Karen Quaid, a Federation Agent who was treading a fine line with her penchant for hard liquor and good times.

By setting up the FuBarr she sealed her own fate and was given the choice of cleaning up her act or leaving the Federation. Being the way she was and spurred on by the success of her new venture, Quaid set about with her new life.

The thinking behind the FuBarr was to provide a place for Agents to meet up and relax away from the confines of the Spire. To this end it was very successful but with her banishment from the Corporation, custom dried up as the punters were instructed not to frequent it.

Never ones to miss an opportunity, an Ai-Jinn division known simply as 'The Laundry' approached Quaid and suggested they take over the running of the bar in Detroit and she move to Old Hong Kong where the customers would be far less discriminating.

Although initially sceptical Quaid agreed and the move turned out to be a great decision as since then another 62 FuBarrs have opened up across the world. They are all recognisable by the American influence – rich wooden-style interiors, leaded lights, neon beer signs, pool tables and juke boxes. The clientele are predominantly Agents although citizens are not excluded.

As regards safety the Fubarr is extremely unpredictable. The bar can go for weeks without incident but when a fight does break out the casualties are enormous. One of the reasons for these heated scuffles is that the FuBarr is open to all Agents, not just those of the local corporation. You'll find a division of Samurai ad Technica seated next to an Ai-Jinn Tiger Patrol or an E.I. Nuke listening intently to a Federation Agent talking about refinements in ammunition technology. Even Comoros Agents frequent the FuBarr, the temporary cease-fire a hint at what the future may hold.

POLICIES

There are a few unspoken rules in the FuBarr, but everyone learns them pretty quickly.

1. Fights are to be taken outside.
2. All damages are to be paid for by the instigators
3. Vendettas are put on hold in the bar.
4. No drinks on the pool table.
5. The UIG are fair game.

STAFF

The FuBarrs are normally staffed by ex-Agents of considerable ability. The company is overseen by the Ai-Jinn and as such the employees tend to be vetted by them. However, this does not mean that the bars are run exclusively by Ai-Jinn staff. The majority are ex-E.I., Ai-Jinn and Federation Agents although a number of Comoros and Shi Yukiro proprietors are currently active.

UIG

The UIG almost never enter the FuBarr and if they do it tends to be Marshall squads, Malenbrach or Rangers. There is a general hatred of the law and its one of the few occasions you will get to see 30+ miscellaneous Agents from various corporations bring their combined might to bear on a single enemy.

THE FUBARR IN YOUR GAME.

You can pop a FuBarr in to any Old City. They tend to be fairly quiet places in general where Agents can hang out and maybe find out some non-sensitive information. It can make for a good meeting point or you could even have Agents which would normally be rivals, realising they are following the same goals and working together.

TAU HADES GAMMA

SAMPLE MINING COLONY

Mining makes up a large part of the Ai-Jinn's activities although unfortunately the Earth's bounties have waned considerably over the past few hundred years. This is a bonus for the Ai-Jinn, however; anyone can mine the Earth, only they can mine in space.

The Ai-Jinn still have a few Terran extraction facilities but most of their operations are located in space; several in the Sol system with a few further afield.

Massive mining crafts such as *The Rat & Dragon* spend years at a time on round trips dropping off miners and machinery and picking them up for the return journey to Earth. Those who work deep in asteroid, moon and planetary mines generally only do so to either avoid the authorities or for the substantial pay cheques they receive.

Even using the FarDrive it is a time consuming business travelling around the galaxy and those who enlist on mining trips generally commit to spending a few years of their life deep in space.

TAU HADES GAMMA (THG)

Setup
Located near Proxima Centauri, Tau Hades Gamma is an asteroid, 700km in diameter that has a wealth of valuable and easily accessible ores and minerals. The mining complex comprises 2 main structures, each of which is built of prefab units.

The first facility, named the Dunai Mine, features a hard-bore mine which was created by *The Rat & Dragon*. The ship used an enormous drill mounted on the underside to drive a primary shaft into the asteroid.

The second facility, named the Kao Len Mine, incorporates a large open cast mine which is worked by finers (see the Eastern Bank). The ore is collected by large cargo-crawlers and taken back to the Dunai Mine where it is stored in the hoppers to await collection.

It takes about 6 months to fill all the hoppers, at which point a mining craft will come to empty them and relieve any miners who have fulfilled their contracts.

Life on Tau Hades Gamma
As you might expect it's pretty desperate. The pre-fabs which the facility is constructed from are anything but luxurious. The floors are tread-patterned alloy, the walls wipe-clean, grey plastic and the ceilings low with stark lighting.
Miners are expected to start work at 8:30 am (THG time) and work through to 6:00pm. They get one hour for lunch and 1 day off per week. Most miners skip the day off, considering the extra money more desirable than a day sat in the rec room, sat in plastic chairs watching bad films.

Meals are extremely basic but nutritionally complete and alcohol and drugs are banned from the facility. The miners' work is hard

despite the low gravity and they tend not to need exercise as their exertions in the mines keeps their muscles healthy. The need to wear magnetic boots all the time can also make day to day tasks tedious.

It's not surprising that most people who sign up to work on THG don't do it again. Although the pay is a massive incentive; around 60,000¢ for 6 months work (+ six months total travel time). The conditions and mind-breaking effects of living in the colony are too much for most people. It's not enough money to set you up for life and it doesn't have the atmosphere and diversity of Dreddoth. On the plus side however, the Ai-Jinn will take anyone and not disclose their passenger manifest to the UIG. This is the main contributor to the fact that many of THG's workers are criminals or desperados looking for a little time out.

PLOT IDEAS
1. An aggressive alien species has been unearthed in the mines. The activity has disturbed their hibernation and they are ready to feed.
2. The Ai-Jinn believe one of the miners is a spy for a rival corporation. Determine who it is.
3. THG always has a contingent of security. Its now the Division's turn to be that security. A six month shift on THG is not going to pass quickly.
4. The Ai-Jinn have quarantined THG. As a rival Division you have been set the task of finding out why.
5. The latest shipment of ore is back from THG. The UIG have done random samples and confiscated all the ore. Find out what's so special about this shipment.

> *Given the exponentially scaling expense of installing new equipment or extending existing facilities in a deep-space environment, the Ai-Jinn will typically only construct a single mine building on a given asteroid or planetary body. These are initially built to sufficient scale to accommodate all projected industrial operations.*
>
> *Such are the provisions of the Interstellar Mining Accord, but the words hardly do justice to the dreadful, magnificent reality. The Ai-Jinn mines are vast, angular cyclopean structures, inevitably blackened by reeking smoke and grime. If what little still remains of human rights legislation held any sway off Earth, the conditions inside those gigantic, oppressive ziggurats of ceaseless industry would violate every rule in the book. An estimated five-eighths of all off-planet miners either transfer home within two years or are driven clinically insane in the noisome darkness within those massive, sheer walls.*
>
> *First-time observers often comment that those obscene structures look more like tombs than mines; for a significant number of their inmates, they eventually serve as both.*
>
> *-from UIG Annual Report on the IMA, 2501*

SECTION 9

ANTAGONISTS

AI-JINN IN GUAN YU ARMOUR

AI-JINN AGENT IN GUAN YU ARMOUR
Rank 3 / Level 12

COMBAT
HP	38
Shield	60
AV	11
Defence	7 (Multiple Defence)

WEAPONS
Strike	AT 15, Dam 6, Rate 2
Plasma Short Sword	AT 15, Dam D6+12+XS
Shotgun	AT 12, Dam 2/3D10, Rate 1
Plasma Cannon	AT 13, Dam 5D10+5, Rate 1, Ignore AV
Combat Talons	AT 15, Dam 11, Rate 2, Ignore 2 AV
Heavy Frags	AT 11, Dam 6D6, Rate 1

STATS
Str 12, End 8, Agi 8, Ref 7, Int 6, Per 7, Pres 7

SKILLS
Assess Tech 5, Attitude 6, Close Combat 7, Computers & A.I. 3, Cybernetics & Robotics 3, Drive 3, Heavy Firearms 6, Light Firearms 4, Looking Good 4, Medicine 2, Observation 5, Support Weapons 4, Street Culture 2, Tactical Firearms 5

LICENSES
A range of licenses based on the speciality of the Agent though he will have most of the licenses needed for the equipment he carries.

TRAININGS
Clanger, Guan Yu Use, Mastered Weapon - Short Sword, There is only Ai-Jinn, Dual Weapon Fighting (Shotgun and Plasma Short Sword), Multiple Defence, Shotgun Pulping

EQUIPMENT
100%	Selection of grenades, some heavy
100%	Plasma short sword is integrated in the Guan Yu
50%	Shotgun is double barrel if you have the rules
50%	Plasma cannon is condition 6
100%	Varied cybernetics

GUAN YU UPGRADES
Hard Ion Field, Combat Talons, Integrated Weaponry, Optical Package, Environmental Baffles.

DESCRIPTION
The Guan Yu equipped Agent is more conspicuous than a normal operative but far more resilient. The nature of Ai-Jinn training means that these suits are far from impedeing and grant the

Agents more advantages than problems. Most suits are black but some are decaled with Ai-Jinn insignias, personalised logos, camouflage or symbolic icons. The user generally stands a foot taller when wearing the suit but normally shows little signs of hindrance despite the suit's archaic appearance.

COMBAT
Guan Yu equipped Agents almost always operate in groups because it is not normally practical for only one Agent to wear heavy armour. They will not generally employ drastically different tactics to normal, simply enjoying the many advantages the suit offers.

ALTERNATIVES
There are dozens of potential Guan Yu setups. The one listed here would be considered non-specialist. The most common are as follows.
Scout - Light, fast with good optics and long range weapons.
Assault - Moderately strong with tactical firearms and close combat weapons.
Heavy - Heavy weapons, extra armour and good shielding.
Close Combat - Dual close combat weapons, often combat talons and integrated plasma weapons.

AI-JINN SLAVE BIO - YILEPSID

YILEPSID - AI-JINN SLAVE-CLASS COLONISER BIO

Rank 0 / Level 5
Value 85,000¢

COMBAT

HP	38
Shield	0
AV	0
Defence	6

WEAPONS

Stone Axe*	AT11, D8+11, Rate 2
Power Strike	AT11, D4+11, Rate 1
Bite**	AT11, 11 Mashing, Rate 1
Bow	AT 11, D6, Range Medium, Rate 1

*Breaks if maximum damage is rolled.
** May be made in addition to unarmed attacks at a -4 penalty.

STATS

Str 11, End 12, Agi 5, Ref 5, Int 5, Per 6, Pres 4

SKILLS

Arts & Culture 4 (Tribal Crafts), Athletics 5, Close Combat 6, Medicine 2, Observation 5, Psychology 3, Stealth 4/8 in frozen tundra, Tactical Firearms (Bows Only) 5

LICENSES

None, though Yilepsids are sentient and possessed of roughly human intelligence, all BIOs are officially property of their licensed creator and as such may not possess UIG citizen status or hold licenses.

TRAININGS

Domestic Trade (Tool Making, Tanning, Cooking, Hunting, Shaman), Unarmed Combat Specialist, Survival

EQUIPMENT

100%	A pouch of dried Graan meat, 10% chance it is flavoured with herbs.
100%	Stone tool, usually an axe.
100%	Hunting bow made from laminated bone and twisted Grann tendons.
70%	Tanned leather armour (+1 AV versus primitive attacks).
10%	Piece of tribal art worth D4x100¢

SPECIAL ABILITIES

Cold Resistance - Yilepsids are particularly well adapted to the cold and gain +4 to their Endurance for purposes of calculating their resistance to the effects of cold weather.

DESCRIPTION

One of the first successful BIO templates that the Ai-Jinn attempted to create on Ornus, the Yilepsid species are 7-foot tall humanoids with thick, shaggy white fur covering most of their bodies, small eyes protected by skin folds and large, expressive mouths filled with thin, needle-sharp tearing teeth. While seeming fairly dense by human standards, Yilepsids are merely uneducated and are in fact one of the most intelligent BIO species created to date, and the only BIO species on Ornus made capable of manifesting telepathic abilities. Indeed, it was one of their number who first realised the Ai-Jinn's deception and started the Maranathan Rebellion which may soon threaten the Ai-Jinn's control over Ornus. It is for this reason that very few Yilepsids are ever allowed permanently in the Ai-Jinn's Ornus bases, instead being either released back or culled. Most Yilepsids live in small tribal bands that roam the wastes of Ornus following the migratory patterns of the Grann, low-metabolism pack herbivores able to subsist on Ornus' few hardy lichens and mosses.

COMBAT

Yilepsids are not aggressive by nature - the Ai-Jinn made them to be docile and pliable workers, not combat machines like most BIO's - but if threatened they will lash out with stone tools or, if unarmed, their own fangs and fists. Yilepsid bites are particularly vicious, their mouths and throats having been designed for rapidly stripping and gorging large chunks of flesh from their meals. However, most Yilepsids will not fight humans due to their belief that humans are spirits or gods and will instead avoid them or try to offer chiminage in the form of hand-crafted art objects and dried meat. Some Yilepsids may wear tanned leather armour, giving them a +1 bonus to their AV which does not apply against powered melee weapons and firearms, though it will still protect from punches, crossbows and thrown weapons.

ALTERNATIVES

Maranathan Rebel

This Yilepsid is a member of the Maranathan Rebellion, they don't know what humans are but they know that they aren't gods and they are not going to put up with exploitation anymore. A Maranathan Rebel will likely have 1 to 2 ranks in Assess Tech and higher ranks in one or more firearm skills, they may even possess low levels of Drive or Pilot. In addition they have a 60% chance to be carrying a condition 7 firearm from the following list: Kinetic SMG, Laser Rifle, Snipers Rifle, Machine Pistol, Machine Gun.

Shaman

A Yilepsid Shaman has visited the spirit world, carried away in a great basket atop the back of one of the flying stone beasts of the humans, and returned with great magical gifts bestowed upon him by the human spirit-people after enduring the ordeals of faith. A shaman has the Telepath training and 3 telepathic skills rated at D10 each, usually Prescience, Biokinesis and Telekinesis.

AI-JINN SLAVE BIO - ANGROL

ANGROL - AI-JINN SLAVE-CLASS COLONISER BIO
Rank 0 / Level 8
Value 110,000¢

COMBAT
HP	42
Shield	0
AV	1
Defence	7

WEAPONS
Power Strike	AT14, D4+14+3, Rate 1
Bite*	AT14, 7, Rate 1

* May be made in addition to unarmed attacks.

STATS
Str 14, End 10, Agi 7, Ref 7, Int 4, Per 7, Pres 6

SKILLS
Attitude 5 (Intimidating), Athletics 8, Close Combat 7, Observation 6, Psychology 5, Stealth 5.

LICENSES
None, though Angrols are sentient and possessed of roughly human intelligence (though only just), all BIOs are officially property of their licensed creator and as such may not possess UIG citizen status or hold licenses.

TRAININGS
Restrain, Unarmed Combat Specialist, Survival

EQUIPMENT
100%	Crude hide clothing.
80%	Half-eaten Grann haunch.
30%	Bits of carved bone, shiny rocks etc.

SPECIAL ABILITIES
Fast Climber - Angrols can climb at the same rate as their move speed up vertical surfaces and even from horizontal surfaces such as ceilings and rock overhangs provided there are sufficient handholds.

DESCRIPTION
Barrel-chested creatures roughly 8-foot tall, somewhat more bipedal than gorillas but still more comfortable when knuckle-walking. Angrol faces are simian but with jutting tusks and a wider jaw-structure, skin tones tend toward whitish-greys with the occasional blue-black mutant. Angrols were originally intended to be a combat BIO species but were given enhanced intelligence and repurposed as worker BIOs on colonisation projects where their powerful frames and brachiating abilities would serve the Corporation well carrying heavy loads up gantries and scaffolds where machines and droids were too clumsy to be trusted.

Unfortunately, much of the original war programming still remains within the Angrol genome and they are one of the most violent and aggressive of the slave BIOs produced on Miller-Urey. Before being put to any useful work Angrols must be broken and any tendencies to rebellion neurochemically castrated by Ai-Jinn handlers, a brutal and tortuous procedure that leaves the poor creatures docile, obedient and too terrified of humans to ever raise a finger in their own defence.

COMBAT
Angrols use few tools and almost never use weapons, preferring to wrestle down their prey and beat them to death with their meaty fists, which are dotted with keratin knobs that make their blows all the more brutal. In the wild they might wear Grann furs haphazardly lashed to their bodies with lengths of gut or twisted hide but that is roughly the limit of Angrol technology, though some may trade meat for better-made clothes and tools with other BIO tribes.

ALTERNATIVES
Maranathan Rebel
Being one of the less intelligent and so less useful of the slave BIOs, the Angrols have suffered perhaps the worst from human exploitation and readily join the Maranathans once they are shown evidence of the plight of their brothers in bondage. A Maranathan Angrol has a 60% chance to be wearing scavenged combat armour, giving them +3 AV, a 50% chance to be equipped with a Condition 7 Combat Chainsaw that they have trained with enough to gain the Powered Melee training and a 30% chance to have a working Self Charging Shield (20 HP, EMPS 15).

Tamed Angrol
A common sight around the Ai-Jinn's Ornus bases carrying heavy loads, performing construction and generally acting like living forklifts. Tamed Angrols have had their wills broken through a combination of torture and neurochemical alterations and many bear signs of mutilation such as lash-marks, burns and rows of circular scars at the base of the neck where probes were inserted into the brain. If spoken to, the wary and sad-eyed creatures will address all humans as Sir or Miss unless told otherwise and will shy away like whipped dogs from any unannounced physical contact. Even if attacked they will not defend themselves, instead curling up and shielding their head as best they can.

AI-JINN SLAVE BIO - TALGIN

TALGIN - AI-JINN SLAVE-CLASS COLONISER BIO
Rank 0 / Level 3
Value 80,000¢

COMBAT
HP   26
Shield   0
AV   0
Defence   4

WEAPONS
Dart Thrower*   AT13, Dam D6, Medium, Rate 1
Bite**   AT12, Dam 3, Rate 1
Strike   AT12, Dam 2, Rate 2

*May be poisoned.
**May be made in addition to unarmed attacks at -4 penalty.

STATS
Str 5, End 6, Agi 8, Ref 9, Int 7, Per 8, Pres 5

SKILLS
Assess Tech 3, Athletics 6, Close Combat 4, Crime 5, Lying &
Acting 4, Mechtronics 2, Medicine 3, Observation 6, Science 2,
Stealth 7, Support Weapons 3, Tactical Firearms 5 (dart thrower
only).

LICENSES
None, though Talgins are sentient and possessed of roughly
human intelligence, all BIOs are officially property of their licensed
creator and as such may not possess UIG citizen status or hold
licenses.

TRAININGS
Aptitude, Jury-Rigging (simple mechanisms only), Survivial

EQUIPMENT
100%   Hide clothing, lined with fur.
100%   Condition 6 Crossbow and quiver of 10 bolts.
80%   Stone knife.
70%   Cave insect rations.
40%   Primitive climbing equipment.
10%   Condition 3-5 tech item dropped by Ai-Jinn personnel,
        e.g. Plasma cutting torch, night-vision goggles, music
        player.

DESCRIPTION
Small, 3-foot tall, humanoids made from the rodent genotype,
Talgin most closely resemble hairless molerats out of all Earth's
fauna. They were created by the Ai-Jinn to work in cramped
service-ducts, repairing machinery and replacing broken
components and have been equipped with long, spindly fingers
suited to fine work and an intense curiosity which gives them an
innate talent for technology.

Talgin have long, dextrous fingers and large, luminous eyes, all
part of their adaptations to increase their technical ability. Of all the
BIO tribes, the Talgin are both the most sophisticated and the least
suited for Ornus' environment. They dwell primarily underground in
tunnel networks and emerge only when protected by multiple
layers of heavy fur clothes, facial swathes and snow-blindness
protectors - simple slotted pieces of bone tied over the eyes - to
shield their delicate senses.

Unlike other coloniser-BIOs who subsist mainly on Grann, the
Talgin find the large creatures difficult to take down and more
trouble than it's worth to emerge from their tunnels into the harsh
cold and light. As a result they feed primarily on cave-dwelling
insects and fungi. Those Talgin who have been brought into the Ai-
Jinn's Ornus bases for study have proven remarkably tractable,
serving willingly and even happily due to their genetically
programmed technophilia.

COMBAT
Talgin are ill-suited for combat but if threatened they will fight off
any aggressors with crude, tubular weapons made from wood or
bone that contain a piece of gut-string under tension held back by
a simple lever. These simple crossbow-analogue weapons fire
poisoned stone-headed quarrels with surprising accuracy.

ALTERNATIVES
Maranathan Rebel
Talgin make up the smallest number of the Maranathans, the
rebels can show them far fewer examples of Talgin being treated
cruelly by the Ai-Jinn than they can for the Angrols. Indeed, most
Talgin would consider the chance to explore human technology
worth any degree of slavery. Some however decide to join the
Maranathan Rebellion out of resentment of the humans hoarding
their technological treasures. Maranathan Talgin increase their
Assess Tech, Mechtronics, Medicine and Science scores by 1-2
points and may even possess knowledge of Computers & A.I. or
Cybernetics & Robotics. They will typically be equipped in a
support role, carrying explosives and intrusion devices.

Collaborator
This Talgin has joined the Maranathans but has no true loyalty to
their fools' cause. When the humans come to punish them for their
impiety he plans to aid them, perhaps even convincing them to
take him to the spirit world with them. He already has the rebels'
supplies rigged to explode. He will feign typical Maranathan
resentment of all humans but if there is an opportunity to aid them
he will take it, begging, fawning over and sometimes downright
worshipping them all the while.

SCOUT CLASS CYBERUN

SCOUT CLASS CYBERUN - THE EYE OF HORUS
Value - 10 Million credits

COMBAT

Hit Points
Loco	50
Hull	500
R. Hardpoint	0
L. Hardpoint	0
Shield	700HP
AV	15
Defence	6
EMPS	Immune
Activations	5

WEAPONS
2 Plasma Cannons	AT 19, 5D10+5 Dam, Rate 1, Ignores AV
Minelayer	AT 19, 30D10 Dam per mine, Rate 3
Sniper Rifle	AT 19, 2D6+1 Dam, Rate 2

STATS
Strength	50
Endurance	50
Agility	10
Reflexes	8
Perception	11
Intelligence	7
Presence	6
Cyberlin A.I.	5

SKILLS
Assess Tech 6, Attitude 7, Close Combat 6, Computers & A.I. 7. Cybernetics & Robotics 6, Looking Good 5, Mechtronics 6, Observation 12, Pilot 8, Stealth 8, Support Weapons 8

BUILD
Locomotion	Bipedal Inverse (80mph)
Hull	SCC Rogue H5
R. Hardpoint	Weapon Mounting
L. Hardpoint	Weapon Mounting
Processor	Datanetica FG90 (8 Systems)

WEAPON SYSTEMS
Right Hardpoint
2 x Plasma Cannon
1 x Snipers Rifle

Left Hardpoint
Mine Layer (Carries 30 Mines)

NON-WEAPON SYSTEMS
Sensory Array
Scout Array
Augmented Vision Suite
Flare Launcher
Hard Ion Shield

DESCRIPTION
An extremely light cyberlin used for scouting with minimal defence capabilities. The scout is commonly deployed on the border lands between rival corporations or in desolate areas where sensitive assets are present such as labs or silos.

The scout tends to be weak in combat and so will normally flee rather than fight. Its advanced sensory array allows it to pick up threats from a great distance giving it adequate time to retreat or, if necesary, open up with its ranged weapons.

If forced to flee it will often pepper the retreat path with mines to cripple its pursuers.

(The image shown here has no weapons fitted).

Note: Picuture is an example of the class and does not represent the exact Cyberlin detailed.

RANGER CLASS CYBERUN

RANGER CLASS CYBERUN - THE LAST MOUNTAIN
Value - 15 Million credits

COMBAT
Hit Points

Loco	100
Hull	700
R. Hardpoint	50
L. Hardpoint	50
Shield	1000HP
AV	20
Defence	7
EMPS	Immune
Activations	6

WEAPONS

2 x Assault Cannon	AT 19, Dam 4D10, Rate 1, Special
Ordnance Laser	AT 19, Dam 15D8+15, Rate 1
Ordnance Plasma	AT 19, Dam 15D10+15, Rate 1
2 x Manipulators	AT 15, Dam 50, Rate 1

STATS

Strength	75
Endurance	75
Agility	5
Reflexes	8
Perception	10
Intelligence	8
Presence	7
Cyberlin A.I.	7

SKILLS
Assess Tech 6, Attitude 7, Close Combat 7, Computers & A.I. 6. Cybernetics & Robotics 5, Looking Good 7, Mechtronics 5, Observation 8, Pilot 9, Support Weapons 9

BUILD

Locomotion	Tracks (70 mph)
Hull	SCC Arbiter
R. Hardpoint	Manipulator
L. Hardpoint	Manipulator
Processor	Illian Ghost V2.2 (10 Systems)

WEAPON SYSTEMS
Right Hardpoint
1 Tsunami Assault Cannon
1 Tempest Ordnance Laser

Left Hardpoint
1 Tsunami Assault Cannon
1 Hurricane Ordnance Plasma

Note: Picuture is an example of the class and does not represent the exact Cyberlin detailed.

NON-WEAPON SYSTEMS
Sensory Array
Scout Array
Augmented Vision Suite
Hard Ion Shield
Jump Unit
Lock on Disruptor
Shield Regenerator

DESCRIPTION
The ranger class was designed to patrol large areas of ground around sensitive assets and deter intruders. Their jump packs make them quick to respond and their paired assault cannons make them extremely effective at neutralising groups of infantry.

Although ranger class cyberlins are primarily a deterrent, they can make formidable opponents if the need arises.

BATTLE CLASS CYBERUN

BATTLE CLASS CYBERUN - THE FURY OF MENCATH
Value - 25 Million credits

COMBAT
Hit Points
Loco	300
Hull	1100
R. Hardpoint	100
L. Hardpoint	100
Shield	1500HP
AV	25
Defence	10
EMPS	Immune
Activations	8

WEAPONS
Assault Cannon	AT 20, Dam 4D10, Rate 1, Special
CAC Cannon	AT 20, Dam 40D10+100, Rate 1
Rail Cannon	AT 20, Dam 15D10+30, Rate 1, Ignores 25 AV
Mine Layer	AT 20, Dam 30D10 Dam per mine, Rate 3
Manipulators	AT 19, Dam 100, Rate 1

STATS
Strength	100
Endurance	100
Agility	5
Reflexes	9
Perception	10
Intelligence	9
Presence	9
Cyberlin A.I.	10

SKILLS
Assess Tech 6, Attitude 10, Close Combat 10, Computers & A.I. 6. Cybernetics & Robotics 7, Looking Good 9, Mechtronics 6, Observation 9, Pilot 10, Support Weapons 10

BUILD
Locomotion	Quadrupedal (28mph)
Hull	SCC Dominator C10
R. Hardpoint	Convergent Artillery Cannon
L. Hardpoint	Manipulator
Processor	Takata R50 DX (11 Systems)

WEAPON SYSTEMS
Right Hardpoint - Convergent Artillery Cannon
Mine Layer
1 Sirroco Rail Cannon
Left Hardpoint - Manipulator
1 Sirroco Rail Cannon
1 Tsunami Assault Cannon

NON-WEAPONS SYSTEMS
Sensory Array
Scout Array
Augmented Vision Suite
Lock on Disruptor
Shield Regenerator
Auto-Repair Systems (Elite)
1 x Armour Plating on Hull
Gravity Rams
Hard Ion Shield
Electronic Counter Measures

DESCRIPTION
The Battle Class represents the most agressive level of cyberlin construction. They are typically used to guard a corporation's most important assets or for full on conflicts. At the present time inter-corporation cyberlin battles are very rare but they are not uncommon in the freestates.
The Battle Class will normally open up with its assault cannon to destroy the enemy's shields, then send in volleys of rail cannon fire and deliever heavy blows with the CA cannon. Although this model would function better at range it can do terrible damage with its manipulator which may well be equipped with a plasma sword as on page 78.

Note: Picture is an example of the class and does not represent the exact Cyberlin detailed.

ANTAGONISTS

RED TALON MK VII P-TANK

RED TALON MARK VII SUBMERIBLE P-TANK
Value - 300,000 Credits

VEHICLE STATISTICS
HP   250
AV   15
MPH   65
DM   -1

Length 4.8 Metres
Height 2.6 Metres

Tpyical Driver Stats
Weapon Action Total   15
Piloting Action Total 15

Typical Weapon Configuration
Linked Rail Guns   AT 15, Dam 6D10, Rate 2, Ignore 15AV
Plasma SMG   AT 15, Dam 6D6, Rate 1, Ignore AV
Laser SMG   AT 15, Dam 6D8, Rate 1, Ignore Shields

DESCRIPTION
The P-Tank is a lightweight, highly customisable tank which can can be easily retrofitted with a variety of weapons to enable it to function in a range of environments.
The P-Tank has two key attributes which differenciate it from other vehicles in its class.

Self Destruct
The internal reactor can be set to overload. This causes the tank to explode creating a massive zone of destruction. The pilot is almost always killed. For this reason piloting the P-tank carries with it great risk and although some see death in the line of battle to be an honourable end, many secretly dread being assigned to a P-tank battalion. This threat is often held over Ai-Jinn employees, another sucessful loyalty enforcer.

Pressurised
The P-tank is a sealed pressurised unit capable of existing for 7 days without a source of air. Up to 10 scrubber units can be attached to the basic tank, each one adding another week's worth of clean air for the pilot. (The 'p' in P-tank stands for pressurised.) This system allows P-tanks to be used in space, often as fixed weapon platforms attached to asteroids or planetoids.

RETROFIT OPTIONS
The P-tank has several retrofit options so that it can operate in a variety of environments and in a range of capacities.

UNIVERSAL RETROFITS - All P-Tanks features the following.

Self Destruct
D10x100 Damage in a 100 metre blast radius.

Internal Weapon Cache
1 pistol, 1 Kinetic SMG, 2 Frag Grenades, 4 Spare Clips

TURRET RETROFITS
The turret weapon can be any of the following. The tank can obviously have less so could be equipped with a single tactical firearms for its main turret weapon. Costs are based simply on the price of the weapons.

1 Heavy Weapon
2 Linked Heavy Weapons
3 Linked Tactical Weapons
1 OverRisk Weapon

Or a specialist weapon if desired; however, the vehicle is too small to reliably attach Ordnance Weapons

SPONSEN RETROFITS
The P-Tank has two side sponsons. Each can accomodate the following; Costs are based simply on the price of the weapons.

1 Tactical Weapon
2 Linked Tactical Weapons
1 Heavy Weapon
2 Linked Light Weapons

DRIVE RETROFITS
The standard caterpilla drive can be replaced with one of the following.

Wheels - Increase speed to 110mph and DM to 0; cannot tackle very rough terrain. (No cost involved in this)

Hover Drive - Decrease speed to 55mph and increase DM to +1. This upgrade costs 100,000 credits. The vehicle can travel up to 1 metre off the ground allowing it to travel over very rough terrain.

Gravity Rams - 30,000 - The P-Tank can be dropped from aircraft and land without being damaged.

HULL RETROFITS
The hull can be modified in the following ways.

Heavy Armour - 10,000¢ - Decrease speed to 45 MPH, +8AV, -1 DM.

Light Armour - Free - Increase speed to 85 MPH, -6AV. +1 DM

Camouflage - Free - A custom camouflage gives the tank +4 to stealth based checks.

Stealth Field - 50,000¢ - The tank becomes almost invisible and silent granting observers a -8 to detect it.

Vacuum Seals - 5,000¢ - The tank is upgraded with airlock seals to allow pilots to get in and out in space envionments.

INTERNAL RETROFITS

A.I. Pilot - 100,000¢ - A rare upgrade as the Ai-Jinn enjoy the fear piloted tanks instill. The driver's stats remain unchanged for system purposes.

Passenger Compartment - Free - The inside of the tank is modified to allow another passenger. As a result both crew are very crowded and there is very little room for personal equipment.

SatBlanket - One tank in the swarm is fitted with a heavy SatBlanket to help disguse the swarm's activities.

The P-tank, most common models shown here, neatly embodies several different aspects of Ai-Jinn design philosophy. They're extremely ugly, they're very functional, they can be deployed pretty much anywhere. Most importantly – and y'all need to get this through your heads, ladies and gentlemen – the Clangers can churn out seven of these things in the time that it takes us to produce a single Stormscythe-class MBT. I cannot sufficiently stress the point that if we ever get suckered into a war of attrition with the Ai-Jinn, we are going to lose.

But there's a philosophical difference at work here too. The Ai-Jinn will blow these damn things up at the drop of a hat; for additional collateral damage, to cover their tracks, and sometimes just because it works out cheaper than an airlift. Hence their unofficial name of zi sha shui tong – 'suicide bucket'.

So P-tank pilots are usually fanatics... but they're very seldom veterans. By contrast, every Federation tank crewer is expected to leave this place with sufficient skill to account for at least those seven P-tanks before losing his or her own vehicle. Just don't ever drive too close to the sons of bitches.

-from Lectures at New West Point
attr: Col. Jack Danes, Western Federation

JN'09

P-Tank 1/10, Primary Command Unit from Swarm 10. The solve surviving unit which fought in the Corporate Wars

APPENDIX I - SAMPLE NAMES

SURNAMES

Cai	Lee
Cao	Li
Chan	Liang
Chang	Lim
Chao	Lin
Chen	Liu
Ch'en	Lu
Cheng	Luo
Cheu	Ma
Cheung	Ong
Chew	Ooi
Chien	Pan
Chin	Peng
Chiu	Qian
Chong	Shen
Chow	Siu
Chu	Song
Cui	Soong
Deng	Sun
Du	Tan
Fang	Tang
Feng	Teo
Fong	Wang
Gan	Wong
Gao	Woo
Goh	Wu
Guan	Xiao
Guo	Xie
Han	Xu
He	Yang
Ho	Ye
Hsia	Young
Hsiao	Yuan
Hsieh	Zhang
Hsu	Zhao
Hu	Zheng
Hua	Zhou
Huang	Zhu
Hui	
Jian	
Jin	
Kam	
Kan	
Kao	
Kim	
King	
Koh	
Kuan	
Kuang	
Kwan	
Kwang	
Lam	
Lau	

FEMALE CHRISTIAN NAMES

An	Li
Bo-Bae	Li Hua
Cho	Li Mei
Dae	Li Ming
Ha-Neul	Li Na
Hea	Li Qin
Jin	Li Rong
Joo-Eun	Li Wei
Kyon	Lian
Min	Lien
Moon	Lin
Shin	Lin Yao
Soo	Ling
Sun	Lixue
Yon	Mei
Cho	Mulan
Hea	Park
Hei	
Chan Juan	
Chang	
Cong	
Da-Xia	
Fang	
Fang Yin	
Fen	
Feng	
Huan Yue	
Hui Ying	
Jia Li	
Jiang Li	
Jiao	
Jin	
Jing	
Juan	
Jun	
Lee	
Lei	

MALE CHRISTIAN NAMES

Chen
Cheng
Chi
Cong
Dewei
Fai
Guang
Ho
Jun
Kong
Kuan-Yin
Lee
Lei
Li
Lian
Liang
Lok
Long
On
Park
Shaiming
Shen
Sheng
Shing
Sying
Ye
Bae
Chin
Gi
Ha-Neul
Ho
Jin
Joo-Chan
Jung
Kwan
Seung
Sun
Yong
Chin
Chul
Hyun-Ki
Hyun-Shik
Soo
Yul

APPENDIX 2
GANG NAME GENERATOR

This generator is just for fun. Some combinations may not work but it should no doubt provide some entertainment.

ELEMENTS - D6

1. Roll Adjective + Descriptor
2. Roll Colour + Descriptor
3. Roll Adjective + Descriptor + Terminator
4. Roll Colour + Descriptor + Terminator
5. Roll Adjective + Colour + Descriptor + Terminator
6. Reroll

If no terminator, the descriptor becomes pluralised.

ADJECTIVES - D20

1. Dancing
2. Furious
3. Great
4. Invincible (warning: may be taken as a challenge)
5. Killer
6. Laughing
7. Mighty
8. Silent
9. Terrible
10. Whispering
11. Glorious
12. Famous
13. Indestructible
14. Notorious
15. Rampaging
16. Unstoppable
17. Murderous
18. Inhuman
19. Ravaging
20. Drunken

COLOUR - D20

1. Black
2. Blue
3. Green
4. Indigo
5. Orange
6. Purple
7. Red
8. Saffron
9. White
10. Yellow
11. Pink
12. Bronze
13. Midnight
14. Luminous
15. Dark
16. Scarlet
17. Crimson
18. Cereulean
19. Golden
20. Silver

DESCRIPTOR (PLURAUSE IF WITHOUT TERMINATOR) - 2D10

1. Sword
2. Assassin
3. Bandit
4. Cat
5. Devil
6. Dragon
7. Flame
8. Immortal (warning: again, sounds like a challenge)
9. Jester
10. Knife
11. Legend
12. Lotus
13. Monkey
14. Ox
15. Pirate
16. Pistol
17. Scorpion
18. Serpent
19. Titan
20. Warrior

TERMINATOR - 1D20

1. Agency
2. Association
3. Brigade
4. Gang
5. Group
6. Hong
7. Initiative
8. Organisation
9. Society
10. Triad / Yakuza / Tong
11. Clan
12. Band
13. Crew
14. Cartel
15. Posse
16. Pack
17. Syndicate
18. Tribe
19. Cabal
20. Family

APPENDIX 3 - PULPING

Reprinted from Machines of War for your convenience.

MAIN BODY PART DESTRUCTION TABLE

Target	Pen	Dam	Description
Hand	-6	8	Anything requiring the use of two hands is impossible. Rolls such as climbing which partially use the hand are made at -4. Agents are ambidextrous.
Foot	-6	10	Reflexes and Agility are reduced by 3 points with regard to movement. Running is impossible and walking is slow.
Shin	-4	14	The shin is destroyed although the foot can be recovered. Agility is reduced by 4 points. Any locomotion other than hopping and crawling is impossible.
Thigh	-4	18	The thigh is destroyed although the shin and foot can be recovered. Agility is reduced by 4 points. Any locomotion other than hopping and crawling is impossible.
Groin	-4	16	The groin area is destroyed. Agility is reduced by 2 points. Even Agents may wince at this!
Abdomen	-4	24	The abdomen is destroyed. The hips and legs are separated from the upper body but can be recovered. You can only move by using your arms. Agility is reduced to 1.
Chest Even	-2	24	The cardio-respiratory system is destroyed. This will kill anyone without I.C.E technology instantly. Those with I.C.E suffer 3 points of bleeding damage a round until healed.
Shoulder	-4	14	The shoulder is destroyed and the corresponding arm falls off. Anything which requires two arms is impossible. Rolls such as climbing, which partially use the hand are made at -5. Agents are ambidextrous.
Upper Arm	-4	14	The upper arm is destroyed. The lower arm can be recovered. Anything requiring the use of two hands is impossible. Rolls such as climbing, which partially use the hand are made at -4. Agents are ambidextrous.
Forearm	-4	14	The forearm is destroyed, the upper arm and hand can be recovered. Anything requiring the use of two hands is impossible. Rolls such as climbing, which partially use the hand are made at -4. Agents are ambidextrous.
Head	-4	25	YES! The head is totally destroyed, blow apart, pulped, it's gone, instant death, no coming back from this! Even a cerebral link won't help!*

Target	The part you are trying to pulp
Pen	Penalty to target the part
Dam	Damage needed to pulp the body part
Description	The effect of a successful hit.

Fingers? - Fingers are too fine to be a reasonable target for destruction. If the situation warrants it the GM should be able to decide the effects of smashing fingers and thumbs.
*Those lucky enough to have Agent Backup can of course, be brought back as normal.

Body Part Destruction (also known as Pulping) is a result of certain attack types or unfortunate circumstances.

WHEN CAN I PULP?

Normally the weapon or attack you are using will tell you whether it is considered a Pulping attack. Alternatively the GM can designate that the current situation warrants the use of the Pulping Table. *E.g. Getting trapped in a hydraulic metal press.*

SYSTEM

If you have the opportunity to make a Pulping attack simply look up the relevant penalty on the table opposite. The penalty relates to how hard it is to target the body part in question and applies to your action total. If you hit, look up the body part on the table, if you dealt the damage needed after AV reduction, the respective body part is pulped.

CYBERNETICS

Cybernetics are not necessarily made of reinforced metal and as a result do not make a body part harder to pulp unless they carry an inherent AV bonus. If this is the case then this is taken into account with the basic Pulping system.

Location of Cybernetics

You may need to know where certain cybernetics are located to see if they were damaged during an attack, if so consult page 72 of Machines of War. If you don't have it you'll need to use your imaginaton.

EFFECTS OF PULPING

A Pulped body part is irrecoverable; it cannot be reattached with Compound-H. Any underlying cybernetics are also destroyed. If a component was only partially hit it may be possible to repair it. The chewed mess left behind is considered a mashing wound and bleeds at 1HP point per round.

DAMAGED CYBERNETICS

Sometimes cybernetics become damaged, this is not necessarily a drop in condition. Imagine you had StealthSkin and had your arm blown off, you would need to repair it. Below are some basic guidelines to fixing damaged cybernetics. This rule should not be overused and the GM should feel free to ignore it if he feels it may damage the group's play style.

RANDOM PULPING

D100 Roll	Dam	Part Pulped
01-05	8	Hand
06-11	10	Foot
12-19	14	Shin
20-29	18	Thigh
30-39	16	Groin
40-50	24	Abdomen
51-70	24	Chest
71-77	14	Shoulder
78-85	14	Upper Arm
86-92	14	Forearm
93-00	25	Head

DAMAGED CYBERNETICS

Minor Damage
Something small impeding the function of the item.   Cost - 10% of new price
Cracked lens on a visual upgrade, coffee spilt in a neural jack, stealthskin compromised by the loss of a limb, wolf jaw bent

Moderate Damage
Something significant making the item fairly ineffective.   Cost - 50% of the new cost
Bones snapped on an alloy skeleton, Body Space door broken off, Reaver Body Plate cracked.

Heavy Damage
The item is basically useless. At this point it's almost worth getting a new one.   Cost - 75% of the new cost
Cybernetic Arm broken in two, Alloy Skull smashed open, Videoskin burnt and ripped.

CYBERLIN RECORD SHEET

Name _____   Value _____   Processor _____
Class _____   Pilot _____   Max Systems _____

Locomotion _____   Hull _____   Activations per Round _____
Speed _____ Agility _____   HP _____ AV _____   Immersion Type _____

STATS

Strength (L*) _____
Strength (R*) _____
Endurance _____
Agility (Loco) _____
Reflexes (Pi) _____
Perception (Pi) _____
Intelligence (Pi) _____
Presence (Pi) _____
Cyberlin A.I. _____

L = Left, R = Right, Loco = Based on
Locomotary System, Pi = Based on Pilot's
STAT

	Type	HP	Strength
Hardpoint Right			
Special			

	Type	HP	Strength
Hardpoint Left			
Special			

Notes

WEAPON SYSTEMS

Weapon	AT	Dam	Rate	HP	Hardpoint	Special

NON WEAPON SYSTEMS

System	Function

Damage Record

Hull	Locomotion

Right Hardpoint	Left Hardpoint

VEHICLE RECORD SHEET

VEHICLE 1

Vehicle _____ Value _____

Owner _____ Pilot / Driver _____ Colour _____

STATS

Top Speed _____
Driving Mod _____
Armour Value _____
Internal A.I. _____
Drive / Pilot AT _____
Condition _____
_____ _____
_____ _____
_____ _____

Hit Points

UPGRADES

System	Function

VEHICLE 2

Vehicle _____ Value _____

Owner _____ Pilot / Driver _____ Colour _____

STATS

Top Speed _____
Driving Mod _____
Armour Value _____
Internal A.I. _____
Drive / Pilot AT _____
Condition _____
_____ _____
_____ _____

Hit Points

UPGRADES

System	Function

HP   The vehicle's HP (Hit Points). Indicates how much damage the vehicle can take until it cannot be used. If it is reduced to 0HP or less the vehicle is useless and each round stands a cumulative 10% chance to explode, i.e. 10% on the first round, 20% on the second and so on. Explosion of a vehicle deals 3D10 damage and is a Blast with a radius of vehicle HP / 10 metres, e.g. 40 HP = 4m blast.

AV   Armour Value of the vehicle

SPEED   Top speed of the unmodified vehicle (miles per hour).

DM   Driving Modifier. You gain this to your Drive or Pilot Action Total while using this vehicle.

EMPS   Civilian vehicles have EMPS 22, if affected they simply stop. Military vehicles are immune to EMP.

RAMMING   D6 for every 10mph you are travelling at. Round down.

INDEX

In a vast cavern of ice, buried deep beneath the bottom of the world, the single most powerful man alive stood contemplating a grim future.

Jaime Van Dyer, Speaker for the Exchange, mouthpiece of gods, closed his wrinkled eyelids against the great blank screens set into soaring glacial walls. In his mind, he replayed the debate that had raged over the last three days, until all of the Exchange but him had succumbed to exhaustion and quit the Archon Chamber.

All projections showed that competition for dwindling terrestrial resources would push the world into outright war within two years, the Exchange had argued. If Hyperion could not be controlled, then surely the Six must now see that the limitless resources of deep space were the escape valve, the only way to avoid the looming disaster.

The Archons had returned an overwhelming chaos of fragmented half-answers, the massive screens periodically hinting at a blur of mighty faces, then shattering back into swirling colour. The Six referred obliquely to unspecified dangers lurking in the cold dark of space, spoke of the importance of careful control, repeated old warnings of the need for balance. None of it was new. Balance? the Exchange had queried. The Ai-Jinn continue to build an unbreakable monopoly over raw mineral resources, their stock prices making ever more ground against their rivals. They continue to amass war materiel, outstripping the other Corporations combined on a daily basis. The balance is breaking. The secrets of the Far Drive must be shared or there will be war; war for dominance or for resources, either way it will consume the world.

But the Archons had said nothing. The great screens of the gods had faded to black; their whispering, thundering voices had gone, leaving only the querulous arguments of the Exchange to fill the frozen silence.

Impotent, frustrated, and with the civilisation under his stewardship sliding inexorably towards its final catastrophe, he felt the first tear slide down his cheek; it moved sluggishly in the frozen gloom. The single most powerful man alive – Jaime Van Dyer, Speaker for the Exchange, puppet of gods – stood in a cavern of ice, feeling alone and very, very old, and wept for a world he could do nothing to save.